Uneasy Virtue

Uneasy Virtue

The Politics of Prostitution
and the
American Reform Tradition

BARBARA MEIL HOBSON

Basic Books, Inc., Publishers   New York

To the Meil family, Peter, and Jenny

Library of Congress Cataloging-in-Publication Data

Hobson, Barbara Meil
  Uneasy virtue.

  Includes indexes.
  1. Prostitution—United States—History—19th
century. 2. Prostitution—United States—History
—20th century. I. Title.
HQ144.H62 1987   306.7′42′0973   87–47520
ISBN 0–465–08868–6

Contents

v

PART III

A National Crusade and Its Aftermath, 1900–1930

PART IV

Recent Challenges and Debates, 1970–

Illustrations follow pages 76 and 199

Preface and Acknowledgments

THIS BOOK BEGAN with a quest for knowledge about the prostitution muddle in the United States. Despite nearly universal criticism of the nation's prostitution policies, no alternatives seemed to be forthcoming. As a historian, I naturally began to search for answers in the past. But in the mid-1970s, when I started, little published work was available.

Much of the first wave of my research required detective work and dogged persistence. An important source of information for me—descriptions of all Massachusetts institutional records and their storage locations—had probably been considered boring and unproductive by the original research team employed by the Works Progress Administration in the 1930s. Yet from their work, I traced one set of records to a subcellar of the minimum security prison outside of Boston. There, strewn on the floor, were registers of inmates from the 1850s; the records had survived many years of neglect and even a fire. I located other registers of prostitutes at an orphanage that once had been connected to a society responsible for a refuge for fallen women in the early nineteenth century. Scholars who are used to comfortable modern archives would balk at the places in which I conducted much of my research. Sometimes I was locked in an empty cell block of a prison or seated on a crate in an airless vault in the subterranean levels of a courthouse.

But these arduous tasks had rewards. Through my research in court and prison records, and my studies of reform movements concerned with prostitution, I found a history with numerous divisions and competing agendas grounded in many of the same gender and class issues that concern us today. I also recognized a set of policies and legal conventions that seemed impenetrable to successive campaigns for reform.

In the midst of my historical research, I heard about a major political debate over prostitution in Sweden; a large-scale government commission had been appointed to investigate prostitution issues, past and present, in that country. Through a grant from the Swedish government, I spent the summer of 1982 speaking to police, prosecutors, social workers, members of the government commission, and prostitutes who had been involved in the Swedish debate. This research visit transformed my book and my consciousness about prostitution in my own country. As an American, my approach had been unwittingly based on certain assumptions about the sex commerce industry and the treatment of prostitutes. I recall an interview I taped with the former chief of the Stockholm police: he referred repeatedly to "prostitution crime" for several minutes, until I interrupted him and asked what he meant by such a phrase since it was not illegal to be a prostitute in Sweden; he laughed at my cultural bias and explained that prostitution criminals in Sweden were pimps and business owners in the sex industry. I later traveled to Germany and Holland and found different cultural traditions and other social and political forces shaping prostitution politics: Germany had a strictly regulated prostitution system, while Holland had evolved a laissez faire prostitution policy.

To understand the American response to prostitution, I had had to go to Europe to explore different social contexts and ways of talking about prostitution. Most important, I learned that to study prostitution was to confront a society's definition of social justice, its aims for equality between men and women. At the same time, I realized that prostitution policy was intricately bound to the questions of how active the state should be in promoting these goals and of what the costs and benefits of state intervention were.

The reader who expects a political agenda will be disappointed in this book. Still, one cannot be neutral about prostitution, and my perspective pervades the discussion of the historical and present-day debates. The insights and revelations of prostitutes I interviewed—although I don't quote most of them—helped me to understand what was and was not sold in the exchange between a prostitute and her customer. A long interview I had with Jeanne Cordelier, who wrote an autobiography about life as a prostitute in France, deeply affected my thinking about prostitution. Her descriptions of prostitution were disturbing and uncomfortable, making it clear that prostitution can never empower women or provide them with economic autonomy.

This book could never have been written without the institutional support that provided me with time to devote to research. I am particularly indebted to the National Endowment for the Humanities for awarding me a research grant that enabled me to build upon and expand the scope of my dissertation. The Swedish Institute funded my first research in Sweden, and the Gertrude Philipson Fund gave me a grant to travel to Holland and Germany. I was fortunate to be able to do my research and writing in stimulating and supportive research environments, the Mary Bunting Institute, the Henry A. Murray Research Center at Radcliffe College, and the Swedish Center for Working Life. I am deeply grateful to the research support staff of the Murray Center and to its director, Anne Colby, who were all extremely helpful in the final stages of this book. I would also like to express my gratitude to the Swedish Center for Working Life for giving me a wonderful place to complete the European research for this book and to the Swedish Delegation for Social Research for allowing me to take a leave from my other projects to finish this book.

For this kind of research, the importance of librarians familiar with the range of sources cannot be overstated. I had the advantage of having access to the extraordinary resources and staff of the Schlesinger Library at Radcliffe College. Eva Moseley, curator of manuscripts, provided me with all kinds of research materials and suggestions about other places to look. I also owe a great deal to Judith W. Mellons, manuscript associate at the Harvard Law Library, who went to great lengths to track down materials for me. Kerstin Söderholm, librarian for the Swedish Center for Working Life, helped me in so many searches.

For sharing their unpublished data with me, I would like to thank Theodore Ferdinand and Gunilla Johansson. Carroll Smith-Rosenberg was kind enough to allow me to use computer material coded by one of her students. I am indebted to Robert Bloom, administrative assistant to the chief justice of the Massachusetts Supreme Judicial Court, who cut through red tape and enabled me to have access to municipal court records for statistical analysis; and I must pay homage to Steve Karbowski, my indefatigable research assistant, who coded thousands of cases with me in the damp lower levels of that courthouse.

Too many persons to name here contributed to this book by their comments, suggestions for research strategies, and reading of my manuscript. I would like to single out Eric Schneider, Janet Golden, Paul Wright, Allan Brandt, Susan Reverby, and Ava Baron for their suggestions during the book's various stages. I am deeply indebted to Lynn Weiner, whose careful readings of the manuscript were invaluable. In our endless conversations about prostitution and the Swedish welfare state, Hanna Olsson shared her experiences and provocative insights with me. I owe a great deal to Fred Stemvers and Hans Menlenbroek for sharing their knowledge of the complex issues and parties involved in Dutch prostitution policy. Diana Long's support and interest in my work over the last years have kept this book going at times when I found myself losing energy. I would also like to thank Sam Bass Warner, Jr., for suggesting that I write this book in the first place.

For her engagement with and commitment to this book, I thank my editor at Basic Books, Judith Greissman, a rare exception in an industry that has become impersonal and disengaged from its authors. From our first two-hour meeting at Radcliffe to the completion of this book, she challenged and stimulated me and shaped my thinking. The fine editorial eye of Nola Healy Lynch sharpened and brought clarity to the manuscript; I feel extremely lucky to have had the benefit of her sensitive and intelligent reading. I am also grateful to Paul Golob for tying together all the loose ends.

This book is dedicated to my family: to my parents, brother, and sister, who have encouraged me to do research and to write. I thank Jenny, my daughter—always supremely considerate—whose copious sleep during her first year allowed me to complete this book. And, most of all, this book could never have been written without the support, patience, and care of Peter Hedström, who shared home and child care responsibilities so that I could continue my work. Despite his own demanding research, he always found time to listen, to share his keen insights and broad knowledge, and to read through the many versions of the manuscript.

Uneasy Virtue

Introduction:

The Two-Way Mirror

PROSTITUTION is a perplexing and controversial subject. Even the nature of prostitution is difficult to define—is it a sexual relationship or a work contract, private act or public commerce? Prostitution will always lead into a moral quagmire in democratic societies with capitalist economies; it invades the terrain of intimate sexual relations yet beckons for regulation. A society's response to prostitution goes to the core of how it chooses between the rights of some persons and the protection of others. In nearly every society past and present, the state has sought to control the prostitution economy through the female prostitutes themselves. Prostitutes have been marked as outsiders by state policies of licensing or criminal penalties. They have been stigmatized through caste and status distinctions; most often they have been forced to work and reside in segregated areas of cities.[1] Yet prostitution has been resistant to nearly all efforts to suppress it.

In this book I reveal how essentially contested prostitution policy has been over the last century and a half, and I show how the differences in approach go to the heart not only of a society's organization of class and gender but also of the state's role in regulating morals and markets. The study of prostitution becomes a two-way social and ideological mirror. On the one side, we see a prostitution economy that expresses social and sexual inequalities within society—women are overwhelmingly the sellers of sex and men the buyers. The class and gender bias within the controls and penalties aimed at prostitutes reflect these inequalities.[2] On the other side, we see that reform movements have continually sought to alter prostitution policies, but the strategies they have proposed and the influence they have achieved have been shaped by sexual politics and class interests.

This book is not about the prostitution culture or the secret lives of prostitutes, their patrons, or pimps. Nor do I look at the psychological dynamics in prostitution or its relationship to prostitution and venereal disease or AIDS, except in the context of sexual politics. I have not dealt with male prostitution because I have focused throughout this history on the response to prostitution rooted in concerns about women's sexuality and female roles. And I have not taken the case study approach of deviant groups and subcultures, which has been the most common way to study prostitution.[3]

This book is about the politics of prostitution. I have defined politics in the broadest sense: as a social institution that embodies the relations between sexes and classes; as a body of laws and legal practices; as a reform movement linked to other movements; and as a phenomenon with historical and cultural traditions that frame the discourse and guide the search for alternatives. Prostitution politics in the United States has long been highly volatile and divisive. For a nation with a tradition of intervention in moral concerns yet committed to free market principles, prostitution poses a dilemma. The American response has been one of radical swings in policy between all-out campaigns against prostitution and sufferance of its existence. Nevertheless, one thread has remained constant: a rejection of legalization and of official regulation of prostitution. (Only in the last decade has there been a departure from this position and only in one state, Nevada.)[4]

Throughout this book I present the diverse actors and their agendas on prostitution policy. Police and courts responded to prostitution as disorderly conduct or public nuisance; consequently, they evolved strategies to control the most visible and noxious forms. Reacting against this position were religious reformers and feminists who sought to expand the meaning of prostitution to include general sexual misconduct or exploitation. They advocated the suppression of all types of sex commerce, and the most radical demanded criminal laws that would be applied to all violators, regardless of sex and social class. Prostitutes, those most affected by conflicts over prostitution policy, had no public voice or group to represent their point of view until the 1970s.

Feminist groups have been the most constant and vocal actors in the struggles over prostitution policy. Prostitution embodied one of the clearest examples of women's lack of access to economic and political power. But beyond feminists' agreement on the general principles lay ideological differences over rights versus protection and over the importance of gender and class identity.

Throughout the nineteenth and early twentieth centuries, different American feminist groups espoused the cause of the prostitute: female moral reformers, temperance and purity groups, prison reformers, and suffragists. All asserted women's collective identity—that they had similar mentalities, moral natures, and maternal instincts. But gender consciousness did not break through class differences: middle class reformers could not grasp the motivations, moral codes, and survival strategies of poor women—that prostitution could appear as a viable alternative to low wages and lack of employment options. Feminist ideology supposed that men, not women, were promiscuous; that men, not women, sacrificed moral values for monetary gain. They resolved this paradox by asserting that no woman freely chose prostitution—that extreme coercion, desperate poverty, or mental derangement explained this phenomenon. Consequently, they advocated protection rather than punishment, which translated into policies that imposed strong controls over young women's lives, work, leisure, and relationships.

Historically, the main goal of the feminist attack on prostitution policy has been to achieve the equal application of laws. Feminists have sought stricter enforcement of laws against keepers and pimps, and most important, criminal penalties for men who buy prostitutes' services. But even when such laws were enacted they were never enforced. The activism surrounding prostitution most often had the unintended consequences of increased penalties and greater social stigma against prostitutes.

I take the position in this book that the inability of American feminists to make any change in the prostitution system has been a result of their lack of political and economic empowerment. But I also emphasize that conflicts within the feminist movement over issues of class, race, and sexuality have inhibited the development of any coherent strategy toward a new prostitution policy.

This book begins in the first decades of the nineteenth century, with the rise of the industrial city. During that pivotal period, as prostitution became increasingly an urban phenomenon, cities in Europe and the eastern United States developed more uniform policies for dealing with prostitution. Intense migrations increased both the supply of prostitutes and the demand for their services; but their visibility disturbed the new class of businessman who demanded order in the workplace and in the streets.

Prostitutes appeared increasingly threatening to the social organization of middle class Victorian society, in which male and female roles and spheres of activity were rigidly delineated. Men were the producers, who took part in the public world of work and politics; women were the caretakers of home and family. The Victorian ideology of domesticity portrayed women as more chaste, spiritual, and passive than men. In trading her sex in the marketplace, the prostitute blurred these lines between masculine and feminine and between commercial and private spheres.

The book moves in concentric circles from local to national and international prostitution politics. The first part, "Policing the City," traces the evolution of prostitution policy and the reform agendas in the first half of the nineteenth century, focusing on one municipality, Boston. To explore the day-to-day policing of prostitution and the treatment of chastity offenders in courts fills an important gap in our knowledge, since we know very little about how prostitution policy was carried out in cities during the pre–Civil War era. Boston is a logical place to begin this study: in the 1820s it conducted a full-scale municipal campaign against vice; other cities followed suit in the next decades.

The second part of the book, "Prostitutes and Their Keepers," steps back and explores the social reality of prostitutes—their motivations, economic options, and possible futures. This reality is set against the prevailing medical and legal analysis of prostitution as pathology and sexual deviance.

Part three, "A National Crusade and Its Aftermath," highlights the nationwide campaign against prostitution in the first decades of the twentieth century and analyzes the forces that coalesced in the last all-out campaign to rid American cities of commercialized prostitution. The principal actors were a wide range of reformers, and new theories of social science and psychoanalysis were crucial in redefining female deviance in this era.

The final section, "Recent Challenges and Debates," reflects upon the unsuccessful challenges of feminist groups, civil liberties lawyers, and prostitutes themselves to change the course of prostitution policies in the United States. Since the search for alternatives has led many reformers to look to Europe for answers, I examine the different approaches to prostitution in Holland, Germany, and Sweden, and I contrast American images of European prostitution with the actual politics of prostitution in those countries today.

This book highlights three periods when prostitution reform became a public concern: during the evangelical religious movement of the 1840s; as a part of the Progressive reform era in the first two decades of the twentieth century; and in the 1970s at the height of the latest feminist movement. In each case I have emphasized the range of social constituencies and political agendas involved in prostitution reform. Generally, studies of campaigns against prostitution in the United States have tended to write them off as symbolic crusades—and, to some extent, they were. But in these campaigns there were real issues at stake: for religious reformers to tolerate prostitution was to turn one's back on sin; for feminists to accept prostitution as a necessary evil was to institutionalize women's inferior status; and for doctors to ignore prostitution was to leave alone what they believed was a major veneral contagion. (In view of our fears about AIDS today, the anxiety over venereal disease at the beginning of this century appears more comprehensible.)

At several points in the book, I contrast European policies with American. Overall the enforcement of prostitution laws was more rigorous and wider in scope in American cities than in European cities (where a system of criminal laws controlled prostitution). In contrast, European countries with licensed prostitution imposed greater controls on prostitutes and consistently punished those who did not comply. When American municipalities adopted European-style registration schemes, however, they took a less active role in regulating prostitution. The rules were more informal and the punishments for those who refused to comply less stern. This perhaps reflects the American ambivalence toward recognition of prostitution as a legal activity and the state as manager of sex commerce. In one instance I use the European example as a foil to show how different prostitution reform agendas can have different outcomes: I compare the American campaign in the Progressive Era with the Swedish crusade against prostitution in the mid 1970s; underlying the campaigns' different policies and results were different cultural traditions, political ideologies, and legal practices.

Much of the today's policy analysis and legal scholarship looks at prostitution in a historical and political vacuum. I argue implicitly in this book for the importance of viewing prostitution policies in their social and cultural contexts. What may work in one society or era may not work in another. A prostitution policy in one setting may be totally transformed in another. It is equally true that changes in policy may not affect day-to-day practices.

If there is any message in this book, it is that the search for an alternative prostitution policy will be stymied if reduced to technical and legal procedural strategies. Both short-term remedies and long-term solutions must be tied to general social policies on poverty, nonmarital pregnancy, child support, and women's inferior economic position. Ultimately prostitution politics must confront masculine and feminine constructions of sexuality. I have cast prostitutes neither as passive victims enslaved by procurers nor as heroic rebels rejecting social conventions. The individual causes of prostitution are complex and varied—whether prostitution be a strategy for survival, a means of escaping an oppressive family situation, or the result of a desire for economic mobility—and the opportunities for exploitation are numerous.

While one recent tendency is to analyze prostitution as an employment option for poor women, it is naive to divorce prostitution from sexual politics. Prostitution is both work and sex, and prostitutes are sexual actors who play out the drama of power and submission in sexual exchanges. In their daily lives they face violence from pimps, customers, police, and psychopaths. And criminalization makes American prostitutes even more vulnerable to these occupational hazards.

This book comes at a time when American prostitution policy has come under attack from the most established sources—judges, police, and lawmakers. All agree that the system does not work, that it has little effect on sex commerce, that it is a drain on taxpayers' money, and that it makes a mockery of the legal process. The farce is played over and over again in American criminal courts: arrest, guilty plea, fine—prostitutes move in and out of the revolving door of the criminal justice system. This book will not break the current impasse over prostitution policy in the United States. But in tracing the long history of this contested domain, I hope to open up the debate and reverse the tide of cynicism.

PART I

Policing the City,
1820–1860

I

The

Discovery of Prostitution

IN AUGUST 1823 Mayor Josiah Quincy and a posse of volunteers mounted a raid on a notorious center of vice in Boston known as the Hill. It consisted of three or four blocks in the West End of the city. The mayor's raid was the final assault in a campaign against saloons and dance halls. Throughout the month, Quincy brought twenty-three liquor license violations before police court. He was able to initiate this action under the broad licensing power the state legislature had granted him the year before. Quincy was not interested in controlling drinking per se, but rather he wanted to close down the rowdy hangouts of prostitutes, gamblers, and vagrants. The raid marked the beginning of a policy of mass arrests of prostitutes that continued throughout the fall of 1823. This campaign loaded the courts with more than a hundred cases.[1]

Although eighteenth-century Boston magistrates and ministers had complained of sexual vice in the city, it was not until the first decades of the nineteenth century that reformers "discovered" prostitution as a dangerous urban social problem and mobilized a broad segment of the population—what one might call the respectable classes—against it. They published reports on the rising tide of vice, hired city missionaries to study the problem, and organized citizens' petitions to rid their neighborhoods of disorderly houses.

In those early decades of the nineteenth century, other East Coast cities were experiencing similar urban reform pressures against public prostitution. Both New York and Philadelphia had periodic sweeps of prostitutes and raids on the haunts of vice, but they were less dramatic than the Boston mayor's frontal attack. Moreover, in those cities it took longer to develop the professional police, courts, and penal institutions necessary to implement a policy of repressing sex commerce. When put into effect, the social control machinery had the same results in every city. Places where prostitutes solicited were off-limits to respectable women, were in the least desirable neighborhoods, and were associated with crime and violence.

Why did vice in the city suddenly come to be seen as a threat to the social order? This development occurred during a period when East Coast cities were radically changing in size, neighborhood composition, and institutions. A constant flow of persons moved in and out daily. This transient population probably did increase petty crime and public prostitution, but a sea of anonymous faces also made the city *appear* less safe and less manageable. At the same time, urban reformers were creating higher expectations about order and decorum, and an emerging business elite sought to impose new standards of discipline in the workplace, the marketplace, and the streets. They were the key actors in the religious dimension of this urban reform movement, and they attacked the evils of drunkenness, licentiousness, and idleness among the working poor. In Boston the sense of alarm and urgency regarding vice and crime in the city occurred during a period when the face of the city was changing, and a particular group of reformers was instrumental in shaping its identity.

The Changing Face of the City

The 1820s was a critical decade for Bostonians: the town became a city. After years of debate and rejected proposals, the reluctant citizenry finally accepted incorporation in 1822, long after New York, Philadelphia, and Baltimore had approved a municipal form of government. With a population of about 45,000, of whom 8,000 were possible voters, a more centralized government seemed imperative. Between 1790 and 1820 Boston had become a metropolis with a diverse and rapidly growing community. In 1790 Boston had 18,000 inhabitants; the 1820 census listed 43,000;

and by 1825 the population had reached 57,000. While other cities, such as New York and Philadelphia, were actually growing at a faster rate, the impact of the population explosion may have been greater in the narrow peninsula of Boston. Surrounding mud flats and waterways had long forced new residents to cluster in densely populated areas. Beginning in the 1790s hills were cut down and coves filled in to allow more living space; however, only with the post–Civil War massive land fill projects in the Back Bay did the city expand outward.

Two sections of the city, the North End and the West End, became the most densely populated. They had the most transients and the highest concentrations of taverns and brothels. The North End, the oldest part of the city, had once been the home of the illustrious Mathers, Paul Revere, and some of the richest colonial Bostonians, but by the late eighteenth century it was already in a state of decline. It had the lowest tax base and the greatest proportion of rural migrants and foreign immigrants.[2] The West End was also in transition, but moving up. Businessmen and professionals began moving into the areas around the Hill, and on the east side elegant mansions were being built in a section that was becoming the most fashionable in Boston: Beacon Hill (still the home of Boston's upper crust). For West End residents, disorderly houses represented more than a nuisance; they were a threat to property values, a point made in a petition signed by over a hundred persons in 1820.[3]

For years citizens' complaints of disturbances on the Hill had been virtually ignored by the selectmen. Brothels, dance halls, and gambling houses operated seven days a week without interference. One observer in 1816 said that the area was infested with "drunkards, harlots, spendthrifts, and outcasts." A former head constable testified that if any officer entered one of those haunts of vice, he risked his life, for "highbinders, jailbirds, and women of the worst character inhabited the Hill and murder was committed with impunity there." He told Mayor Quincy that it would take military force to bring law and order.[4]

The constable's image of a dark underworld of crime and violence did not capture the ambiance of the Hill. A modern observer might see it as colorful area where jugglers, women of easy virtue, ballad singers, and libertines paid homage to the joys of the flesh and strollers could find places for drink, sex, and gambling that were always open. On Southac Street, considered to be the most infamous in Boston, there was a mixture of classes, races, and households. Blacks lived next door to whites; commercial establishments were adjacent to residential buildings. Nearly half the shops were groceries selling liquor. (Small groceries had the reputation for being working class hangouts—centers for raucous drinking and carousing.) Southac Street also had several dance halls, the major meeting places of prostitutes and their patrons.[5] From contemporary descriptions, the Hill resembled Hogarth's eighteenth-century working class London with its rowdy street life, nightly brawls, drunks reeling in the streets, and prostitutes calling to passersby.

For the respectable, pious citizen, the Hill was the throne of Satan. One city missionary, calling it a sink of iniquity, captured its Bacchanalian character:

Five and twenty or thirty shops are open on the Lord's day from morning to evening, and ardent spirits are retailed without restraint, while hundreds are intoxicated, and spend the holy Sabbath in frolicking and gambling, in fighting and blaspheming; and many in scenes of iniquity and debauchery too dreadful to be named.[6]

From one perspective, removing public prostitutes and closing the grog shops was part of a larger set of municipal improvements promised by Quincy. The mayor spent public funds lavishly on cleaning and widening the streets and on improving walks and waterworks. In his third mayoral address Quincy congratulated Bostonians for the growth and prosperity of their city. In only four years (1821–25) real and personal property tax revenue had risen dramatically, despite a lowered tax rate.[7]

Set against the prosperity and progress of the city, vice and crime appeared more pernicious and noxious. William Collier, an urban missionary, compared the Hill district to an "insidious serpent" in a household surrounded by opulence, literature, and "every external accomplishment." West End petitioners appealed to the same pride in the city when urging action against the Hill. They insisted that prostitution, if a necessary evil in this age and state of society, "be placed under certain regulations of law—confined to certain limits, and even licensed as has been done in certain corrupt communities, but not in Boston."[8]

An 1818 account from one of the earliest investigations of prostitution in Boston cataloged the range of sexual liaisons. Some women were dance hall pickups. Clerks, mechanics, apprentices, and captain's mates went to the dance halls, which were open from six to midnight every night except Sunday; from there women took men to their lodgings. Other women, who did not wish to mix with the multitudes in halls, had prearranged rendezvous and went directly to houses of assignation. The highest class of sex partners lived in elegant apartments in quiet neighborhoods; they were the mistresses of wealthy men. Sexual services appeared to be readily available and aboveboard transactions.[9]

Houses of ill fame were small-scale and informal settings for sex commerce. Often other tenants who were not prostitutes rented rooms in the same building. Women might trade their sexual services for noncash payment—food, rent, or clothes. In this era, there was less of a distinction between paid and kept women.

The Puritan settlers who had come to Boston in the seventeenth century put into effect strict moral codes and vigilant policing of sex. Employers monitored the behavior of servants; neighbors kept a watchful eye on each other; and courts punished all sorts of sexual offenses, from fornication to lewd flirtations. With this kind of surveillance, open bawdyhouses could not exist in the colony. A specific statute against brothelkeeping was not passed until 1672, immediately after Alice Thomas was convicted of being a common bawd for having allowed notorious persons of both sexes to congregate in her house.[10]

By the end of the eighteenth century, however, there was a general loosening of controls on sex that led to a certain toleration of bawdy-houses. Sailors who landed in Boston's bustling port had no trouble locating rowdy taverns with loose women, nor did British soldiers quartered there. Eighteenth-century libertines, celebrating the ladies of pleasure on the Hill, dubbed it Mount Whoredom.[11]

Defendants challenging the legality of Quincy's antivice campaign identified with this libertine tradition. One man caught in the brothel raids proudly stood up to the judge in police court and proclaimed his right to frequent whorehouses. Another, John Bowden, having been found guilty of selling liquors in a house noted for its lewd, wanton, and lascivious persons, took his case all the way to the state's highest court. In his appeal he challenged the law that allowed the police court to sentence to the house of correction persons found guilty of selling liquor without a license. That statute made an action criminal in Suffolk County (Boston) that was not illegal in the rest of Massachusetts. The justices of the State Supreme Judicial Court, who rejected Bowden's appeal, concluded that certain kinds of behavior were more dangerous in an urban setting. They reasoned that the indiscriminate sale of liquor could produce moral contagion, which they believed was as threatening to the well-being of a community as a cholera epidemic.[12]

Those calling for the destruction of brothels maintained that the city's growth and prosperity had its costs. A large metropolis, with its impersonality and numbers, encouraged vice. It also attracted a growing class of marginal persons—transients, chronic paupers, and criminal types—who appeared to be promoters of vice. They perceived the city as a magnet not only for the enterprising but also for the idle and vicious, and there were no longer mechanisms to remove the undesirables.

Colonial towns dealt with persons without resources and family ties by "warning" them out: officially giving them notice that they would not be supported and expelling them. After the Revolution new poor laws allowed towns routinely to ship vagrants back to their home communities. This administrative procedure became nearly impossible to carry out in a city the size of Boston with the numbers of migrants moving from country to city and from neighborhood to neighborhood.

During the first decades of the nineteenth century, increasing numbers of people were leaving New England farm communities as economic opportunities dwindled. Most of the rural migrants were single, and a significant portion were single women or widows, who posed a dual threat to city managers. Not being attached to a family who would monitor their sexual behavior, they could produce bastards the state would have to support. Because women had so few job opportunities in the preindustrial city, female transients were also considered prime candidates for prostitution.[13]

How to deal with persons on the fringes of society became a primary concern of city and town governments; the strategies they adopted would be shaped by new attitudes toward dependence and deviance. By the second decade of the century, city officials from the large East Coast cities had studied and put into effect remedies to deal with a class of wandering poor. Mayor Quincy was a key figure in two studies of pauperism in Massachusetts, one sponsored by the state legislature and the other by the Boston City Council. Both reports contained a new terminology that classified the poor into two groups. The sick, infirm, or widowed, who could not be blamed for their poverty, were the worthy, deserving, or virtuous poor. Those whose poverty was the result of indolence, sensuality, and vice belonged to the unworthy, undeserving, or vicious class of poor. Implied in these highly charged terms was a belief that the majority of poor persons were criminals or potential criminals. While serving as a municipal court judge, several years before he became mayor, Quincy had made this connection. He maintained that vice, crime, and poverty were so often found together that they were in some sense inseparable; individuals who exhibited a propensity for one vicious trait were most likely to have a propensity for other vices.[14]

In these policy debates, prostitutes were therefore not singled out as a distinct class of deviants, or treated as such; that process occurred several decades later. Prostitutes were viewed as belonging to the vicious classes: the idle, dependent, and dissolute. However, the policies that emerged during this period laid the groundwork for the response to prostitution as a gender- and class-specific crime. Most important, the criminal law applied to prostitutes in the first wave of repression defined prostitution as a status or style of life rather than as the act of selling one's sex. Workhouses and other penal institutions that came of age in this era were aimed at the potential as well as the practicing prostitute.

Courts and Penal Institutions

A document entitled *Miscellaneous Remarks on the Police of Boston,* published in 1814, had one of the earliest proposals for a strong centralized police force to control the "notoriously dissolute and inefficient members of society." According to the author, likely a town official, the city was being inundated by vagrants, beggars, and swindlers, who were preying upon the benevolent impulses of Boston's public and private charities. His proposed solution, mandatory police registration for all persons entering the city, would have required all boarding houses and hotels to report strangers.[15] This kind of police state was clearly unacceptable to Bostonians, who had rid themselves of British tyranny only a generation before. Nevertheless, by the second decade of the nineteenth century, the city had developed a set of social controls that worked through police, courts, and penal institutions.

During his five-year tenure (1823–28), Quincy instituted a series of measures to carry out his law-and-order campaign. He strengthened the constabulary by appointing a city marshal accountable only to the mayor. Both the constables and the watch—the evening patrol recruited from the citizenry—were awarded pay raises. The North End and West End were each assigned a permanent constable to patrol their streets daily. The creation of a police court in 1822 made it possible to process quickly large numbers of defendants. This nontrial court consisted of three rotating justices holding sessions five days a week. In police court cases, facts were rarely disputed; the court heard and summarily disposed of cases, and guilty outcomes were almost certain. Over 90 percent of the women brought before the court on the charge of lewdness were sentenced to three to six months' imprisonment.

In 1820 the municipal court docket showed only four cases of lewd and lascivious behavior and four prosecutions against keepers of bad houses. In 1822, in the docket of the new police court, there were just five cases of lewdness and three cases of keeping bawdyhouses for the entire year, out of 1,168 entries. In most of these cases interested parties brought the actions to court. With only one exception, the lewdness cases in the 1822 police court docket were brought by the husbands of the accused. Not a husband but a father charged one Ann Gilmore with keeping a house of ill fame because she had enticed his sixteen-year-old daughter into prostitution. Only after the next year's raid on the Hill and Quincy's initiation of a policy of repression against prostitution did prostitution become a significant part of court business. The number of prostitution cases reached three hundred a year in the mid-1820s; the prosecution rate for Boston's population would never be higher.[16]

Quincy's policy of mass arrests of prostitutes and brothelkeepers represented a radical break with the past. Throughout his years as mayor, court dockets were filled with consecutively numbered prosecutions for prostitution and brothelkeeping, many of them with the same arresting officer, evidence which suggests that there were periodic sweeps of prostitutes in vice districts.

Increased police and court activity brought about the need for facilities to keep persons who were sentenced for misdemeanors. As early as 1787 the state had empowered counties to establish penal institutions for idle and disorderly persons under the Vagabond Act, which covered rogues, vagabonds, jugglers, common pipers and fiddlers, runaways, stubborn children, common drunkards, common nightwalkers, pilferers, and persons lewd and lascivious in speech and behavior.[17] But Bostonians did not want to have their tax monies spent on such facilities. Finally, in 1822 they approved funds for a workhouse (the House of Industry) to be built at the edge of the city at South Boston Neck. A year later a prison (the House of Correction) was placed in a section of the new courthouse, and the city council set aside funds for building a larger facility.

These two institutions gave city managers and private charitable organizations a powerful weapon for disciplining the poor who refused to live by middle-class codes of hard work, chastity, and sobriety. It would have a profound effect on women involved in nonmarital sexual relationships. Unwed mothers who applied for public charity now faced confinement in the workhouse. This deterred many women from seeking support or reporting their illegitimate offspring. The Boston House of Industry listed only 9 cases of bastardy in a year when the Philadelphia overseers of the poor, who dispensed only direct payments to unwed mothers, noted 269 cases. The Philadelphia overseers concluded that more punitive measures were needed to discourage departures from virtue.[18]

In England the revised Poor Law, approved in 1834, had the same punitive impact. Previously, unwed mothers had been able to sue alleged fathers for child support, but the new law made it more difficult for women to bring paternity charges. It also forced unwed mothers into dependence upon church relief, since all monies collected for bastard children were administered through church treasuries. British poverty commissions, like their counterparts in the United States, insisted that the system of benefits to unwed mothers was an inducement for women to have illegitimate intercourse; under the new law penalties for unwed motherhood were increased. As was true of their American sisters, poor English women with bastard children and without family support or private charity were forced into workhouses.[19]

Confining poor women to institutions shifted the onus of responsibility for nonmarital sex exclusively to the female gender. This policy linked women's sexual nonconformity to criminality in two ways. First, some unwed mothers faced with the prospect of the county workhouse tended to seek the refuge of the brothel. Second, unwed mothers were often housed in the same institutions as prostitutes and other minor criminals. (Boston committed first juvenile prostitutes and soon after professional prostitutes to the workhouse to ease overflow in the house of correction.)

For women who practiced prostitution either as a full-time trade or occasionally, the threat of arrest meant being officially labeled as a public woman and having the stigma of a convict's record. Women hauled into police court became public prostitutes, known to constables, judges, and their own neighbors.

The mayor had no illusions about eradicating prostitution in the city. His aim was to drive it underground, or, as he put it, to make it skulk around like filth in drains. But this was no easy task in cities where bawdyhouses had become institutions and where profits were to be made from the prostitution trade by liquor interests and surrounding shops. Public officials, the judiciary, and urban reformers considered prostitutes, through their visibility and solicitation, to be active agents in the spread of vice. These women were viewed as recruiters of all classes and ages: single men and married men, apprentices and their masters, the innocent and the licentious, the pious and the irreligious. The images of pollution and contagion that pervaded the reform literature of this era reveal the anxiety of reformers over their inability to contain the evil effects of prostitution. The use of courts and prisons was one facet of the strategy to drive prostitution underground. Another strategy, promoted by urban reformers, was to infiltrate vice districts through missionary work with hopes of coverting the sinner and, more important, of mobilizing the respectable poor to cast out vice from their neighborhoods.

The Benevolent Army

Quincy's policy of suppression against the Hill district was preceded by six years of religious agitation. These moral activists paved the way for law enforcers to close down public resorts for illicit sex, gambling, and drink. Though Quincy himself came from an aristocratic old Boston family, his supporters were from a new elite composed of businessmen and professionals. The business community reaped the greatest rewards from the mayor's civic improvements of streets and sewers and from his moral cleanup. These were "the men of property and business" who, Quincy believed, were best suited to investigate claims and discipline lawbreakers. Over the next decades the reformers would dominate city politics and the boards of public and private institutions.

This elite organized in 1816 the Boston Society for the Moral and Religious Instruction of the Poor, the first of many evangelical reform societies that sprang up during a period of religious activism in American cities. Its officers were middle class, self-made men: manufacturers, publishers, doctors and lawyers, and shopkeepers. In their writings on sexual immorality, they wove together moral and economic consequences. For example, the society estimated in one report that if two thousand prostitutes were each paid $1.25 a day, then wage earners were spending

$912,500 a year for licentiousness. They reasoned that to pay for moral depravity, individuals would be tempted to defraud their employers, creditors, and families. One concerned father wrote to the *Boston Gazette,* cautioning other parents to guard the moral welfare of their sons to insure their financial future: "What will it avail for us to accumulate property sufficient to establish them to settle them in life if during the period of their minority, they are exposed to the artful machinations of the profligate?"[20] For these religious reformers, prostitution not only condemned the outcast woman and her companions to a life without salvation, but it also allowed sons to squander the fortunes of their fathers and undermined the discipline of the worker.

Reformers were undeniably motivated by evangelical impulses to rescue abandoned sinners, but mixed in were their notions of law and order and fear of the lower classes. Missionaries spoke with great compassion about the plight of prostitutes, often entreating them to find some means of escape from a life of sin. The Female Missionary Society found the ideal solution, a quiet retreat where their fallen sisters would find peace and redemption. The Penitent Females' Refuge, founded in 1822, was a secluded refuge, with all the earmarks of a prison—walls, a mandatory term, and a strict regimen. Prostitutes who came there were removed from temptations, but they were also isolated from their communities, treated as moral lepers who could spread their sinfulness to others.

The first surveys of prostitution in Boston were done by religious reformers who, in trying to determine the extent of vice, were really seeking to establish the lines between respectable and unrespectable, virtuous and vicious, and saved and sinner. Dudley Rosseter and James Davis, the missionaries hired by the Female Missionary Society, suggested that there were incredible numbers of prostitutes in Boston—over 2,000 in 1817. That would be one out of every fourteen women between the ages of twenty and forty-five. However, this figure included nonmarital sexual relationships that today would not be considered prostitution.

The chief of police of metropolitan London produced a study of crime that used a similarly broad definition of prostitution. Patrick Colquhoun, in his *Treatise on the Police of the Metropolis,* reported that there were 50,000 "unfortunate females" who made their living wholly or chiefly by prostitution. Since metropolitan London had less than a million inhabitants in 1796, the year the report was published, Colquhoun's numbers translated into an extraordinarily high ratio. Like Rosseter's and Davis's prostitutes, Colquhoun's included all types of "lewd and immoral women." Many women cohabiting with men were not mistresses but common-law wives; these couples could not sanctify their relationships because few among the lower classes could afford divorce in England.[21]

In linking nonmarital sex with prostitution, both Colquhoun and the Boston missionaries hoped to give all illicit sex a criminal aspect. They sought to divide the upstanding workingman's family from the rough urban poor. In Boston the missionaries descended upon the city's poor neighborhoods like a swarm of locusts.

The first mission in the Hill district was a former beer house on Southac Street. Part of it was set aside for prayer meetings and religious services. John Gamble, a recently arrived Irish Presbyterian minister, became the resident minister; several respectable workingmen rented other rooms in the house. City missionaries began making neighborhood rounds; sabbath schools and mission houses attempted to become alternative institutions to the brothel and saloon. These Christian foot soldiers were not always received hospitably by the sinful brood that they were trying to convert. James Davis told of an incident wherein a brothelkeeper threatened to break his neck if he ever came again. At the Southac Mission, several neighborhood residents threw a large rock through the window, nearly hitting the minister. Yet, unlike the next generation of evangelicals, who brought their message to hostile Irish Catholic enclaves, this first wave of urban missionaries were not in an enemy camp.

Though the urban poor lacked religious education and did not attend church, they belonged to an Anglo-Protestant tradition. Only a genera-tion earlier, many of these so-called heathen had lived in rural communi-ties, where the church was the dominant social institution. One brothel owner who was approached by a team of missionaries refused to host prayers in his house, saying that it would be unsuitable; yet he claimed that he highly approved of the mission house and was willing to subscribe three or four dollars in support of the minister. When asked if he expected to pay this from the fruits of a house unsuitable for prayer, he admitted to a pang of conscience, but defended himself by saying that there had always been and always would be such houses.[22]

William Jenks, who became the guiding force in the City Missionary Society, reported in his diary that missionaries were successful in rousing local residents to protest against sexual immorality. One incident he describes occurred after he had been called to the funeral of Nancy

George, a woman who had been living with a man who was not her husband. During the service, Jenks exhorted those assembled to uphold the holy institution of marriage and warned of God's revenge against sinners. Jenks noted the next day that some had understood his message; a mob assembled and destroyed several houses of assignation in the same area.[23]

The Bawdyhouse Riots

Prostitution policy begins in neighborhoods, then and probably now. Two years after Quincy's raid, a large-scale mob action against brothels in the North End took place. It was organized and orchestrated by neighborhood residents without the knowledge or support of the municipal officials.

The Beehive was a three-story, cone-shaped building on North Margin Street, owned by a widow, Marm Cooper, who lived with her two daughters and a rotating population of prostitutes and their patrons. It was the first brothel to be attacked by the mob, which grew to 300 persons and rioted for three nights. The men in the mob wore blackface and carried pitchforks, tin pans, drums, and whistles. The rioters had as targets specific brothels and were well enough organized to outwit the mayor and constables who twice tried to outflank them. A great deal of property was destroyed, but no persons were injured.

Newspapers treated the rioters humorously. Featherbeds that had been ripped open and hurled out windows "bestrode the air like gossamer," in the *Courier*'s synopsis. The staid *Centennial* was more indignant, referring to the riot as "unmanly proceedings" and to the victims of the moral onslaught as the "frail sisterhood." But the rioters took themselves seriously and went about systematically destroying several brothels in the same vicinity, despite the mayor's curfew and appeal for order.[24]

Who were the faces in the crowd? Unfortunately, no overall picture of the rioters exists and only nineteen persons connected with the riot appear in the court records. What all the rioters had in common was residence in the North End; some lived within earshot of the brothels.

They were artisans, small tradesmen, and laborers—for example, coopers, housewrights, mariners, and truckmen. Hosea Sargent, who was charged with two counts of disorderly behavior for two consecutive nights of rioting, was a victualer who lived and worked in the North End. A defendant in another trial was a merchant who had refused to help the mayor quell the disturbance.[25]

These men were not at the lower end of the social scale: all made bail, which ranged between three hundred and five hundred dollars. It is even more indicative of their status that the defendants were represented by counsel and appealed their case to the State Supreme Judicial Court on both substantive and procedural issues. From the court testimony, it is clear that the rioters perceived themselves as public servants acting against immoral and criminal conduct; they felt that the law's delay and failure to prosecute prostitutes and brothelkeepers justified their actions.[26]

No doubt they had noticed that the mayor's efforts were concentrated in the West End, rather than in their neighborhood. The North End had seen an exodus of respectable residents over the previous twenty years. Churches had moved to more fashionable areas and property values had dropped. A contemporary editorial in *Bowen's Newsletter* asked why inhabitants of the northern part of the city seemed to show so little interest in improving their streets and architecture, noting that the principal streets were long neglected.[27]

For those trying to maintain respectability in a declining neighborhood, the mere presence of brothels must have been a source of anxiety. A saloon owner, for example, might lose his liquor license if a prostitute was found hanging about. Or a respectable working man might fear that his own wife or daughter might be mistaken for an immoral woman by a potential customer or by a policeman. Prostitution was becoming known as criminal activity, a fact that would have a strong impact on creating norms and boundaries between respectable and unrespectable. Individual behavior was not the only issue as places of leisure, streets, and entire neighborhoods became identified with "immoral" activities.

Over the next forty years, mob actions against brothels took place in many industrializing cities. Bawdyhouse riots in Portland, Maine; Cincinnati; St. Louis; and Minneapolis had common features. First, the riots were local, and, with the exception of Portland's, nonviolent. Second, they were in cities where prostitution had not yet been established in particular locales or zones in the city. Finally, they were in cities where a prostitution policy had not yet been settled.[28]

Zones of Immorality

The municipal campaign against vice in Boston in these early decades of the nineteenth century was the beginning of a process of demarcating the social landscape of American cities. It pushed sex commerce to the fringes of the cityscape, both geographically and in relation to other legitimate businesses or respectable neighborhoods. In a sense it made the visible invisible. The process would occur over and over again in other cities, though the strategies and outcomes would differ according to the power of competing interests: who profited from prostitution, how institutionalized it had become, and what the earlier traditions toward policing sexual morality had been.

In New York and Philadelphia, municipal campaigns against prostitution emerged in the 1830s and 1840s. In New Orleans in the 1850s, a reform slate of small businessmen won municipal elections with an antiprostitution platform. However, once in power, they could not make any headway against the powerful prostitution interests—landlords with ties to the police and influential merchants who profited from prostitution trade. Nor could they keep the support of the working class, who wanted to drive prostitution from their neighborhoods but did not want to carry the tax burden for more law enforcement.[29]

In frontier towns across America, aldermen were quick to develop a prostitution policy that isolated sex commerce from the social life of cities. Prostitutes in Virginia City, Nevada, had been included in social events and integrated into the life of the city in the very early years of the Comstock Lode. But it did not take long before a series of licensing ordinances was passed, restricting prostitution activities to specific areas. Soon after, vagrancy and disorderly conduct laws required prostitutes to cover windows and banned provocative clothing. As was true in Boston, the antiprostitution forces consisted of small businessmen opposed to houses of ill fame in commercial districts and working class people residing near bawdyhouses and concerned about their neighborhoods. According to one historian, San Francisco's prostitutes in the frontier years (1849–52) were respected and admired, politely mentioned in the press, and welcomed to meetings at the schoolhouse. But in the next decade, as more families moved to San Francisco, law enforcers designated a zone for prostitutes, the Barbary Coast. Respectable folk would not have to be offended by a prostitute's soliciting or by the presence of brothels near their homes. Police ignored discreet high class brothels in residential neighborhoods; but contacts with prostitutes had to be made on the sly because the prostitute, even the elegant courtesan or madam, was beyond the social pale.[30]

Boston was exceptional in that urban reformers during the Quincy years were able to consolidate their power in city government and gain wide community support for a policy of repression against vice. But in other respects Boston was typical of urban metropolises: police and courts did not devote resources to the suppression of prostitution unless pressured from the outside. They merely sought to keep the trade beyond the view of respectable folk.

Yet the neighborhoods of vice were close enough to the urban centers that businessmen or male visitors to the city could easily stray five or ten city blocks off the beaten track to find them. Boston's Ann Street was a ten-minute walk from the banking and commercial district; New York's Five Points was sandwiched between the wharf area and the commercial center; Philadelphia's St. Mary's Street was situated near the waterfront but still close to the city's center.

Prostitution was a fact of everyday life and poverty in working class communities, not considered a moral outrage or an offense to one's sensibilities as it was for middle class residents. But a woman who went out on the town—who became a known prostitute—brought shame to a working class family, and she often sought the anonymity of other cities.[31] The possibility of arrest and a public record—even if it were remote—turned the most casual and informal bartering of sex into a risky venture. Just appearing in the court docket and being subject to public investigation and exposure damaged a woman's reputation. Massive raids against houses of prostitution were uncommon in American cities, but prostitution cases were a daily part of court business. Once a woman had a public record, she found it harder to cross social boundaries between respectability and disrepute, legal and illegal activities, and public and private identities.

The prostitution trade became more and more concentrated in particular districts or notorious streets in metropolitan American cities. A prostitute's soliciting in a neighborhood signaled its decline and social deterioration. Women walking alone at night on streets like Ann Street risked their reputation and their safety. The streets themselves became ways of identifying prostitutes who lived and worked in these districts. Prostitutes were not quarantined to specific locales or houses as they were through government regulation in European cities, but American public officials had the same goals of insulating the public from the spectacle of vice. Driving prostitution underground in effect meant pushing the open trade to the outer fringes of city life and into the neighborhoods of the poor and ethnic minorities.

2

Crime,

Justice, and Reform

STUDIES of prostitution have tended to classify the prostitution policy of a nation into one of two classes: intolerant and tolerant systems. They have placed the American system of criminal penalties among the most intolerant and European countries with licensed prostitution among the most tolerant.[1] Recent studies of regulated prostitution in nineteenth-century European countries, such as France, Italy, and England, however, reveal that this is a false dichotomy. Legalized prostitution, these studies maintain, was not an expression of society's acceptance of prostitution but instead epitomized a policy of isolation and stigma toward the prostitute.[2] Rather than being either intolerant or tolerant systems, prostitution policies represented variant forms of controlling or segregating prostitution—making it invisible. Given this broad framework, regulation and criminal sanctions are not polar opposites but are quite similar in intent and consequences.

The real differences between legal and illegal prostitution can be seen in the kinds of markets and institutions that emerged in sex commerce. Contrary to what we might expect, the American response to prostitution produced a more open and flexible prostitution market than did European regulation. Regulating prostitution gave authorities greater power to restrict the businesses where prostitution trade could occur, to circumscribe the hours when women could solicit, and to determine who the managers of prostitutes could be. Begun in 1810, the Paris morals police implemented increasingly strict regulations that prohibited prostitutes from frequenting cafes, taverns, or theaters—traditional meeting places for prostitutes and their customers. Nor could the women display themselves as merchandise: all windows in supervised brothels had to be closed.

Not only the players but also the play of erotic life could be directed and supervised by the morals police. According to Alain Corbin, French officials sought to sever prostitution from the pleasurable: "The brothel under police supervision was the antithesis of the house of clandestine debauchery. . . . Far from being this sort of school for pleasure, the brothel must act as a safety valve without the temptation of erotic refinements."[3]

In contrast, sex commerce in American cities offered a range of erotic services in a range of settings. Criminal sanctions seemed to have given prostitution a seductive quality, the aura of forbidden fruit, that could not be gratified by state-supervised brothels. Some brothelkeepers even used the illegality of prostitution as a market strategy. They required customers to have special admission cards and represented their establishments as discreet exclusive clubs for pleasure seekers. Others openly advertised sexual services, particularly in cities where men stayed briefly in transient occupations or for conventions. In Louisville, for example, the Grand Old Army Reunion rated an entertainment guide, which had five pages listing theaters, parks, and operas and twenty-three featuring ads for brothels.[4]

Brothelkeepers who kept their establishments free from violence, theft, and general rowdiness may have had little interference from police. In some cities keepers actually paid for this protection, to carry on business as usual. While laws forbade prostitutes from any public soliciting, in practice they could be found seeking out trade in the gathering places that were off-limits to their French counterparts: cafes, saloons, and theaters.

Prostitution was linked to other urban entertainments. Most gambling places and many saloons had back rooms suitable for assignations, and dance halls were meeting places for prostitutes and their customers. Not only the third tier in theaters—a well-documented rendezvous for prostitutes and their customers—but also small vaudeville halls with bawdy shows (some featuring nude dancers) attracted prospective buyers of sexual services. These were places where race and class taboos could be broken—erotic zones that attracted pleasure seekers and provided men who were concerned about their reputations with a place to live out their secret lives.

As an administrative procedure, the European system of regulating prostitution was more efficient than the American system of using criminal courts. With regulation, police had sweeping powers to intervene in the lives of women suspected of being prostitutes and to curtail their sphere of operation. Nor was it necessary for the state to prove beyond a reasonable doubt that a woman was a prostitute before registering her. Under a criminalized prostitution policy, arrests and prosecutions, when carried out, were cumbersome, time-consuming, and expensive. Furthermore, trials and their outcomes were unpredictable; sometimes defendants jumped bail, used the law's delay to their advantage, or played upon the sympathies of juries to win acquittals.

Nevertheless, the use of criminal sanctions to control prostitution created a peculiar set of conditions under which sex commerce in American cities evolved. The laws themselves allowed law enforcers extraordinary discretion, since in nearly all American cities during the nineteenth century no statutory proscription existed against prostitution per se. Vagrancy or disorderly conduct charges were generally applied to women who publicly sold sexual services. The fluidity of the criminal justice system produced extreme stratification in the prostitution class system. The streetwalker—the most visible practitioner and most vulnerable to police harassment—was at the bottom of the prostitution hierarchy. The prostitute working a fashionable brothel and least vulnerable to police control was at the top. Criminalization also widened the gap between the peddlers of sex (prostitutes) and their managers (brothelkeepers), who were rarely touched by the legal hook of the state.

The dissociation between law and practice led to ideological tugs of war between police, who often adopted a policy of unofficial regulation of prostitution (keeping prostitution in specific areas and at certain levels), and those who sought strict enforcement of laws and a fairer application of them to both sexes and all classes. During the first half of the nineteenth century, control strategies and legal conventions were not yet fixed. Consequently, prostitution policy was highly sensitive to pressures from reformers and neighborhood groups. Antiprostitution agitation was heightened by reaction to waves of immigration and the involvement of poor immigrants in sex commerce. Within prostitution policy all the contradictions in class and gender politics were aired over and over again in the public discourse.

More than any other category of criminal behavior, illicit sexuality is the paradigm case to demonstrate the degree to which criminal facts are social facts. The rises in rates of prostitution-related crime over the last century and a half mark the points at which prostitution surfaced on the political agenda, and the dips in arrest rates show when the public interest waned. In addition, what constituted a prostitution offense and who was charged were determined by informal rules and procedures, not by statutes. American cities in the nineteenth century varied in both the kind and degree of controls they applied to prostitution. Yet certain conventions in prostitution policy were more or less universal: (1) the laws governing sex commerce formed boundaries between public and private sexual nonconformity, between peddlers of sex and their managers, and between brothelkeepers and their landlords; and (2) the policing of prostitution had gender and class biases.

From Indoor to Outdoor Sex Crime

In Boston norms governing the criminal justice system's view of prostitution took shape in the first decades of the nineteenth century. Most important, law enforcers shifted their interest from indoor, or private, to outdoor, or public, chastity offenses, which in turn institutionalized the class and gender biases within the policing of sex.

The regulation of private morals had been a major concern of colonial courts, particularly in Massachusetts. Even though, compared with earlier tribunals, eighteenth-century courts were less vigorous in their pursuit of fornicators and adulterers and more lenient in punishments meted out to them, significant numbers of these cases continued to appear in the dockets. But in the decades after the Revolution, prosecutions for sexual misconduct mainly dealt with paternity suits and child support. Premarital pregnancy became an administrative or financial issue for the courts. Fornication, previously one of the major crimes prosecuted in the courts of sessions, dropped to insignificant levels—an average of five cases a year between 1790 and 1820.[5]

Cases of fornication in urban courts often involved issues other than sex outside of marriage, often interracial sex. From the daily accounts of police court in Boston newspapers, it seems that both men and women were brought before the court and charged with fornication when nonmarital sex involved an interracial couple. A typical example reported in the *Boston Daily Bee* was the case against Samuel White, a "dyed in the

31

wool Ethiopian," and Susan Wentworth, a "delicate snow-white female."
Both were charged with "cohabitation, amalgamation and several other
tions" and sent to the house of correction for twelve months.[6]

With the growth of the city and in the numbers of its transients it was
not possible to control private, discreet liaisons. The city provided couples
having illicit affairs with a veil of protection from both informal and
formal systems of control. Church fathers could not admonish transgres-
sors who were not church members; neither could keepers of virtue keep
track of moral offenders where neighbors no longer knew each other.

The shift of official interest from private to public illicit sexuality
mirrored changes in the priorities of urban law enforcers. Policemen and
municipal court judges were coping with a quantity of disorder—thefts,
riots, and assaults—that strained the resources of city budgets. Those
policing the city were forced to concentrate on safety in the streets and
the appearance of order and decorum in the business districts and respectable neighborhoods. A prostitute's soliciting or a brothelkeeper's beckon-
ing to a passerby might interfere with the flow of traffic in the shopping
area or bring the angry protests of property owners. Generally, nineteenth-century law enforcers adopted a policy of maintenance in regard
to chastity crime. Depending on individual mayors, police chiefs, and
social conditions, maintenance could mean driving prostitution underground, confining it to specific areas, or prosecuting only its most disorderly or lowly haunts.

No new laws were passed in Massachusetts in response to this shift in
concern from private to public sex crimes. Statutes applied to prostitutes—proscribing lewdness and nightwalking—dated back to the colonial period and became part of the Massachusetts legal code after the
Revolution. But they had had a different meaning and application earlier.
Lewdness might have referred to any gross sexual misconduct or display.
Nightwalking, the offense most prostitutes were charged with, had been
part of the general law (the 1787 Vagabond Act mentioned earlier), which
covered a range of marginal types: fiddlers, peddlers, and many others
who in their speech or behavior disturbed the public peace. No mention
of solicitation by prostitutes appeared in the text.[7] Prostitution in effect
represented a deviant status and not a specific act.

The identification of prostitution with vagrancy had its roots in the
British common law. Since the fifteenth century, prostitutes had been
treated as a species of vagrant easily prosecuted and convicted in British
local courts. New World colonies adopted the same definitions and

practices. Clearly there were advantages to a law that could be applied so generally to different types of persons living on the social fringes. An individual arrested for vagrancy was charged with *being* a vagrant and posing a *potential* threat to the community. In the case of a prostitute, no proof was needed of the sale or offering of sexual services. The nightwalking statutes *assumed* that a woman on the streets after dark intended to solicit.[8] Many states even today use vagrancy laws, rather than solicitation or prostitution laws, to prosecute prostitutes; a practice that attests to the usefulness of such a legislative strategy.

By the nineteenth century, England had restricted vagrancy to illegal conduct rather than status and had instituted separate prostitution statutes. These laws required that a woman have loitered in a public place and annoyed the inhabitants or passengers before she could be arrested as a common prostitute. The law was therefore dependent on the public view of prostitution; a businessman, visitor, or resident in a community had to testify that he or she had been offended by a prostitute's soliciting. Though magistrates might ignore this clause, London streetwalkers appeared to be less subject to harassment than were their counterparts in American cities. In comparison, American statutes gave police and prosecutors wide latitude to control sex commerce.[9]

Gender, Class, and Race

When public lewdness and nightwalking became exclusively chastity crimes, a gender and class bias that had always existed in the treatment of moral offenders became official policy. Whereas eighteenth-century gentleman fornicators had been fined, while their female partners had been whipped, nineteenth-century gentlemen of vice were completely ignored by urban courts. By the 1830s prostitution openly practiced in the haunts of upper class men—theaters, oyster bars, and genteel brothels—was not disturbed by those policing the city. Abolitionist William Lloyd Garrison excoriated the toleration of vice after being escorted by a Boston policeman on a guided tour of Tremont Theater's third tier.[10]

When police conducted vice raids, they sought out lowly dance halls and disorderly houses in high-crime areas. Police were mainly concerned with protecting patrons from theft and assault. Brothels were looked upon by police as establishments where seedy characters and criminal types congregated, places not substantially different from gambling houses or rowdy taverns. The task of law enforcers was to maintain safety and order for the city's respectable citizens, not to regulate sexual morals.

Laws against lewdness and nightwalking made no reference to gender. In theory, a man or a woman could be charged with either crime, and in the early years of the nineteenth century men represented about one-fourth of all defendants in public lewdness cases. In 1826, a year in which chastity offenses dominated the lower courts, there were 213 cases of lewdness and nightwalking; 26 percent involved men. The 1830 figure was slightly higher, but in 1840 fewer than 15 percent of the patrons of vice were tried. By 1850, no men at all were prosecuted for either crime.[11]

Outcomes and penalties revealed even greater discrimination in favor of men. Customers of prostitutes had a lower conviction rate than the women they patronized. Many cases were dropped before trial. Of those men found guilty, more were fined than imprisoned. Only 22.4 percent of male chastity offenders (not including brothelkeepers) were sent to the house of correction in Boston, compared with 71 percent of women. The few men who were sentenced for lewdness tended to be charged with other crimes, such as drunkenness and vagrancy. As early as 1826, court docket entries give some evidence that male chastity offenders, most probably gentlemen, were being protected. In two cases where a defendant was found guilty and fined, no names were printed in the docket book.[12]

With the exception of brothelkeeping, prostitution offenses came to be identified with the female sex in the first half of the nineteenth century. Edward Savage, a policeman who joined the Boston force in the 1850s and became chief in 1871, remarked that there was no such thing as a male nightwalker and there had not been for years.[13] The decline in prosecutions of men formalized the prevailing norms in nonmarital sexual encounters, that women and men had different standards of accountability and that only women should suffer the adverse social consequences and public degradation.

In Boston the police court docket of July 23, 1830, lists a raid of brothels in which nine men and fourteen women were charged. All the men were fined four dollars, but the women received four to five months in the house of correction. An 1842 descent on the haunts of vice on Ann and Richmond Streets (near the site of the notorious Beehive Riot) netted thirty or forty individuals. Local newspapers reported that seventeen persons were sent to the house of correction for four months each and seventeen were fined four dollars apiece. No breakdown of penalty by gender was necessary; readers understood the rules of the game.[14]

An 1866 case appealed to the Maine Supreme Court clarified the gender-specific character of a prostitution offense. The chief justice defined a prostitute as

a female given to indiscriminate lewdness for gain. In its most general sense, prostitution is the setting oneself to sale, or of devoting to infamous purposes what is in one's power. In its more restrictive sense, it is the practice of a female offering her body to an indiscriminate intercourse with men, the common lewdness of a female.[15]

The high court judge had both declared prostitution to be a female offense and codified certain assumptions about sex commerce: that women were the initiators in prostitution exchanges and that *female* promiscuity was linked to a criminal enterprise.

On the surface, prostitution arrests might appear to have been random. A prostitute happened to be on the street at the very moment police were rounding up ladies of the night, or a women in a brothel might be arrested if a fight erupted. But in actuality, the results were not haphazard and were fairly predictable. Police directed most of their energies toward the most conspicuous forms of prostitution and concentrated on the areas with clusters of brothels. The working class, the most recent immigrants, and blacks tended to live in these areas, and prostitutes from these backgrounds were more likely to be on the street or in the roughest establishments. Class, ethnicity, and race were spokes in the wheel of discretionary justice.

At midcentury, Irish prostitutes made up the bulk of women charged and convicted in the East Coast cities of Boston, New York, and Philadelphia. Prostitution districts existed in the Irish sections, which had the lowest standard of living and the highest crime rates. Similarly, in the smaller city of St. Paul, the Irish and Scandinavians (that city's major immigrant groups) were overrepresented in the prostitution arrest statistics.[16]

Race was a key factor in the arrests of prostitutes in certain cities. For example, in Austin, Texas, over three-fourths of the women charged were black. But these skewed statistics also reflected the socioeconomic position of black prostitutes. They belonged to the class of prostitute most vulnerable to arrest; they tended to be alley prostitutes, streetwalkers, or women living in ramshackle cribs.[17] Prejudice against racial and ethnic minorities was and still is a factor in the deployment of justice, from arrest to conviction. Yet it is almost impossible to distinguish the effects of race from those of class.[18]

Only in rare instances was race itself a separate issue. Such was the case in the 1860s and 1870s when California created special laws aimed at Chinese prostitutes and brothelkeepers. During this period, San Francisco police arrested Chinese prostitutes but ignored prostitution when other ethnic groups were involved. Race also was the overriding factor when law enforcers singled out racially mixed brothels in New Orleans in the 1850s; black madams who violated racial taboos were easy targets. But here again the effects of race and class are difficult to disentangle since these brothels were more likely to be of the lowest grade.[19]

The class nature of prostitution crime demarcated the lines within the prostitution trade in a way that did not happen in societies with regulated prostitution. Whether a prostitute could ply her trade indoors or outdoors, in protected houses or crude shelter, reflected a prostitute's income and status, and determined her ability to avoid arrest.

Two Levels of Justice

Discretion in the legal system produced different treatment for female and male sex offenders and for streetwalkers and genteel prostitutes. It also created distinct sets of procedures for those behind the scenes of the prostitution trade.

In practice, the relationship between prostitution and brothelkeeping are symbiotic, but the criminal law treats them differently. Prostitution cases were some of the earliest examples of the sort of routine justice that has become standard in today's urban courts. Conviction rates for prostitution crimes in Boston during the first half of the nineteenth century ranged from 80 to 90 percent, which is extraordinary compared with the 65 percent rate for all crimes. Furthermore, few prostitution cases were appealed and almost none were dropped before trial. However, it is important to remember that these figures relate only to those caught in the web of the criminal justice system—the most visible and vulnerable. The kept mistress or the refined prostitute in a genteel house rarely appeared in the prisoner's box.[20]

Brothelkeeping in the early nineteenth century was the business of municipal courts (the equivalent of today's superior courts), even though the police court had jurisdiction. The prosecution of keepers therefore required a greater commitment of the state's resources than did trials of prostitutes in police court. To try a case in municipal court, county prosecutors had to obtain a grand jury indictment, which not only extended the duration of a case but also increased the chances that charges might be dropped before trial. Moreover, cases in the higher court were almost always tried by a jury. Few brothelkeepers were brought to trial or sentenced compared with the high percentages of prostitutes in the first half of the nineteenth century (see figure 2.1). In the case of brothelkeeping, defendants had a much higher chance of acquittal from a jury of their peers than did prostitutes before a police court judge.

FIGURE 2.1

Commitments to House of Correction, 1823–61,
per 100,000 of the Population Aged 15–50

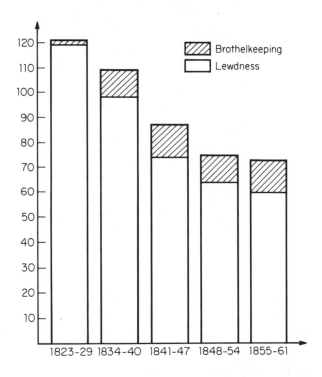

SOURCE: Register of Inmates, Boston House of Correction and House of Industry, 1858–65.

Outcomes of brothelkeeping cases reflected the difference between the two courts. In the first half of the nineteenth century, conviction rates for brothelkeepers averaged 57 percent. This difference was the result not of acquittals, since only a small percentage of keepers were found not guilty, but rather of the number of cases never reaching the trial stage. While some of these nonresolved outcomes represented a defendant's leaving town—a default—the majority reflected a district attorney's decision not to prosecute. Cases either were not prosecuted or were left on file— indications of prosecutorial discretion. These decisions probably reflected a prosecutor's realism about a jury's willingness to convict. They also mirrored the court's ambivalent attitude toward the managers and proprietors of brothels.

In these early years, when sex commerce was not highly organized, those charged with keeping were not necessarily managing a house, nor did they own a prostitute's labor. Often they were collecting rents, albeit high ones. One newspaper referred to brothelkeepers arrested during a raid as proprietors, the implication being that they were owners or at least the main lessees of a house.[21] Prosecution of keepers raised sensitive issues about those who profited from prostitution in general: Were landlords different from the furniture sellers, wine dealers, or dressmakers who did business with prostitutes?

In some sense early brothelkeeping cases resembled what we today call white-collar crime, and there is some evidence that the court viewed them that way. Brothelkeeping was an offense with many unresolved cases and rarely carried a prison term, both characteristics of white-collar crime. In fact, before 1842 almost no keepers were tried or convicted (see figure 2.2). An account of a police court trial in the *Boston Daily Bee* illustrates how institutionalized the different treatments for prostitute and keeper were. Fanny German and Mary McQuade were arrested in a dance cellar on Ann Street. McQuade was the renter or keeper of the establishment that the *Bee* called the "worst hole on Ann Street." Pronouncing them both guilty, the judge sentenced German to the house of correction, but fined McQuade four dollars.[22] Even though McQuade was tried in police court, and not charged with nightwalking, she was still treated as a keeper—fined rather than imprisoned—which suggests that in this period fines were the legal convention for keepers, even those of the worst sort.

That law enforcers virtually ignored the brothelkeeper is not surprising in light of prostitution policy in the years after the crackdown of the

FIGURE 2.2

Prosecutions for chastity offenses 1822–50, in absolute numbers

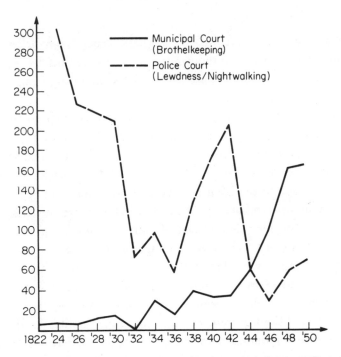

SOURCE: Boston Police Court Dockets, 1822–50; and Boston Municipal Court Dockets, 1822–50.

1820s. Policemen on the beat were concerned with keeping prostitution from becoming too visible and noxious rather than eliminating it or driving it underground as Mayor Quincy had attempted. Immediately after Quincy left office, the number of prostitution cases plummeted. Although periodic crackdowns were common, all-out assaults on the vice trade were extremely rare. Once the policy of maintenance had been established, to put prostitution on the political agenda would require intense public pressure. Pressures did build, until the mid-nineteenth century witnessed a full-scale war against prostitution in Boston. During that time a public debate on prostitution emerged, many new laws governing prostitution were passed, and a professional police began an all-out assault on the brothel district. Most important, law enforcers turned their attention to the keepers of brothels. Brothelkeeping cases soared while nightwalking cases actually declined, a dramatic reversal that would never again occur (see figure 2.2).

The Reform Agenda

More than any other factor, what set this period apart from earlier decades in Boston was the arrival of thousands of Irish immigrants fleeing famine. The small foreign population had been steadily increasing from the 1820s onward, but during the late 1840s Boston experienced its first large wave of immigration. Between 1845 and 1850 Boston's foreign-born population increased from 24 to 34 percent of the city's population; by 1855 foreign-born families outnumbered native-born families and comprised 53 percent of the city's residents. The massive influx of Irish placed a strain on existing housing, on the labor market, and on pauper and penal institutions. Although city officials, public and private welfare agencies, and the popular press had long complained of laxity in morals and rising levels of crime and poverty, the arrival of so many immigrants at once lent an intensity and urgency to these issues.[23]

The 1840s and 1850s were also a period of reform ferment. All kinds of movements to eradicate age-old evils and to offer radical alternatives sprung up: abolitionism, temperance, feminism, popular health movements, utopian communities, and antiprostitution. Underlying the fervor for reform was a millennialist current in evangelical religious activity that dynamic preachers and revivals spread throughout New England. Those who called for the perfection of mankind on earth perceived all illicit sexuality as an evil to be publicly condemned. Mass meetings protesting sexual vice, such as one held in Faneuil Hall in 1846, were filled to capacity.[24]

This tide helped a reformist slate capture the majority of the state legislature, and reform advocate Josiah Quincy, Jr., son of the former mayor, was elected mayor in 1846. Quincy the younger came to office with far more expectations than his father had had twenty years earlier. Quincy senior crusaded against vice yet never believed that the city could rid itself of prostitution, gambling, or saloons. Quincy junior and his supporters had grander goals (or illusions) about eliminating crime and vice in the city.[25]

During the following years, reformers greatly extended the power of the state to intervene in the private lives of its citizens. In 1851 the Massachusetts legislature enacted, over the governor's veto, a stringent liquor control bill just short of prohibition. Compulsory school attendance became law a year later; truancy cases were to become a powerful weapon in the battle to control the morals of the immigrant poor.[26]

The moral reformers brought the prostitution issue to public attention, and the most vocal among them were women. Female moral reform groups' vehemence against prostitution was motivated by gender issues as well as religious fervor. Prostitution embodied the degradation and exploitation of their sex. According to the female reformers, the truly guilty parties—procurers, keepers, and patrons—were being ignored by those policing the city.

Reformers began to see the fruits of their labors at the end of the 1840s. Certain types of prostitution had been previously ignored but were now no longer tolerated. In 1847 the city council enacted a law forcing theater owners to hire a policeman to prohibit liquor sales and solicitation by prostitutes on the premises.[27] The law destroyed the venerable third tier in Boston theaters. Not only were new laws passed but old ones were more strictly enforced. Brothelkeepers were pursued more vigorously by police, more often brought to trial by prosecutors, and sentenced in larger numbers by judges (see figures 2.2 and 2.3).[28]

Prostitution became a central issue on the social and political agenda. Both the official reports and the popular press carried the message that prostitution had reached dangerous levels. Even grand juries in Boston—customarily silent on general matters of law and society, in contrast to those of many other cities—became vocal in 1849–51. The grand jury of 1851 issued a warning on the rising tide of crime and vice in Boston, particularly in a section of the North End centering on Ann Street. The officer assigned to that street estimated that it contained 227 brothels, 26 gambling dens, and 1,500 places where liquor was sold. During their investigation, members of the grand jury heard testimony about the area referred to as the Black Sea, where "the depraved of both sexes and all colors constantly congregated, and robberies and assaults are so common that it is not always safe to pass through there even in the day time."[29]

During this period the reform coalition in city government appointed a tough law-and-order police chief, Marshall Tukey. The police force began a series of intensive raids against Ann Street brothels and gambling houses in the spring of 1851. On March 8, eighty-six gamblers were arrested in a raid; six days later police made another assault on gaming establishments. April 23 was the culmination of the spring offensive against vice. Fifty police (the entire day force) and an equal number from the night watch organized a descent on various dance cellars, rum shops,

FIGURE 2.3

*Brothelkeeping and Nightwalking Cases in Suffolk County Courts
per 100,000 of the Population, 1830–1920*

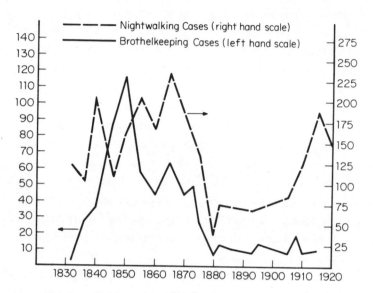

SOURCE: Boston Police Court Dockets, 1822–50; Boston Municipal Court Dockets, 1822–50; Boston Municipal Court Dockets for the Latter Half of the Century, 1870–1920, sample data. See also *A Record of the Enforcement of the Laws Against Sexual Morality Since Dec. 1, 1907* (Boston, 1909), pp. 5, 12–13; and George E. Worthington and Ruth Topping, *Specialized Courts Dealing with Sex Delinquency* (New York, 1923), pp. 148–49.

and brothels on Ann Street. They netted sixty men and ninety-five women; thirty-five of the men were indicted as keepers of brothels and disorderly houses. The women were tried in police court as common nightwalkers and lewd persons.[30]

It is impossible to know whether the number of brothels was really multiplying in the 1850s or whether they were becoming more noxious or bigger establishments. What does seem apparent is that a new consciousness toward the brothel as a social and economic institution was emerging. The laws passed at midcentury reflect an awareness of prostitution as an increasingly commercialized trade with more middlemen and merchandisers. For example, city ordinances passed in 1847 required employment agencies and cab drivers to obtain licenses, since many were believed to be agents in the prostitution trade seeking out clients and potential prostitutes.[31]

In day-to-day legal practice, police and court personnel recognized a growing differentiation in the business of prostitution. In 1851 the attorney general's reports began listing keeping brothels and letting brothels as two separate crimes. The 1855 brothel law formalized this distinction. It contained a section specifically on renting houses of ill fame, which stated that landlords could be penalized if they failed to evict persons known to be operating such a house. Though this crime carried a prison term and fine, the few persons charged were not sentenced. Courts themselves apparently recognized the changing character of prostitution in the city, as several cases appealed to the Massachusetts Supreme Judicial Court in the 1850s and 1860s demonstrate. Two cases concerned the nature of evidence that constituted proof a house was used for purposes of prostitution. In both cases, defendants—accused keepers—had been convicted on the testimony of police that the house had a known reputation and that women living there were known prostitutes. The high court upheld the conviction, saying that the character of the women was proof enough that the house was of bad repute. However, in a different case, *Commonwealth v. Lambert*, the court drew the line between public prostitution and private sexual behavior and maintained that although Maria Lambert leased rooms to unmarried couples she was not a brothelkeeper. In so ruling, the high court made formal what was already convention in the policing of sexuality.[32]

This classification of keepers and landlords clearly delineated brothelkeepers as managers of prostitutes involved more directly than landlords in the business of prostitution. Landlords merely collected rents, but keepers took a share of the profits and thus had a vested interest in expanding the prostitution market. During the 1850s a tenfold increase in the maximum fine—from three hundred to three thousand dollars—testified that prostitution had become a lucrative business for those who managed it. Tukey had urged steeper fines for brothelkeeping, claiming that the business was not affected by criminal prosecution or moderate fines.[33]

A more specialized and institutionalized prostitution trade was evolving gradually, parallel to the increasing rationalization of the general economy throughout the nineteenth century. Brothels were becoming more commercial enterprises, with printed cards for distribution; directories to the more fashionable houses were sold. The *Directory to Seraglios* published in 1859 covered New York, Boston, and other cities. It listed the name and address of the house and gave a brief description of the furnishings, food, wines, and ladies. This directory provides a rare piece of evidence that houses passed from keeper to keeper in this period: a former Boston house of Miss Matty Callan was listed under another woman's name; Miss Callan had moved on to New York.[34]

Perhaps the most threatening facet of prostitution to law enforcers as well as to Protestant reform groups was that in this period brothelkeeping, like prostitution, was becoming more and more identified as an immigrant venture. Considering that it took some capital to run a brothel, the fact that over 40 percent of the brothelkeepers in the house of correction records were first-generation immigrants is significant (see table 2.1). Blacks were also overrepresented in the records of brothelkeeping arrests. For immigrants and blacks denied access to legitimate commercial ventures, brothels, gambling, and saloons were marginal businesses that allowed some movement up the economic ladder. Over the next half-century other immigrant groups, such as Italians and Jews, would seek the same routes for mobility, and their arrival in vast numbers would greatly expand the prostitution market.[35]

Not only were brothels managed by immigrants; they also found shelter in immigrant neighborhoods. Streets such as Ann Street gave Irish enclaves in the North End the appearance of an alien city, a haven for criminals and a place where the innocent and young were corrupted. The city's brothelkeeping statute that defined the crime as a public nuisance had to be revised, in part because neighbors were unwilling to make complaints against places of prostitution. The new law allowed any person to initiate action against a keeper and stated that it was unnecessary to

TABLE 2.1

Social Characteristics of Brothelkeepers Confined in the House of Correction, 1858–65

Average Age	30.3 years
Native-born	54.6%
Foreign-born	44.7%
Married	68.5%
Single	31.5%
Male	37.0%
Female	63.0%
Literate	56.4%
Illiterate	41.7%
	(N = 108)

SOURCE: Register of Inmates, Boston House of Correction and Boston House of Industry, 1858–65.

prove that individuals in the community suffered from the presence of a brothel. This revision of the common nuisance law gave police and reformers the green light to take action against the lowest class of brothels in immigrant neighborhoods.[36]

During the Civil War and the years after, intense public debate on prostitution waned. The ravages of war had dampened the reform fervor; stability, not moral crusades, was the order of the day. Prostitution crime rates continued to be high, but the pattern of policing prostitution returned to the standard practice of concentrating on the streetwalker and not the keeper (see figure 2.3). Brothelkeeping arrests dipped and night-walking cases rose, particularly during the Civil War years, when anxieties over women's situation increased, since their protectors and controllers—fathers, brothers, and husbands—were away.

After Tukey, Boston police chiefs did not become involved in moral crusades until the early twentieth century. Raids in 1858 and 1871 were aimed at cutting down the volume of vice and expelling new faces rather than closing down every house of ill fame. The main concern of police was once again maintaining the peace and removing prostitutes from shopping areas and respectable neighborhoods. Brothels in Boston were still clustered in two neighborhoods—the North End and one small section of the West End. Police surveys of brothels in the 1860s or 1870s listed none in the shopping or commercial districts or in the middle class neighborhoods.[37]

From an 1866 description of Ann Street by a group of Protestant missionaries taken on a tour by a policeman, little seemed to have changed in the fifteen years since the Tukey raids. Descending into one of the many dance cellars, they entered "by way to hell," and found the "squealing of fiddles" and "disorderly shuffle of many feet." Prostitutes, bounty jumpers, housebreakers, and con artists—all known to the police escort—were dancing. Blacks and whites mingled together and the "swarthy faces of negresses glistened with excitement and sweat." Thirty years later, Benjamin Flower, editor of the reform journal *The Arena,* would take the same tour and portray the same scenes of Boston's underword of crime and vice in a book called *Civilization's Inferno.* [38]

The campaign at midcentury had merely skimmed the surface of the Black Sea. That brothelkeepers had been sentenced to prison during the decade perhaps temporarily forced many in the prostitution business to lie low until the wave of repression passed, and it did. Ten years after Tukey's raids, another police chief, Josiah Aimee, summarized law enforcement policy in Boston when he appraised the ability of the police to control moral ills: "This class of houses are found in all large cities and are of that class of evils impossible to suppress and difficult to control." He insisted that prostitution could never be eliminated by the strong arm of the police and was best cured by the "cultivation of virtue."[39]

Accommodation

The decade of the 1870s marked the beginning of a long period of toleration of prostitution during which the prostitute was rarely prevented from practicing her trade. In 1878 the newly formed Watch and Ward Society (previously the New England Society for the Suppression of Vice) complained that not only genteel establishments but also most brothels and gambling houses were being ignored by police. The official statistics support their claim. Prostitution cases became a minuscule proportion of daily court business (1 percent or less of the caseload in municipal court). Boston police actually began noting in their reports numbers and locations of houses of prostitution in the city, which indicates that they had begun to accept as normal certain levels of prostitution.[40]

The relaxation of controls was not a response to smaller numbers of prostitutes or fewer establishments. Surveys of brothels by police and a study by census takers in the 1880s suggest that, on the contrary, prostitution was on the rise in the late nineteenth century. There is also some support for the argument that prostitution was becoming more established and institutionalized in these decades. Prostitutes who were arrested appeared to be professional operators with networks to lawyers and bailbondsmen. They were savvy about how the court system worked and were able to use the law's delay and make bargains with prosecutors. Of the classes of offenders who came before municipal court* judges in the late nineteenth century, they had the highest percentage of appeals. Aware that their chances were much better in the trial court, many women

---

*After the Massachusetts court reorganization at mid-century, what was called police court was renamed municipal court. The middle-level court, formerly municipal court, became superior court.

actually pleaded guilty in the lower court so that their appeals could be processed more quickly. And the strategy paid off, since the majority of cases were dropped before trial; others resulted in fines or probation rather than imprisonment. Prosecutors in the trial court did not want to waste resources building cases against prostitutes.[41]

Boston did not have a segregated zone of prostitution, but everyone knew where to find the red-light district in the North End. A strong regulationist movement never took hold in the city. Police and courts abandoned the idea that prostitution could be suppressed, and instead adopted a policy of management. Both inside and outside the criminal justice system, prostitution had come to be seen as a part of urban life, but most respectable folk had little contact with the brothel district.

In some American cities, prostitution policy approached the institutionalized systems of Europe. Police sometimes kept an informal register of prostitutes. St. Paul was exceptional in that prostitution had a semilegal status; keepers and prostitutes were routinely given fines that were in effect licensing fees that helped to pay for municipal services. Beginning in 1863 madams were arrested and formally convicted once a month under a city statute that carried a maximum fine of one hundred dollars and thirty days in jail. In practice, they were fined a general fee of twenty-five dollars, plus ten dollars for each prostitute in their brothel; they were never sentenced to prison. Law enforcers and brothelkeepers made an accommodation that allowed the former to maintain some degree of control over the brothel district and the latter to continue business as usual without community censure and police harassment.[42]

To interpret this informal system of regulation as a sign that prostitution was tolerated or accepted by the general community, however, is to ignore the importance of the public reenactment of guilt and conviction in the courts. This ceremony every month confirmed the relationship between prostitution and criminal activity and affixed a deviant status to madams and prostitutes. St. Paul and many other cities adopted a de facto licensing of prostitution. But when St. Louis put into effect a system of regulation in 1873, an outpouring of public criticism, both locally and nationally, forced its repeal. In legalizing prostitution, the city council had ignored the complicated play of forces in prostitution politics. Municipal officials and law enforcers had to strike a delicate balance between competing interest groups: pressure from reformers for elimination of prostitution on one side, and pressure for a laissez faire policy from legitimate businesses that accrued profits from prostitution on the other. Even within prostitution neighborhoods, one found some residents who complained about disorderly houses and solicitation by prostitutes, and others who resented police interference with their places of leisure.[43]

During the intense campaign against prostitution in Boston in the pre–Civil War era, social pressures tipped the balance in reformers' favor. For a brief period, it seemed as if they would be able to reshape the law and legal apparatus so that all moral offenders would be equally punished and the gender and class bias could be eliminated in the policing of sex. But the public policy toward prostitution expressed social and sexual norms that were firmly planted, and by the 1870s the legal procedures and traditions were established. A policeman on his rounds, when he plucked the flower on the streets, rarely took the stem or branches, and the system never touched the roots. Law enforcers went after the easiest and most visible target, the public prostitute; they often ignored the keeper, almost always passed over the clients, and never adopted measures that touched the social and economic causes of prostitution.

3

Predator and Prey

IN the 1830s and 1840s evangelical women involved in moral reform societies in American cities and towns transformed the social and political meanings of prostitution. Prostitution reform had been equated with rescuing the sinner and the source of the problem attributed to individual failings and weaknesses. Female moral reformers constructed a sexual politics around prostitution. They linked prostitution to male dominance in economic, political, and social life, and viewed the sexual double standard as an extension of the imbalance of power between the sexes. Female moral reformers analyzed prostitution in the broad context of sexual exploitation in nonmarital and marital sexual relations. Thus prostitution was one result of male sexual aggressiveness, and sexual coercion in marriage was another. The man was not held accountable in either case; neither visiting a prostitute nor raping a wife was a crime.

Though they did not call themselves feminists, these reformers recognized that prostitution expressed class and gender inequalities. They had a strong impact on antiprostitution campaigns in this era and had a lasting influence on feminist debates and strategies regarding prostitution over the next century. Most important for the future of feminism, they analyzed prostitution in terms of women's lack of protections rather than their lack of equal rights.

The roots of female moral reform were to be found in women's benevolent endeavors on behalf of their unfortunate sisters. A plethora of female charitable associations sprung up in the Northeast at the turn of the nineteenth century: societies for the benefit of widows, orphaned children, poor seamstresses, and women in need of employment. Prostitution itself was not outside the sphere of interest of evangelical women, who organized rescue homes and hired missionaries to preach to fallen women. More common were the preventive institutions—religious homes for poor or orphaned girls, who were considered prime recruits for prostitution.

The growth of a consumer economy provided middle and upper class women with more leisure time for these associations. Domestic ideology, which elevated women's caretaking role and affective nature, made them appear supremely suited for charitable works. Separate women's religious groups and institutions reinforced self-consciousness about women's special attributes, sources of community, and common interests.[1]

Female moral reformers gave new meaning to gender identity and community within the Christian sisterhood. For them, women were bound together not only by their shared experiences but also by common grievances against men's sexual aggression, both outside and inside marriage. In order to protect their sex, women had to form an alliance, a moral counterforce, that would compel men to adopt the same codes of behavior and accountability as were applied to women. Female moral reformers consequently reserved some of their harshest criticisms for women who accepted a sexual double standard and were thus traitors to their sex: "The world contains women who punish the faults of their own sex with unrelenting severity, and yet value a man in proportion to the number of women whom he has destroyed."[2]

They maintained that sexual liberalism, which they referred to as sexual license, always translated into sexual exploitation of women. Whereas most reports and studies of prostitution had analyzed the problem in terms of supply, they perceived prostitution as an issue of demand. Thus their task was controlling male sexual behavior. Although they accepted women's culpability in the existence of the sexual double standard, female moral reformers placed the burden of responsibility on men, who controlled the legal, economic, and political institutions. Unlike feminists of other times, they did not presume that women should take over or even share these sources of power.

Eighteenth-century advocates of women's rights, such as Mary Wollstonecraft in England and Judith Murray Sargeant in the United States, based their arguments on "natural rights" regardless of sex. The equal rights feminism of the American suffrage movement, which called for property rights, education, and full citizenship, flowed from this tradition.

Female moral reform ideology represented another current in feminism. It assumed that women's influence and participation in public affairs sprung from gender differences. Female moral reformers accepted the main contours of the ideology of domesticity, which determined that women had different mental, moral, and sexual natures from men and therefore had different spheres of influence. Yet they extended the definition of domestic influence beyond the physical boundaries of the hearth to include the exploitation of women in sexual and economic relations outside the home. This assertion of women's domestic influence in public policy became the wellspring of women's activism throughout the nineteenth and early twentieth centuries.

Moral Reform Societies

From the mid-1830s to the Civil War years, moral reform societies were the mainstay of antiprostitution. They were staunchly religious, militant in their tactics, and unpopular among the ruling elites of cities. Moral reform was not exclusively a women's movement; male ministers, in fact, had been the pioneers. In earlier religious reform activism, women had merely been foot soldiers; in moral reform they became dominant.

Moral reform differed from the first wave of missionary and reform groups of the 1820s. In contrast to the campaigns against public vice of the previous generation, male and female moral reformers aimed primarily at private illicit sexuality, particularly the discreet upper class houses of ill fame, where the fashionable libertine could indulge his lust without jarring his sense of refinement. Moral reformers' obsession with private illicit sexuality is understandable. In their lifetime they had witnessed dramatic changes in the policing of sex. Police, courts, and judges were totally uninterested in discreet sexual liaisons, and enforcers defined their task as the suppression of the most visible forms of vice—public drunkenness, open solicitation by prostitutes, and raucous gambling houses. Established churches seemed loath to denounce moral delinquents, especially among their wealthy and powerful congregations, and few demanded that adulterers make public confessions.[3]

Reformers had seen the rise of controls to subdue the criminal and wandering poor—courts, police, prisons, and workhouses—but what institutions or structures would challenge the violator who held rank and position? In view of their goal to create a single standard of morality, they naturally wondered who would police those who were supposedly policing others. As they saw it, what ultimately would undermine society was sexual misconduct in the bastions of respectability: the family, the church, and the sites of power—the court, legislature, and police force. The wealthy and powerful were the most dangerous because no political and social structures existed to oversee them.

Moral reform in the early stages of the movement appeared radical and dangerous to the established elites in Eastern cities. Yet its goals and ideology were quite conventional on the surface. Other religious societies had attacked sexual libertinism and promoted sexual purity. Not the message but the medium is what appeared threatening. Moral reformers published vivid descriptions of prostitution in journals for public consumption. Equally disturbing, they accused and sometimes named powerful and prominent patrons of prostitution.

Boston's two moral reform journals, the *Friend of Virtue* and the *Illuminator,* carried numerous articles on crime in high places, which uncovered some notorious seducer in the pulpit, the bench, the state legislature, and even the halls of Congress. One issue of the *Friend of Virtue* accused a magistrate of using his office as a house of assignation. Was it not hypocrisy, reformers asked, that abandoned females who had been invited to this man's chambers could be committed to prison for offenses "against society," whereas he and others like him retained "their offices, trust and place in society"?[4]

John McDowall, the father of the movement, published his firsthand accounts of prostitution in New York City in 1832. The journal caused a furor among respectable citizens of that city. It was confiscated by authorities as obscene literature. McDowall's critics—mainly his ministerial brethren—charged him with spreading moral contagion. Typical of his sensational accounts was the story of a gentleman who asked a well-known procuress to find him an innocent girl who had never been seduced. When he entered the room in the brothel, he found that his own daughter was to be his victim.[5] Accused of writing pornography and spreading licentiousness, McDowall was ostracized by the established clergy and died a penniless, broken man.

Boston had its own moral reform martyr in Joseph Whitmarsh, whose *Illuminator* exposed the sexual exploits of a Boston editor and his employees who occupied the same building as Whitmarsh. Whitmarsh printed their names, addresses, and details of their illicit liaisons. Soon after, he was embroiled in a series of libel suits and was physically assaulted by friends of those he had accused. His journal collapsed within two years, and he disappeared from the Boston resident directories.[6]

In contrast to these early martyrs to the cause, female moral reformers were able to establish societies and networks from the already existing religious sisterhood. They had the advantage of being women speaking to women about sexual exploitation by men, an issue that touched a sensitive chord among women in first half of the nineteenth century and would be a strong current in the nascent feminist movement of that period. Through their journals, networks, and numerous chapters, they not only helped to create a climate against prostitution but also shaped the discourse surrounding the prostitute herself.

The New England Female Moral Reform Society

The New England Female Moral Reform Society is an ideal case study for exploring the discourse and strategies of this movement. It was organized and run by women who, in class background and religious ideology, mirrored other female moral reform societies. Though begun in Boston, the society had a strong rural constituency, which was the backbone of moral reform efforts in America. Also, it had a long and active history as well as an influence on public debates and campaigns against prostitution that few could boast.[7]

Begun in 1836, the society was limited to Boston women and was an auxiliary of a New York society founded two years earlier. In 1838 the members decided to strike out on their own, maintaining New England should have its own independent reform operation with headquarters in Boston. The society changed its name to the New England Female Moral Reform Society and began publishing the *Friend of Virtue,* a bimonthly journal, which continued to be its official organ for nearly fifty-five years. Through the efforts of agents in the field and as a result of the wide circulation of the *Friend of Virtue* (which had 3,000 subscribers by 1841), the society could claim sixty-one auxiliary chapters throughout New

England, concentrated in the towns of Massachusetts, Maine, and New Hampshire.

The board and managers of the society were not the middle and upper class ladies commonly identified with moral crusades and benevolent endeavors. Rather, most were the wives of artisans and shopkeepers, such as clerks, booksellers, printers, housewrights, and masons. Only a few had husbands who were merchants, professionals, or owners of large businesses. Of the husbands listed as ministers, the majority were pastors of small congregations or agents of moral reform societies. The single women in the society were teachers, boardinghouse keepers, milliners, and laundresses. Overall the women were from lower class and lower middle class backgrounds (see table 3.1). The society paid salaries to its agents (who were hired to rescue prostitutes in brothels), to the matron in charge of the Temporary Home for Fallen Women, and to the editor of their journal. For Eliza Garnaut, a widow of a Welsh workingman, the money she earned as an agent of the society was her only source of income. Rebecca Eaton had been a school teacher before she took on the job of editing the *Friend of Virtue*. Compared with other private charitable institutions of the same era, the society was more egalitarian in its organization. Garnaut, Eaton, and even the matron who took charge of the daily operations of the Home sat on its executive board.

TABLE 3.1

Social Backgrounds of the Managers and Executive Committee of the New England Female Moral Reform Society, 1836–60

Occupation	Husband's or Father's N	Working Women N	Total N	Total %
Minister[a]	11		11	18.3
White Collar (Professional/Merchant)	7		7	11.7
Low White Collar	7	7	14	23.3
Blue Collar (Skilled/Semi-Skilled)	16		16	26.6
Laborers/Peddlers	4	1	5	8.3
NEFMRS Agents		7	7	11.7
Total	45	15	60	100.0[b]

[a]Ministers, the dominant occupational group, were made a separate category because of variations in types of work performed and the remuneration for work. For example, some were agents of missionary societies; others were editors of religious newspapers.

[b]Figures do not total 100 percent due to rounding.

SOURCE: *The Boston Directory* (Boston, 1822, 1824, 1826, 1828, 1830, 1832, 1834, 1836, 1838, 1839, 1841, 1851, 1853, 1856).

In religious ideology the managers of the society were at the radical end of the spectrum of evangelical Protestantism. Many were members of the Marlboro Church, where William Lloyd Garrison was a leading force. Called the Free Church, this hotbed of abolitionist, temperance, and moral reform activity opened its doors to all minorities and provided a forum for unpopular causes. The female moral reformers' world view was shaped by their religious beliefs, but equally important was their belief that all women had common interests regardless of class.

Was the gender consciousness within the New England Female Moral Reform Society feminist? That depends on one's definition. When the radical wing of the antislavery movement proposed that women be integrated into the national organization, rather than remain a separate female auxilliary, the majority of the New England Moral Reform Society's members (who were also members of the Boston Female Anti-slavery Society) sided with the conservative, antifeminist wing.[8] Their position was logical and consistent with their assertion of gender differences and their support for separate women's institutions. Within their analysis of gender conflict, there was an implicit radicalism: the view that men held all the power and had none of the responsibility for illicit sexuality. Within their acceptance of women's traditional domestic roles, there was an implicit conservatism, which shaped their remedies for prostitution and poverty.

As stated in the first issue of the *Friend of Virtue,* the primary goals of the society were to protect virtuous women and to rescue their fallen sisters: "to guard our daughters, sisters, and female acquaintances from the delusive arts of corrupt and unprincipled men" and "to bring back to the paths of virtue those who have been drawn aside through the wiles of the destroyer." Implicit in these two statements was the imputation of male guilt and responsibility for a woman's loss of chastity. For female moral reformers, men were always blameworthy, whether they accomplished their purpose by brute force or subtle persuasion. Images of male sexual aggressiveness appeared on nearly every page of the *Friend of Virtue;* upper class libertines and profligates were predators, wolves in the streets, monsters, and vultures. Their female victims were cast as lambs, prey, the unprotected. In the accounts of seduction and betrayal, the authors of the *Friend of Virtue* interwove the themes of male dominance and class exploitation that took shape in fictional and real-life accounts of the wolf in gentleman's garb.

Seduction and Betrayal

The exploiter and the exploited were clearly delineated in the *Friend of Virtue*. Almost without exception, villains were powerful and influential men who had both wealth and social status; victims were women of humble birth, from poor but respectable families, often orphans or the daughters of widows. The paradigm gentleman–destroyer-of-virtue appeared in the "Soliloquy of the Libertine," a narrative of a lowly chambermaid's seduction. Speaking of his intended victim, the libertine lays bare the arrogance of class privilege:

She is young, pretty, graceful and almost elegant. Had she been born in higher circles, she might have been a star of the first magnitude. But she is poor, consequently degraded and designed only to contribute to the pleasures of the rich. She is an orphan too, and that is in my favor, and her brothers are too low in the world to avenge a sister's wrong.[9]

Female reformers characterized the gentleman of vice as the most dangerous villain because he could mask his brutish designs with a cloak of respectability. Advantages of wealth, education, and refinement made him the most artful seducer. Because he could purchase expensive gifts, he could tempt those with few worldly goods. Such were the tactics, the libertine revealed in his soliloquy, that enabled him to transform an innocent young woman into a depraved woman. He brought her fashionable clothes and jewelry and introduced her to the theater and popular amusements; soon she became "disenchanted with the drudgery of an honest life." True to the seduction-and-betrayal formula, the fallen woman is abandoned by her lover within a few months and dies a horrible death as a common prostitute. The seducer feels no pangs of remorse and suffers no economic loss.[10]

The portraits of arrogant and ruthless male predators and of their female prey were morality plays in which individuals became projections not only of good and evil but also of opposing forces of urban and rural; wealthy and poor; competitive, aggressive men and weak, submissive women. A classic example of the genre appeared in the *Friend of Virtue* under the title "Facts More Awful Than Fiction." The victim in that piece was the deaf daughter of a poor widow living in a small New England town, the embodiment of passivity and defenselessness. Her seducer was a Boston merchant, the archetypical entrepreneurial man on the make, who had come to the Vermont town to set up an auction store.[11] These "scenes from real life" were social dramas that expressed class and gender conflict in an emerging industrial society, a society that was creating new sets of relationships between labor and capital, between producers and consumers, and between men and women in matters of sex.

During the first half of the nineteenth century, a changing commercial economy provided artisans and shopkeepers who were able to accumulate capital the chance to become small businessmen. At the same time, a class of men whose fathers had been independent artisans, farmers, or shopkeepers now found themselves working for commercial and manufacturing establishments as junior clerks, journeymen, or factory operatives. Growth in capital investments and industry enabled middle class wives to have more consumer goods, more money to hire servants, and more leisure. The cult of domesticity was an ideology that reflected the growing identification of women's work roles with domestic tasks and child rearing. It created a class division between wage-earning women and housewives. In the 1830s the first wave of female factory operatives had entered the labor force; they were called mill girls. Lucy Larcom, a Lowell mill factory worker, alludes in her memoirs to the class distinction between mill girl and lady and defends the dignity of the working woman:

> It is the first duty of every woman to recognize the mutual bond of universal womanhood. Let her ask herself whether she would like to hear herself or her sister spoken of as a shop-girl, a factory-girl or a servant-girl, if necessity had compelled her for a time to be employed in either of the ways indicted. . . . She is a little inhumane when she puts her unknown human sisters who are so occupied into a class by themselves. . . . She [the employed woman] is really the superior person who is accepting her work and is doing it faithfully, whatever it is.

Glimpses of these changes in class structure can also be found in reform literature. A short story written by a Lowell mill girl in the 1840s featured a young woman who decides to work in the mills to pay off debts after her father dies. In the story her decision alters her future options and affects her social status. Her fiancé, the son of a wealthy farm owner, is no longer interested in marrying her.[12]

Transformations in commerce and industry forced men to delay marriage for years until they could accumulate enough savings to start a household. Prostitution was a way for many wage-earning men to have sexual relations without financial responsibilities. If a respectable workingman's betrothed became pregnant and he lacked the position and resources to provide for a wife, he faced a no-win situation. He was damned if he married her and damned if he didn't.

One story from the *Dedham Patriot* in 1839, reprinted in the moral reform society's journal, reveals one couple's desperate response to premarital pregnancy. It reported the tragic death of Susan Bowman, engaged to Nathan Barker, a Latin teacher at a Boston high school. Barker called a doctor when she became ill, but he remained silent while the physician, unaware that he was treating a pregnant woman, administered medicine that killed both mother and child. The editorial in the society's journal characterized Barker as a murderer who had used his place in society and his accomplishments to gain the confidence of a woman of humble station.[13] The society never considered that his promise to marry her might have been sincere or that societal pressures had prevented the couple from revealing their shame. Nevertheless, a man who could not fulfill his obligations to marry did not suffer the same consequences and disgrace as the unwed mother. Female reformers' conclusion that the double standard afforded men an impregnable wall of protection was in one sense accurate.

In their day-to-day experiences with the seducer and the seduced, female moral reformers cited two universal conditions: (1) although a man became involved with or even attached to a woman of a lower class, he always married a virtuous woman of his own social class; and (2) a man with economic resources more often made a cash settlement with his victim than offered her "honorable reparation." An indignant article in the *Friend of Virtue,* "The Price of Insult," intimated that the going rate for a woman's loss of honor was ten dollars. Although one might assume that the author was exaggerating, the figure was not too far off the one reported by Mrs. Garnaut. In one of the most heart-rending episodes to appear in the *Friend of Virtue,* Garnaut described a night that she spent in a brothel at the bedside of a dying prostitute named Hariot. When Hariot became seriously ill, the doctor who was treating her wrote to her seducer describing her desperate condition; the man, a Dr. C., sent his lawyer to negotiate a settlement. Garnaut lamented that the poor ignorant girl, not knowing what she should have received, agreed to let Dr. C. off the hook for thirty dollars.[14] What female moral reformers saw clearly was that the consequences for women who lost their chastity were greater and the censure toward the unwed mother stronger than it had been a generation earlier. What they failed to grasp was the way in which economic and social forces as well as ideological constraints on women working also restricted the marriage options of men.

Narratives of seduction and betrayal in the *Friend of Virtue,* both fact and fiction, do not reflect the general pattern of illicit sexual unions. Seducers were not always members of the upper classes. As a matter of fact, most studies suggest that the reverse was true: that women had nonmarital sex with men of the same class or of the next class up the scale.[15] And no proof exists of the accuracy of the reformers' perception that women were being seduced and abandoned in unprecedented numbers. Daniel Scott Smith and Michael Hindus's study of New England towns during this period shows that premarital pregnancy was actually decreasing. The researchers concluded that couples were having less nonmarital sex and that an overall change in sexual mores was taking place. But another, equally plausible, explanation is that stricter codes of chastity resulted in fewer *reports* of premarital pregnancy.[16]

Regardless of whether illegitimate pregnancy increased or decreased, attitudes began to change in the first half of the nineteenth century. An unwed mother experienced more isolation from family and community than had her eighteenth-century foremothers. In New England towns in the late eighteenth century, there were strong incentives and pressure for the offending couple to marry and legitimize the bastard offspring. Family, friends, and influential community residents could force the father of a bastard child to provide a single mother with respectability. As towns became more stratified and less closely knit, these informal mechanisms began to break down. Furthermore, increasing mobility made it difficult to force a putative father into marriage. A man living in a New England town could easily avoid his responsibility by joining other young men in migrating to cities and factory towns. When single women who had migrated to the city became pregnant without family support systems, they had little or no chance of pressuring a man into marriage.[17] Given their rural Yankee constituencies, female moral reformers understandably were most concerned about the fates of these women.

The managers of the New England Female Reform society succeeded only rarely in coercing men to marry the women they had seduced. It was difficult to track down seducers (sometimes the women would not identify them). Once a seducer was located, a female moral reform agent could appeal only to his compassion or fear of damnation. The law provided a woman who had "yielded in an unguarded moment" with few remedies, and breach of promise suits were rare among the working class. Women were in the most vulnerable position when the man was of a higher class and presumably more sophisticated in regard to the law.

Female moral reformers always viewed nonmarital sexual relationships as the exploitation of women and never as freedom from sexual repression. They had some justification for this position: premarital pregnancy not only carried a strong stigma for women, it could also produce economic hardship. Women were often dismissed from jobs, particularly those as domestic servants, once it was learned they were pregnant. Even employers in industry often fired a woman who violated chastity codes because she undermined their defense of factory work as respectable.[18] Few charitable organizations would provide support or employment for unwed mothers. In an era when nearly all women gave birth at home, the Temporary Home for Fallen Women, founded by the New England Female Moral Reform Society in 1838, provided single pregnant women a decent place to stay during their confinement and to remain with their babies for a time after the birth. The only other institutional choice in antebellum Boston were the almshouse and public lying-in hospital; both were unsanitary, depressing last resorts for the poorest and most desperate.

The proliferation of ads in pre–Civil War daily newspapers for ways to abort unwanted pregnancies (always camouflaged in the language of cures for women's complaints) suggests that there was a demand for these remedies. A sensational Boston trial of an abortionist in the period also reveals that men and women willing to perform these services were in demand and well known. One witness at the trial claimed that a house in the city was thronged with females at all hours of the night; they had to wait their turns like barber's customers.[19]

Rarely could single pregnant woman anywhere flout sexual conventions and disregard societal pressures to marry. The Scottish lowlands were an exception in the nineteenth century. Richard Smout concludes that a shortage of agricultural workers allowed Scottish dairy maids, who often violated chastity codes, to avoid punishment and keep their jobs after they became pregnant. In Stockholm, Sweden, a striking number of working class women lived with men outside marriage, according to Margareta Matović. Although the laws punished unwed mothers, these women could protect themselves indefinitely by publishing banns for marriage. Such extralegal marriage, Matović concludes, provided women with autonomy in relationships (they kept their earnings and doweries). It also protected working class men, who faced periodic unemployement and often feared the financial responsibilities of child rearing.[20]

But in nineteenth-century New England, where no shortage of labor existed, sanctions against premarital pregnancy could not be offset by a demand for female labor. Neither was there any protection for couples living outside of wedlock, even if they planned to marry. Though women and men lived together outside of marriage—pretending to be married or taking on the public roles of housekeeper and employer—to do so openly was dangerous. It could lead to arrest, imprisonment, or having one's child placed in an institution. Yet husbands were in short supply in New England, with many more women than men of marriageable age. Given this imbalance and given the limited opportunities for women's employment in the first half of the nineteenth century, it is not surprising that women may have taken sexual risks in the hope that a promise of marriage would lead to a formal wedding.[21] In fact, "promise of marriage" was the cause of seduction most often cited by residents of the society's Temporary Home for Fallen Women.

The images of sexual exploitation in moral reform journals—the wolf in gentleman's garb, the male predator seeking out his prey—were ways of comprehending a changing social landscape. These figures were tangible enemies, easier to identify and less disturbing than the more complex issues produced by changing social and sexual norms: the declining power of families and communities to regulate the behavior of young adults, the economic and social pressures that prevented couples from marrying, and the widening class divisions between working poor and middle class.

Sexual Slavery

The procurer was an agent of darkness in moral reform literature. Although the editors of the *Friend of Virtue* portrayed the men in this business as far more odious, they also cited numerous cases of female procurers. The portrait that emerges from the New England reformers is one of pimps and agents for brothels scouring the countryside for innocent victims.

Typical of the accounts of sexual slavery in the *Friend of Virtue* is the following, reported in an 1846 issue. A young woman who had just arrived in Boston by coach inquired of another female passenger if she knew of any employment in the city. Overhearing the discussion, a gentleman stepped forward and said that a woman who did his laundry needed a helper. The young woman accepted his offer and followed him. To her horror, she found herself imprisoned in the house. She finally made her escape by breaking a window with her shoe and catching the eye of a washerwoman living below, whose mistress brought the police to her rescue.[22]

Like the wolf in gentleman's garb, the procurer was a tangible enemy, and sexual slavery offered a simple explanation for the visible and invisible hands in the prostitution market. Surveying the many accounts of sexual slavery in the *Friend of Virtue,* one finds that they touch the pressure points in women's changing work and living arrangements. An article entitled "Slavery in New England" alleged that there were women hired to infiltrate Lowell boardinghouses to tempt factory girls. Railroad stations, stagecoach depots, and steamship ports were said to be the favorite haunts of procurers. Narratives in the *Friend of Virtue* accused cabmen of taking women seeking inexpensive lodgings to brothels. In another instance, a grocer delivering food to a house decoyed a servant to a brothel by promising her higher wages and lighter work.[23]

To analyze the symbolic function of sexual slavery in moral reform is not to deny the existence of cases of imprisonment in brothels or to discount the systems of coercion into prostitution. The following case from the Suffolk County Superior Court in 1863 provides insight into the relationship between fact and fiction. In her testimony against Fanny Moore, a prostitute charged with robbery, another prostitute, Mary Clark, explained to the court how she came to live in a brothel. In a deposition to the prosecuting attorney, she related the facts of her life: "I am seventeen years of age. I came to the city a fortnight ago before [*sic*] from Lowell. I was brought here by Fanny who persuaded me to come here to work saying that she kept a shop. I did not know what sort of house I was coming to."[24] In her affidavit, Mary Clark also revealed why she did not tell her story in police court. She confessed that she was very much afraid of the defendant, who often beat her and threatened to kill her if she testified. Although she did not explicitly state that she was being held prisoner in the house, she admitted that she was not allowed to go out without being accompanied by the owner's wife or the defendant, Moore.[25]

As Mary's brief account suggests, there were women who were tricked into coming to brothels, and once inside they made the best of a bad situation. But surveys of American and European prostitutes in this era argue against the reformers' image of a large-scale traffic in women. What cannot be disputed is the increasing opportunity to become a prostitute. During the first half of the nineteenth century, single women began working outside their homes, in textile mills often in other communities. They had more chances of coming in contact with persons in the trade, greater economic and social pressures that might steer them in that direction, and less oversight from family and neighbors.

The message that the editors of the the *Friend of Virtue* hoped to convey to their readers was unambiguous: country life was wholesome and safe; city life was fraught with dangers. The accounts of sexual slavery reported in reform journals seemed to offer indisputable proof that women who left the protected sphere of home faced hazardous situations where they could be sexually exploited or deceived in their travel, living, and work arrangements.

The journey to the city *could* be perilous, and women traveling alone were often approached by strangers. Railroad stations and other travel depots were, as they are today, the haunts of unsavory characters. In the 1840s the superintendent of one of Boston's railroad stations reported to the society that he frequently had to reprimand men hanging about the station. Once a woman arrived in the city, she could find it extremely difficult to locate a place to board. Single women most often rented rooms not in boardinghouses but in private homes, for which they had to have references or contacts. One young woman who came to the Stranger's Retreat, the society's boardinghouse, claimed that she had walked the streets of Boston for two days in search of rooms.[26]

Reformers also perceived the search for a job as full of danger. Employment agents were always villains in the *Friend of Virtue*. Employment agencies, called intelligence offices in the nineteenth century, had a long-standing infamous reputation, although not all were agents for brothel-keepers. Still, the nature of the establishments laid them open for abuses. Proprietors of legitimate intelligence offices rarely had the facilities or the time to check references of prospective employers. William Sanger, the physician at New York's Blackwell's Island prison, alleged that employment offices were one of the prime recruiting grounds for procurers. From his description, the agencies appear to have been highly impersonal places: a servant seeking employment signed a register listing her qualifications; in another register, the employer had only to record his or her name and address, the duties required, and the pay scale. Sometimes up to a hundred women were in a waiting room hoping to be hired.[27]

Moral reformers treated the exploitation of women workers as an extension of their metaphor of male dominance and female weakness. Their cast of characters featured greedy employers and women in desperate financial straits. Under the heading "Wrongs of American Womanhood," the *Friend of Virtue* published a New York seamstress's personal account of abuses in the needle trades. She noted that in every case women were taken advantage of by ruthless and dishonest employers. For example, the owner would find fault with every woman's caps, no matter how perfectly fashioned, and would refuse to pay any woman for her labor. "These tricks are played by men of no character or reputation, who would not suffer by public exposure, but the poor girls suffer through them." An article called the "Low Price of Female Wages" asked readers to imagine a poor starving widow who came begging for work to a shop where the pay amounted to no more than five or six cents a shirt. No woman, the writers argued, could sustain herself or her children under these conditions. Some went to the almshouse and became chronic paupers; others, too proud to accept charity, turned to prostitution.[28]

In analyzing the economic roots of prostitution, female moral reformers realized the importance of low wages and poor working conditions. Yet their ambivalence toward women working outside the home obscured the possible benefits and opportunities women in the labor market might gain and distorted the sexual dangers they might face. The greatest financial rewards for women were in jobs moral reformers saw as posing the greatest threat to women's sexual purity. These were jobs that often forced women to work and live away from home, sometimes alongside men. Women working in the growing textile factories in towns throughout New England or in the male-dominated trades, such as printing, received higher wages than most other women workers, who did piecework in home industries.[29]

Although the moral reformers viewed work outside the home as fraught with danger, they did not suggest that wage labor unsexed women or degraded them, as orthodox ideologues of the cult of domesticity did. Many of the most active women in the New England Moral Reform Society had been wage earners, teachers, paid missionaries, or boardinghouse keepers. Nonetheless, they still considered motherhood women's true vocation. Not only did they fear for the sexual purity of single women entering industrial employment alongside men, they also looked anxiously at women who by working in factories would forgo domestic training for their future households. Consequently, the society assumed that domestic service was the most useful and the safest employment for women. A domestic worker was in a home setting, wages were assured, and work was not seasonal.

The reformers were not unaware of the unattractive features of service. The *Friend of Virtue* published numerous articles on the needs of domestics and reproved mistresses for their treatment of servants. Yet the articles attacked not so much the drudgery or demanding nature of the tasks as the distant and patronizing relationship between mistress and servant in most middle class homes. For example, editors of the journal condemned the practice of making servants eat in the kitchen, excluded from the family's social life. A minister writing for the *Prisoner's Friend,* another Boston reform journal, went so far as to blame employers for the fall of their domestic employees from virtue.[30]

Despite their criticism of employers' treatment of servants, writers for the *Friend of Virtue* never suggested that there should be more engaging and rewarding work for women, or that domestic service itself was degrading or exploitative. Not only did the society support an employment agency for domestic servants, but they placed the prostitutes rescued from brothels in Christian homes as servants after they left the Temporary Home for Fallen Women. If ex-prostitutes from the home ran away from their domestic service placements to take up prostitution again, the agents of the society faulted their employers for lack of compassion and understanding. The failure was an individual one—the wrong employer— rather the structural class relation between lady and servant.

Many of the reports of entrapment made by inhabitants of the Temporary Home for Fallen Women were histories of disgruntled servants who seized the first opportunity to escape an unpleasant situation, especially when they were promised higher wages and less arduous work. These women were apparently duped or deceived into believing that they were being hired by respectable establishments. Nonetheless, the readiness of women to follow total strangers, and the ease with which they were ensconced in brothels, must have been unsettling to female moral reformers. It raised the nagging question whether life as a prostitute might not appear more attractive—offer more freedom, comfort, and hope—than life as a domestic servant.

The kind of mistress-servant relationship idealized by the society harked back to the Puritan practice of apprenticeship. One's domestic often was a relative or a friend's daughter. In this noncommercial arrangement, a young woman's service had been a training program for marriage, not regarded as degrading. Although there was a servant class, to be a domestic servant was not itself a sign of one's low class position. This was not the case by the early nineteenth century, when the domestic servant was hired help and not an apprentice within the household economy. The sense of mutuality between mistress and maid—ideally, a relationship like mother to daughter—that moral reformers sought to reawaken was not possible in a social setting where ladies contracted the services of women workers.[31]

Middle class codes of propriety assumed that ladies would perform charitable works and domestic tasks that were unpaid. Such codes also divided women's occupations into rough and respectable types of work. Within the respectable category were boardinghouse keeping, teaching, and in the latter part of the century a small number of high status professions. With few exceptions the prescriptive literature on female gender roles suggested that to be a wage-earning woman generally meant a loss of gentility and respectability.

Social forces precluded the resumption of an "ideal" relationship between mistress and maid. A burgeoning popular literature espoused the ideology of domesticity and the cult of the true woman, emphasizing class differences between ladies and working women. Ironically, the ideology of domesticity, which asserted women's shared attributes and sensibilities, in practice underscored their class differences.[32]

Remedies

Female reformers idealistically believed that the vulnerability of all women, regardless of class, to male sexual aggression would create a Christian sisterhood able to transcend class differences in their mutual struggle. The New England Female Moral Reform Society had two strategies for eliminating the sexual double standard. One strategy was to press for legal remedies that would punish men who violated chastity codes. The other, more important, strategy was to use social ostracism— informal sanctions—against the seducer. The society knew that prejudice against the fallen woman was so strong that a virtuous woman who had any contact with her could become morally contaminated; loss of reputation was assumed. They believed that by shutting the libertine out of respectable society they could make others see him as a fallen man, a social outcast. Friends and relatives were urged to admonish or advise the prodigal son, but never to allow him in their home: "Be assured his purpose for visiting the virtuous circle is to secure another victim for his diabolical intentions."[33]

Resolutions passed by the society called on all members to refuse any social intercourse with the libertine, no matter what his standing in society. The opening address of the first meeting of the society proposed a three-point program to end the sexual double standard: no business transactions with a profligate man; no votes for a man whose reputation was in doubt; and no respect to a women who knowingly receives a licentious man. If such a program had been implemented by all women, perhaps female moral reformers would have succeeded in bringing about a moral revolution. But that would have required a prior social revolution, one in which women would have gained greater power in the family and society and one in which women would have identified with other women rather than with men of their own class.

On the legal front, the society managed some tangible successes. On the crest of the reform ferment of the 1840s they successfully pressured the Massachusetts legislature to enact a series of laws aimed at protecting women from sexual exploitation. The moral reformers made no distinction between commercial and noncommercial sexual exploitation or between women's voluntary and involuntary loss of chastity. To protect women against recruiters in prostitution, the society campaigned successfully for two pieces of legislation: a statute that required cab drivers to be licensed was passed in 1847; a similar law regulating employment agencies went into effect a year later.[34]

Most sought after by the society was an antiseduction law. Cases of seduction were civil actions usually brought by parents or guardians. The assumption within a civil case where a parent sued a seducer was that a daughter's loss of chastity left her without prospects on the marriage market. Implicit was the belief that an unchaste woman was damaged goods and that her loss in value affected her parents' standing and wealth.[35] By forcing the system to impose criminal sanctions on men, moral reformers would create a universal standard that defied placing a cash value on women's chastity. A criminal association also would attach a social stigma to the unchaste man and encourage women to ostracize him from respectable society.

The first draft of "An Act to Punish Seduction," proposed in 1845 to the Massachusetts legislature, covered acts of both seduction and abduction. The proposal specified that if an unmarried man seduced a woman under twenty-one and she became pregnant, the man could be sentenced to a maximum of three years in the state prison and two thousand dollars' fine. The proposed law also contained an abduction clause aimed at procurers of both sexes; it carried a three-year sentence as well.[36] For the society, the most important feature of the proposed bill was that it was a deterrent for the upper class man, who would no longer be able to make a cash settlement with his victim. The betrayed woman would have the satisfaction of knowing that her destroyer was to be behind bars; she could receive at least psychic restitution. Finally, such a law would provide moral reformers with a trump card in their struggle to coerce men to marry the unwed mothers who came to the temporary home.

When the law finally passed both houses of the Massachusetts legislature, the section on seduction had been eliminated. Also, the final version included a "presumption of chastity" clause that undercut even its limited applicability. If a defendant could produce any evidence to impugn the character of his female accuser, the case would be dismissed. Furthermore, the seduced woman could be interrogated on the witness stand about any aspect of her private life; any evidence that might cast doubt on her former purity was enough to destroy her credibility. What this meant was that the burden of proof shifted to the woman; she was assumed to be unchaste unless found otherwise.

In view of the huge loophole in the law, and of the elimination of seduction per se, one might suspect that the society's members would have expressed dismay after its passage. On the contrary, they proclaimed it a victory for moral reform and lauded Massachusetts lawmakers as more virtuous than their New York counterparts who had defeated a similar seduction law the previous year. For one thing, the reformers believed that the general language in the bill, which employed phrases such as "enticing away from her father's home," would allow for a broad enough interpretation of abduction to encompass cases of seduction.[37]

Commonwealth v. Cook was the first case to test the scope of the anti-abduction law. In 1846 John Cook was indicted and tried before the Dedham Court of Common Pleas. He was found guilty and appealed his case to the Supreme Judicial Court. Cook was a man of forty, married, with five children, a painter by trade, and said to be of industrious habits. Emily Forrest, the woman he was accused of abducting, was sixteen years old. Her father, Martin Forrest, rented rooms for himself and his family in Cook's house. Emily Forrest had been hired by the defendant's wife to do household chores. After having become attached to the young girl, Cook asked her to elope with him to Philadelphia, which she agreed to do. While living there, they came across a newspaper advertisement requesting information concerning their whereabouts. Soon after, Forrest took up residence in Lowell, Massachusetts; Cook returned home to Wrentham, a town near Boston. He was arrested sixteen days after his return.

Before the passage of the 1845 abduction law, Cook could not have been tried in Massachusetts at all because the act of adultery was committed in Philadelphia. The high court was not ruling on whether Cook had fraudulently enticed Emily Forrest or whether she went voluntarily; rather, it was interpreting the extensiveness of the 1845 statute. It had been asked to determine if seduction was a criminal offense under existing law.

Although the judges of the Supreme Judicial Court prefaced their decision by acknowledging that Cook's actions had "offended their feelings as Christian moralists," they still ruled in his favor. The lower court's guilty verdict was overturned on the grounds that to include instances where women were enticed away for sexual intercourse was to distort the intent of the law. As they construed it, the abduction law covered only cases in which a woman was brought to a house of ill fame or assignation for the purposes of prostitution. Varieties of illicit intercourse were, in the words of the court, "distinguishable in their character and degrees of moral turpitude." There was a tone of defensiveness throughout the high court's opinion. The judges noted that many in the community had strong feelings about seduction, as evidenced by the numerous petitions that had come before the state legislature. Nonetheless, they defended their decision by contending that if the state had wanted a seduction law, it would have enacted one.[38] No seduction law was ever passed in Massachusetts. The original abduction bill was eventually expanded to include clandestine marriages in which a woman under sixteen was taken from her father's home without his consent. Few families, particularly from the working class, sought recourse in the criminal courts in these cases.[39]

Twenty years after the passage of the abduction law, the society asked its members whether it was worthwhile to petition the legislature for stronger laws to punish those guilty of robbing females of their virtue. They admitted that legal action thus far had been ineffectual; the abduction law had not even deterred procurers. Participants at that meeting concurred that there was no point in seeking further legislation. Over the next decades, the only legislation the society lobbied for was compulsory prosecution of male nightwalkers, which would force police to arrest patrons of brothels as well as male street prowlers. In 1872 that bill was enacted, but like other legislation supported by the society, such as the abduction law, it was never enforced. Women still bore the brunt of the penalties against illicit sexuality.[40]

The society never succeeded in redistributing the weight of responsibility and guilt for illicit sexuality that the double standard placed on women. Nor did it expand the enforcement of chastity laws to include patrons of prostitutes. For a brief period, it created a groundswell for repression of prostitution and increased police action against morals crimes; this occurred during the mid-nineteenth-century crusade against prostitution in the city. But, as has been shown in earlier chapters, the enforcement of laws against chastity offenders undercut the aims of moral reform: to eliminate the class and gender bias within the policing of sexuality. The antiprostitution campaigns did not disturb the discreet, elegant haunts of vice nor did it deter libertines from seducing innocent women. The impact of moral reform on prostitution politics waned in the post–Civil War era, as public sentiment and public policy moved toward greater toleration of discreet nonmarital sexual activity and away from the outright suppression of prostitution.

Fact and Fiction

What persisted in moral reform ideology was the image of the fallen woman as an innocent victim preyed upon by evil forces. Journals such as the *Friend of Virtue* or its New York counterpart, the *Advocate of Moral Reform,* were not the originators of this tragic figure. Samuel Richardson's Lovelace stalks Clarissa for over five hundred pages. Charles Dickens's Little Nell is destroyed by a fashionable rake. But female moral reformers placed the seduction and betrayal narrative in a peculiarly American setting in which the victim was a Yankee farm girl and the corrupt city the scene in which the evil deed was accomplished.

From the 1830s to the end of the century, novels in the fallen-woman genre depicted some variation of the innocent lamb being devoured by a sly and powerful wolf. After the introduction of penny presses in the 1830s and 1840s, American readers were inundated with tales of female virtue betrayed. Boston publishers advertised such titles as *The Eastern Belle, or, The Betrayed One: A Tale of Boston and Bangor; The Mysteries of Boston, or, A Woman's Temptation;* and *Tom, Dick and Harry, or, The Boys and Girls of Boston.*[41] A New York reformer and the author of *The Dangerous Classes,* Charles Loring Brace maintained that prostitutes picked up by police or charity workers employed the same formulaic accounts of the fallen woman to gain sympathy. "Often they described themselves as belonging to some virtuous, respectable, and even wealthy family, seduced from the paths of virtue suddenly." A British author of domestic novels, Mrs. Mulock [Dinah Marie Craik], testified to the pervasiveness of the image of the female victim and denounced the exaggerated sentimentalism of her day: "Of late the fashion is to treat such a subject laying all the blame upon the seducer and exalting the seduced into a paragon of injured simplicity, whom society ought to pet, and soothe, and treat with far more interest and consideration than those who have not erred."[42]

The novel of the outcast woman held a fascination for the Victorian audience. She titillated the repressed secret lives of men and women yet did not undermine the ideology of women's innate purity and passionlessness because she neither chose her fate nor revealed any sexual motivation. Richard Henry Dana, a prominent Boston lawyer and novelist, was even drawn himself to rescue prostitutes. Dana would disguise himself as a common sailor and wander through vice districts. During one foray into the brothel area of Halifax, Nova Scotia, he approached a young streetwalker as if to be a customer. His journal entry of July 24, 1842, recounts her sad life: she, a motherless girl, was turned out of the house by a drunken father. She was then placed in service in a baker's home, but she was dismissed after her employer learned of his son's seduction of her. Without any resources or friends, she turned to prostitution. Dana laments the lack of compassion for this young prostitute: "What a dreadful fate has society ordered for a single fault in a woman."[43] Boston police chief Edward Savage described similar types of "scenes from real life" in his memoirs. He recalled many encounters with women "more sinned against than sinning." An entire chapter of his *Recollections* was devoted to the outcast woman, and he featured a long, heart-rending poem written as a letter from a prostitute to her mother. Hers is a tale of the lowly maid enchanted by the ignoble prince: "I know how oft you warned me, mother; / You told me oft the truth. / That village girls were seldom wed / By high and wealthy youth."[44] Unlike Dana, Savage, or reformers involved in rescue missions, the average person had little contact with actual prostitutes. Few readers transferred the sympathy they felt for betrayed fictional heroines to outcast women on the street.

Although the image of the fallen woman as an innocent victim became literary convention, it did not negate the deep-seated prejudice and condemnation of society toward sexually deviant women. The Victorian code, which dictated that a woman who abandoned her virtue had no place in society, was firmly planted in the middle class system of values. The sentimentalized accounts of fallen women in popular literature led to greater censure of women who did not fit the passive-victim model. The counterimage of the fallen angel was the evil temptress or siren of vice.

Two court cases highly publicized in Boston newspapers reveal the extent to which images of fallen women as victim or as viper could influence verdicts in the courtroom. One took place in Boston and involved the murder of a prostitute, Maria Bickford, by her lover, Albert Tirrell; the other occurred in New York City and was the trial of Amelia Norman, charged with the attempted murder of her seducer.

The defendant in the Boston case,[45] Albert Tirrell, was twenty-two years old, the son of a successful manufacturer. He resided in Weymouth, Massachusetts, was married, and had two children. Maria Bickford, the murdered woman, was also in her early twenties. She had been raised in Bangor, Maine, and married a respectable shoemaker in a neighboring town. After three years of marriage she left her husband and moved to Boston with a paramour, who abandoned her in a few months. Bickford, age nineteen, then turned to prostitution and lived in numerous houses of ill fame in New Bedford, Massachusetts, and Boston. From the time Tirrell met Bickford in a New Bedford brothel, he became her constant companion. They traveled together as man and wife, assuming new names as often as they moved. In Boston, or while visiting other cities, they stayed in some of the most fashionable hotels on the eastern seaboard. At one point, they furnished a house on London Street in Boston, which operated as a house of assignation; the name of "Maria Welch" appeared on the door. At the time of her death, Bickford was living in a boardinghouse owned by an elderly couple who charged high rents to unmarried men and women cohabiting.

The prosecuting attorney had a strong case against Tirrell. The defendant was known to have stayed with the victim the night of the murder, and the landlord testified to having locked up the building early in the evening. Tirrell had left Bickford's room before dawn and was not heard from for months; he remained in hiding in the South until he was captured by detectives. The most damning evidence against him was that several articles of his clothing were found clotted with blood in Bickford's room.

The Bickford murder case was not to be decided on the facts alone, however. The Tirrell family hired the brilliant and flamboyant defense attorney Rufus Choate. Choate realized early on that the only way to save his client was to undercut the sympathies felt for the victim, a beautiful young woman. He employed a standard courtroom technique, character assassination. While the ostensible purpose of Choate's line of questioning was to establish that Tirrell was devoted to Maria Bickford, that to kill her would have been an aberration, the desired effect was to portray Bickford as a totally depraved woman, a hardened prostitute.

This aspect of the trial took the form of a melodrama with demons and temptresses, victims and enchanted young men. The defendant's cousins, the Bedford Tirrells, supplied the courtroom with the scenario. They characterized Bickford as a wanton and reckless siren who had depleted nearly all of Tirrell's patrimony with her penchant for jewels and expensive dress. She was said to have been often intoxicated; her promiscuity took the form of flirtations, which aroused Tirrell's jealousy; she sought low and depraved company, demanding that the defendant escort her to dance halls and brothels. He was the devoted partner, abused and degraded by the woman who possessed him.

Choate worked at length to convince the jury that Maria Bickford had no redeeming qualities. Two witnesses were called solely to defame her character. One man revealed that he had seen Maria with a Creole named Frank Carr; another, a black man, testified that she had boarded with him in a house in Keith's Alley, a notorious hub of prostitution.

Choate's strategy succeeded. When the not guilty verdict was announced in the courtroom, the audience, who had come to empathize with Tirrell, let out a floor-shaking hurrah that spread from behind the bar to the gallery and then into the square outside. In order to free his client, Choate had had to prove false the media's image of Maria Bickford as the innocent victim crushed by evil forces. Months before the trial, bogus stories of Bickford's past began appearing in print. A "biographical" sketch printed in Boston's *Daily Mail* attributed Bickford's fall from virtue to a sorceress who prompted Maria to violate her marriage oath.

A spurious novel about her, *The Life and Death of Mrs. Maria Bickford,* was published several months before the trial.[46] All the events leading up to her meeting with Tirrell are fabricated. Its value lies in the material it provides for analyzing stereotypes and images of the heroine molded to appeal to a mass audience. Because there was a real Maria Bickford, it is possible to test these perceptions.

In the fictionalized version, Maria Bickford is depicted as a woman with intellectual accomplishments and poetic sensibilities as well as great beauty. Her tragic and inevitable fate is traced to her first seducer, a thoroughly debauched medical student from Georgia. Throughout the novel, Maria is deceived by men: a ship's captain offers her free passage, but exacts his price while she is on board; a cabbie takes her to a "respectable" boardinghouse that is a brothel. In all situations she is victimized, an unwilling participant in sexual transactions. Compare the fictional heroine with the real Maria Bickford. The real Bickford left her husband for another man (not Tirrell). She had become dissatisfied with her "humble and retired life" in Bangor after having been dazzled by Boston's elegance, variety, and bustle. Her husband, James Bickford, a steady, hard-working, religious man, remained loyal and supportive of Maria even after she had gone through several lovers and become a habitué of infamous houses. He repeatedly implored her to return as his wife and frequently sent her money. The nine men of the jury during Tirrell's trial were shown a woman with incredible power over men who had chosen a life of sin and forsaken an acceptable marriage.

The case against Amelia Norman provides a vivid contrast to the Bickford murder trial. Norman's trial in a New York court in 1844 illustrates how important role expectations were in assessing guilt or innocence. The defendant, at age sixteen and unmarried, came to the city for employment, as many farm girls did in the period. While there, she met Henry Ballard, a rich and influential gentleman who seduced her and kept her as his mistress until he tired of her. In a fit of desperation and rage, Norman attempted to kill him on the steps of the Waldorf Astoria Hotel. At the end of her trial, when the foreman of the jury declared her not guilty, the building shook with applause. Sympathies were clearly with the humble and betrayed. More significant than her poverty and his wealth was the fact that Norman was perceived as a defenseless female, a country girl preyed upon by a worldly and unscrupulous male. The prosecution in the Norman case asked the jury to decide whether it was worse to have their daughters ruined or their sons stabbed by prostitutes.

The jury perceived her as the injured party and chose to vindicate a woman's honor.[47]

Novelists who wrote about the life of a fallen woman had to depict her as an exploited victim in order to create a sympathetic character. Implicit in the fictional formula are expectations about male and female behavior—beliefs concerning women's sexual passivity and submission to male authority. Maria Bickford challenged these assumptions; Amelia Norman did not. As the outcomes of these cases demonstrate, the passive-victim thesis could be a double-edged sword.

In the end, the passive-victim thesis had many more negative than positive effects. Most important, images of fallen women in popular literature and moral reform journals channeled the debate on prostitution away from adverse social and economic structures toward cruel seducers and evil agents. Prostitution, rather than being seen as a social system that flowed from the economic and social dependence of women, appeared as an abberant or capricious set of circumstances that drove a woman off course from her natural life patterns.

The first stage of women's activism against prostitution, begun in the 1830s, had a profound effect on the future strategies to preserve women's sexual purity and on the feminist discourse on prostitution. The legal remedies and institutions moral reformers developed laid the basis for other protective strategies in the following decades. In the 1870s and 1880s, strictly supervised boardinghouses for single women sprang up in hundreds of cities, sponsored by women's Christian associations, and other likeminded organizations. Reformers formed Travelers' Aid societies to meet women traveling alone on steamers and trains and to steer them to respectable boardinghouses and employment agencies run by benevolent groups. Nearly every big city had a network of such protective agencies aimed at the single girl traveling alone.[48]

These were attempts to intercept women at the danger zones in cities and towns, and reformers believed that such a fail-safe system could create a protective shield for the woman adrift from home and family. The same rationale lay behind the the post–Civil War rise of institutions for female juveniles on the road to ruin and for adult women's prisons that sought to "protect" women who violated chastity codes.

For the Christian matrons who spent hours in train and ship depots, or who dared to enter bordellos to rescue their fallen sisters, accounts of women duped, manipulated, or enslaved into prostitution were in themselves protections from some disturbing sides of prostitution. Reformers in daily missionary work encountered women who admitted to selling their sex for the monetary rewards. They also met women who supplemented wages with casual prostitution or bartered their sex for a new dress. To turn to prostitution for survival could be reconciled with moral reformers' assertion of women's innate purity, although editors of the *Friend of Virtue* played down this motivation. But they could not comprehend the idea that prostitution for working class women could be a rational choice for women faced with a field of limited opportunities and options in the labor and marriage markets. The all-inclusive sisterhood that purity reformers envisioned had a rural Yankee evangelical foundation; class and ethnic divisions were not built into the model.

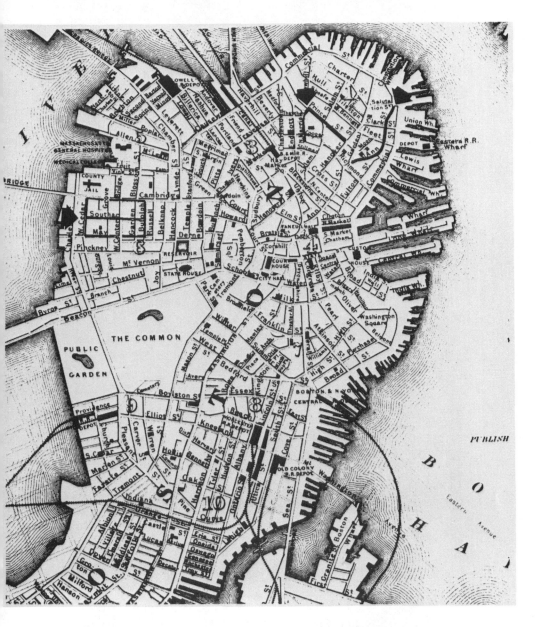

Boston, mid-nineteenth century. The North End vice district is indicated by the arrows at the upper right; the Hill district (West End), where Mayor Quincy's raid took place, is indicated by the arrow at the upper left. (Courtesy of the Boston University Geography Department.)

"The Outcast," an example of the sentimentalized images of poor girls easily seduced into prostitution. Her story appears in the memoirs of Boston Police Chief Edward Savage, *Recollections of a Boston Police Officer: Boston by Daylight and Gaslight* (Boston, 1865).

Portrait of Maria Bickford, a young woman whose 1845 murder (at the hands of her paramour) in Boston's prostitution district was sensationalized and distorted by the press and the courts. (Courtesy of the Social Law Library, Boston.)

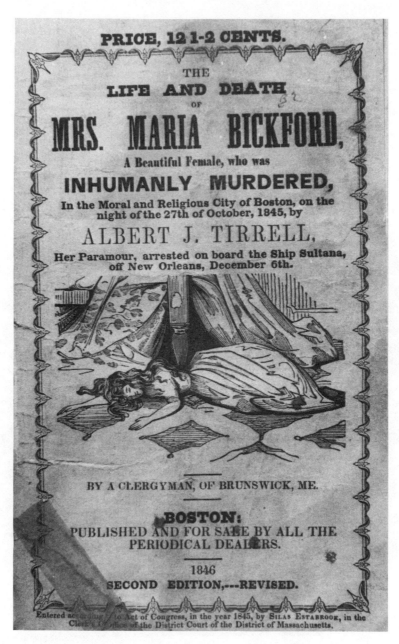

The title page of an anonymous fictional account of Maria Bickford's life. The story follows a conventional nineteenth-century plot line of the innocent country lass seduced and abandoned by unscrupulous men. Maria is seduced by a Southern gentleman and then by a ship's captain, who finds her hiding as a stowaway and demands sex in return for her passage. (Courtesy of the Social Law Library, Boston.)

MISS CATHERINE AUGUSTA LECOMPTE, *alias* KATE ALLEY

ABOVE: A well-known Boston prostitute, who accumulated enough savings to operate her own brothel. RIGHT: More typical of the prostitute's life pattern was Little Hel, who floated in and out of prostitution to other jobs, marriage, and monogamous relationships with men during her prostitution career. Illustrations from *The G'hals of Boston* (Boston, 1850), a popular journalistic account of Boston prostitutes. (Courtesy of the New York Public Library.)

HELEN GURNEY, *alias* LITTLE HEL.

ABOVE: "How the Memphis Firemen Extinguish the Social Evil" (from an 1873 issue of the *Illustrated Police News*). As this cartoon suggests, in real life prostitutes often were treated with derision and humiliated in public, particularly in the police wagon on the trip to the courthouse. (Courtesy of the Boston Public Library.)

RIGHT: In many countries that regulated sex commerce, prostitutes had to submit photographs of themselves to the police. This Stockholm prostitute, from the 1890 police register, rented an elegant set of clothes for the occasion. (Courtesy of Polismusuet, Stockholm.)

PART II

Prostitutes and Their Keepers, 1860–1900

4

Prostitutes

FEW POPULAR NOVELISTS, reformers, or even "experts" writing about prostitution during the nineteenth century recognized the variety in the experiences of prostitutes. Instead they viewed prostitutes as a homogeneous group and reduced their varied histories to formulas. According to the standard scenarios, prostitutes were either passive victims of cruel seducers and scheming procurers or eager recruits seeking a life of indulgence and idleness. But no matter what their stated reasons for becoming prostitutes, supposedly they drifted steadily downward to the dregs of the trade and died in their prime of disease or suicide. Yet the social histories of prostitution suggest a range of experiences and motivations. Rural women came to prostitution by different routes than did urban-born prostitutes; immigrant prostitutes had experiences different from those of American-born prostitutes; younger women were often more vulnerable to the coercive sides of prostitution than were older women.

Scottish physician William Tait, writing in the 1840s, recognized that women became prostitutes for different reasons. Nevertheless, in his study, *Magdalenism,* he argued that the principles governing prostitution were clear-cut and simple. He divided the causes of prostitution into two categories: natural and accidental. By *natural* he meant all the conditions that might be considered internal motivations or deliberate choices— licentious temper, pride and love of dress, dishonesty, desire to have property, indolence, and so forth. By *accidental* he meant external forces, such as seduction, low wages, or poor treatment by parents. Natural/

unnatural, external/internal, or voluntary/involuntary were arbitrary classifications that obscured the complex set of circumstances motivating a woman to become a prostitute. Not one event but a chain of expectations, options, and events led certain women into prostitution.[1]

Most of our knowledge about nineteenth-century prostitutes' lives— their backgrounds, motivations, and futures—concerns women who found their way into the official registers. The social profiles of prostitutes extracted from these records are those not of demimondes listed in the gentleman's guides to elegant brothels, but of women who had to ply their trade in public places.[2] These women rarely recorded their own histories; what we know of them comes from manuscript records of almshouses, prisons, city hospitals, police registers, and private reformatory institutions. In reconstructing the social profiles of prostitutes, I have tried to isolate the characteristics common to prostitutes in the United States and Europe during the nineteenth century as well as to highlight differences. State policy toward prostitution had an effect on the supply of prostitutes; the comparisons I make between American, French, Swedish, and Italian prostitutes are attempts to come to grips with the ways in which regulation systems shaped the experiences of women in the trade.

Some general characteristics of the experience of prostitutes in industrial cities resulted from market forces, work pressures, and the social stigma attached to prostitution. An almost universal social fact about prostitution, both past and present, is the degree to which it is an occupation of young women. During the second half of the nineteenth century, the average age of prostitutes in Boston, New York, and Philadelphia was between twenty-one and twenty-three. Similarly, prostitutes in Paris, London, Bologna, Stockholm, and Amsterdam, during the same period, were between the ages of sixteen and twenty-five, with an average age in the early twenties. Nearly three-quarters of the prostitutes noted in the Boston records were twenty-five or younger; in the city as a whole, census figures show the greatest concentrations of women to be in this age group. However, even in cities with relatively few young women, prostitutes still tended to be under twenty-five.

That prostitutes often retired by the age of twenty-five suggests that prostitution was a transitory phase in the lives of women. Further evidence of this comes from William Sanger's 1858 survey of two thousand prostitutes at New York's house of correction on Blackwell's Island. He found that 60 percent had been prostitutes for no more than three years and that a significant portion had only commenced their careers within the previous six months. French physician and social investigator Alexandre Parent-Duchatelet also emphasized the youth of prostitutes in his extensive study of Paris women in the police registers, published in 1837. He asserted that Parisian prostitutes rarely continued their trade for more than four years. The same was true for Dutch prostitutes, despite the fact that they faced less harassment and control than did women under other European systems of legalized prostitution. These findings on age and duration in the trade of Victorian prostitutes offer some persuasive evidence that prostitution was a stage in a life and not a career or profession.[3]

In assessing the meaning of prostitution in the course of a lifetime, it cannot be overemphasized that it was a temporary stage for nearly all who resorted to it. The age at which most prostitutes abandoned their trade was the age at which most women married. The decision to take up prostitution usually came at a vulnerable point in a woman's life—a time when a daughter was seeking freedom from the restraints of home and several years before the age of marriage. For daughters of the working class, this period was often extended because their contribution to the family economy was vital. Thus, not only was prostitution a way for these young women to rebel against parental watchfulness over social and sexual morals, but it also meant freedom from familial financial responsibilities—a way to live on their own and keep their income.[4]

Nineteenth-century prostitution, like that of today, is characterized by mobility. Jennifer James's study of prostitutes in the 1970s highlights the geographical mobility of women in the trade; she interprets this characteristic as an adaptive strategy for handling police harassment.[5] Prostitutes a hundred years earlier also led peripatetic lives, with increased police activity in one city often leading to a move to another. But the historical record also suggests that prostitutes migrated to find better economic opportunities or to escape family and friends. In the boom and bust towns of the American West, prostitutes followed the floating population of single men. Personal accounts of prostitutes in American cities, as well as the statistics indicating short-term residency in sex commerce, suggest a rapid turnover in brothels and frequent migrations of prostitutes within and between cities. Prostitutes' lives also revealed a fluidity between prostitution and respectable employment. This was common among prostitutes in British garrison towns before the implementation of a system of regulation. But even in cities with regulated prostitution, there is some evidence that prostitutes migrated from city to city and often moved in and out of prostitution.[6]

On the surface, prostitutes in nineteenth-century cities appear to have had similar social and demographic profiles, yet the routes to prostitution and the experiences of prostitutes varied not only between societies but also within them. Swedish historian Gunilla Johansson found considerable differences between prostitutes who had migrated from the Swedish countryside and Stockholm-born prostitutes. The women from rural areas tended to come from more stable families and were from a higher social class than were the Stockholm-born prostitutes. They usually had a previous long-term relationship with a man, began prostituting themselves at a later age, and spent fewer years in the trade than did Stockholm-born women. Even their images of prostitution differed. Prostitutes from Stockholm described prostitution as attractive and exciting, as a life that gave them the opportunity to visit restaurants with their customers. The women from the countryside more often viewed prostitution as the only way to escape boring and low-paid heavy work or as a means to support themselves or their children. Mary Gibson, in her study of Italian prostitution in the nineteenth century, also contrasts the rural and urban-born prostitute, but she finds another pattern—prostitutes from the countryside appeared to be the more disadvantaged group.[7]

In my research on nineteenth-century American cities, the greatest differences in social background, options, and position in the prostitution economy were found to be between native-born and foreign-born prostitutes. These differences reflected the cleavage between immigrant and native-born in American society. Both the migratory patterns and the poverty of nineteenth-century immigrants set them apart from the earlier settlers from Europe. The vast majority of nineteenth-century immigrants lived in the kind of crowded, working class city neighborhoods where the prostitution trade was most often found.

Social Backgrounds

At midcentury in three major American cities—Boston, New York, and Philadelphia—foreign-born prostitutes outnumbered native-born in the official records, although immigrants were a minority of the total population. In Boston, for example, 36 percent of all women, but 55 percent of all prostitutes, were foreign born. Over two-thirds of the foreign-born prostitutes were Irish. The Irish, who emigrated during the famine years, were largely without skills or resources. Compared to their numbers in the city, Boston's Irish were overrepresented in the penal institutions (see figure 4.1). British and Canadian prostitutes formed the next largest immigrant group, but they were less numerous than the Irish.

Predictably, native-born women—45 percent of Boston's recorded prostitute population—were inhabitants of the city and adjacent towns. But a significant number had come from New England towns outside of Massachusetts. Maine and New Hampshire supplied the most prostitutes from New England; rural men and women from those states came to Boston in unprecedented numbers during the 1850s and 1860s (see table 4.1). Only 2 percent of Boston's prostitutes were black, which is not surprising in view of the taboos against even illicit interracial sex in northern cities.

New York and Philadelphia records showed the same high proportions of foreign-born prostitutes. Sanger reported that 61 percent of Blackwell's

FIGURE 4.1

Proportion of Irish Among Prostitutes in the House of Correction, All Inmates of the House of Correction, and All Bostonians

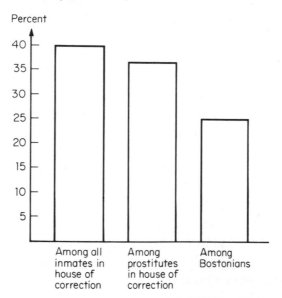

SOURCE: Registers of Inmates at the Boston House of Correction, 1858–65; *Abstracts of Returns of Keepers of Jails and Overseers of the House of Correction, 1855–65;* and Oscar Handlin, *Boston Immigrants: A Study in Acculturation* (Cambridge, Mass., 1959), appendix table 8.

TABLE 4.1

Birthplace of Prostitutes in Boston House of Correction,
1858–65

	Percentage	N
Boston and Environs	23.4	239
Other Massachusetts	4.3	44
Maine	5.2	53
New Hampshire	3.5	36
Vermont	1.2	12
Rhode Island	1.6	16
Connecticut	0.7	7
Other U.S.	4.3	44
Ireland	36.8	376
England	9.2	94
Canada	9.8	100
Other Foreign	0.2	2
Total	100.0[a]	1,023

[a]Figures do not total 100 percent due to rounding.
SOURCE: Register of the Inmates of the Boston House of Correction and House of Industry, 1858–65.

Island prostitutes were immigrants, the majority being Irish. Similarly, more than half of the prostitutes in the registry of the Philadelphia city hospital between 1861 and 1863 were foreign born, again notably Irish. Foreign-born women also comprised a significant portion of the prostitute population in other cities across the country. In Minnesota, Irish and Scandinavian prostitutes dominated the police registers. These were the groups in the lowest-paid occupations. In San Francisco, French, Spanish, and Chinese prostitutes were the first prostitutes to come to the city in the 1840s, and they dominated sex commerce throughout the early decades of settlement.[8]

By its very nature prostitution is a single woman's pursuit. Every study from the nineteenth century to the present confirms this self-evident truth. However, compared with European prostitutes, a surprising number of prostitutes in nineteenth-century American cities—at least in Boston, New York, and Philadelphia—were married. Thirty percent of Boston's prostitutes were or had been married, and in New York and Philadelphia a substantial proportion of prostitutes—between 23 and 24 percent—were or had been married. Consistently, married prostitutes were likely to be foreign born, even if one takes age into account. However, few prostitutes seemed to be living with their husbands, a situation that would become more common at the turn of the century among immigrant couples.

Prostitutes

Prostitution, in fact, offered some women a way out of marriage. A significant number of prostitutes in Sanger's survey cited ill treatment by husbands as the reason behind their decision to become prostitutes. Among the few Philadelphia prostitutes who gave reasons for their failed marriages, most said that their husbands had mistreated them or had failed to provide for them. That so many foreign-born workers—particularly Irish—had to leave their families to find employment on canals and railroads in other cities may account for the high proportion of foreign-born married prostitutes. If a husband died—these jobs had high accident rates—or deserted his wife, prostitution may have provided a means by which the wife could support herself and her children.[9]

Foreign-born prostitutes differed from their native-born counterparts in other respects besides marital status. Most important, immigrant women tended to enter prostitution later in life and to stay in prostitution longer. This was true in the nineteenth century as well as in the early twentieth century. Among Philadelphia and Boston prostitutes in the 1860s and 1870s, the average age of foreign-born prostitutes was higher than that of native-born. Probation records from 1910 to 1920, which mainly concern young or first-time offenders, reveal a similar pattern. Prostitutes over twenty-five were almost always foreign born. These records also show that the foreign-born practiced the trade more continuously than did the native-born, which suggests that they were more likely to be full-time professionals.[10]

Another striking feature of foreign-born prostitutes was their low literacy. Native-born prostitutes were significantly more literate than foreign-born prostitutes: 73.6 percent compared with 55.8 percent. Sanger's study of New York prostitutes also revealed a disparity between native-and foreign-born literacy—75 percent to 60 percent. The majority of foreign-born prostitutes in both cities were Irish—from a country with one of the lowest literacy rates in Western Europe; they were actually more literate than their countrymen back home, though they fell far below the American literacy standard.[11]

Foreign-born prostitutes had a different profile from that of native-born. Immigrants were more likely to be married or to have been married; they tended to be older and to remain prostitutes longer. The foreign-born women appear to have had less education and fewer skills than native-born residents. They most probably lacked the family networks for getting jobs in certain trades.[12] Their situation reflects a general axiom in the prostitution economy: the older the prostitute and the longer she has been in the trade, the fewer her options in the labor and marriage markets.

Speculating as to why so many prostitutes were foreign born, Sanger concluded that many women who emigrated to American cities were trapped into prostitution, unaware of the dangers awaiting them in boardinghouses and on the streets. Yet his statistics argue against him. When asked how soon immigrants became prostitutes after they landed in the United States, few of Sanger's respondents answered that they had taken to the streets within the first year of their arrival. In fact, 60 percent had been in America at least four years before they entered prostitution. Nor did these women come to New York penniless or totally without friends or family. The majority claimed that they had received monetary assistance to emigrate and had relatives or friends already here.[13] The Philadelphia hospital records reveal similar patterns about foreign-born prostitutes there. They tended to emigrate to the United States between the ages of eleven and twenty-one; yet most of these women entered prostitution between nineteen and twenty-five years of age. Tales of women trapped into prostitution the moment they set foot in the new land were at odds with the accounts prostitutes gave and even with the facts investigators gathered. The women seem to have become familiar with American ways and to have assimilated American values and aspirations before becoming prostitutes.

Occupational data on family background argue against the common view that nineteenth-century prostitutes as a group came from the poorest and most degraded homes. Although few prostitutes in the New York survey were from upper or middle class families, neither were they from families in the lowest occupational groups. Most were the daughters of artisans or farmers (see table 4.2). Out of 123 respondents in the Philadelphia register, more than half had fathers who were artisans; about one-fifth were farmers; and the rest were laborers or soldiers.

Again, however, there is some difference between foreign-born and native-born women. Foreign-born prostitutes were more often daughters of unskilled laborers, whereas native-born prostitutes had fathers who were principally artisans. An artisan who did not own his own shop and worked under a master was still respectable in America. However, artisans as a group were losing status in the first half of the nineteenth century, when the craft tradition was breaking down and a general deskilling of labor occurred. This happened earliest in East Coast cities, where large-scale manufacturing and technological innovations transformed the posi-

TABLE 4.2

Father's Occupation, Blackwell's Island Prostitutes

Occupational Group	Percentage	N
High White Collar		
(merchants, professionals, businessmen)	5.9	112
Low White Collar		
(tradesmen, clerks, government officials)	15.1	286
Skilled Workers		
(artisans, mechanics)	33.0	626
Semiskilled Workers		
(soldiers, sailors)	9.3	176
Laborers	13.6	259
Farmers	23.2	440
Total	100.0[a]	1,899

[a]Figures do not total 100 percent due to rounding.
SOURCE: Calculated from listed occupations in William W. Sanger, *The History of Prostitution: Its Extent, Causes, and Effects Throughout the World* (1858; reprint, New York, 1974), pp. 535–36. One hundred six cases unascertained. Occupational rankings are based on Stephan Thernstrom, *The Other Bostonians: Poverty and Progress in the American Metropolis, 1880–1970* (Cambridge, Mass., 1973), appendix B. Farmers were included as a separate category.

tion of skilled workers in the textile and shoe industries. Did daughters of artisans and small family farm owners bring with them expectations of economic and social well-being that could not be fulfilled in a world of narrowing opportunities?[14]

In analyzing the prospects and possibilities for young women, it is important to remember that a complete reversal of circumstances could be brought about by the death or illness of a father. Most of the New York prostitutes Sanger interviewed were orphans; the majority of their fathers had died before the girls reached sixteen. Numerous other studies of prostitutes also include a high proportion of women who had lost one or both parents. Such losses were very common in the nineteenth century, but they had the greatest impact on working class families.[15]

Nineteenth-century studies of the family economy reveal the precarious financial situations of the working class. The serious illness or death of a breadwinner, in an era when few families had savings or private insurance, left families in dire straits. Even in cases where family savings or support from relatives offset the devastating loss of the main family earner, daughters still faced diminished marriage opportunities and greater economic pressures.[16]

Sanger expressed bewilderment at the substantial numbers of American-born prostitutes "in a land where a good education is within the reach of everyone; where industry if properly applied in the right channels, will afford a comfortable maintenance for all." Underlying Sanger's optimism about the opportunities in America, however, was an expectation that most women would marry and have husbands who would provide the family wage. Ironically, Sanger referred to working women as "dependent women." By not living under a father's or husband's roof, he assumed, women would have to look to the state, charitable organizations, or illicit liaisons for subsistence.[17] But for many working class women marriage was not a ticket to a secure life. For some women, prostitution was the only way to avoid becoming "dependent" on public or private charity.

Options and Expectations

Expectations play a key role in a woman's decision to enter prostitution. To underscore the role of expectations in a prostitute's life choices is not to deny the existence of economic necessity as a driving force behind a woman's decision to sell her sexual services. Women's lack of access to skilled jobs and limited participation in the labor force was the bitter root from which prostitution grew in the Victorian city, and the same conditions nourish the prostitution economy today. True, the vast majority of prostitutes were not from the most economically depressed families, nor were they women on the verge of starvation. Still, native-born daughters of artisans were a class of women whose life chances did appear bleaker than had those of their mothers and grandmothers. For foreign-born prostitutes, unfulfilled expectations of a better life in a new land cannot be discounted in evaluating a woman's entry into prostitution. For example, among Sanger's respondents one-quarter of the women stated that their main reason for emigrating was "to improve their condition."[18]

In the first half of the nineteenth century, American women gained access to new occupations in industry; one could find female typesetters, bookbinders, shoebinders, weavers, and so on. But they were also shut out from trades that had once been open to them. More rigid notions of female propriety led to women's exclusion from taverns, shops, and street-stall peddling. Women's home industries were most affected by the transformations in the reorganization of work and technological innovations in this first stage of industrial capitalism. The needle trades encompassed some of the most exploitative work environments for women. Since hand sewing was a skill nearly all women had, there was no shortage of applicants even for the lowest of wages. Sewing, which was mainly contracted labor, allowed women to combine work and family responsibilities. However, homework (called outwork) isolated the seamstress from co-workers and left her powerless to defend herself against a piece-work system that demanded more and more hours of work at lower and lower wage rates. The invention of the sewing machine in the 1850s drove piece rates lower and women often had to work fifteen to eighteen hours a day to earn a subsistence wage.[19]

Yet shining examples of working women's success did exist. Lowell, Massachusetts, mill workers Harriet Hanson Robinson and Lucy Larcom, mentioned earlier, landed skilled jobs, accumulated savings, and took advantage of educational opportunities.[20] But such women represented a small portion of the female labor force. Moreover, in the second half of the nineteenth century, speedups, lower wages, and worse conditions induced many native-born women to leave the mills; immigrant families replaced them. Thomas Dublin, writing about the careers of Lowell mill workers, concludes that by the 1850s even these cases of career mobility for women were disappearing. Ceilings on women's earnings reduced wage differentials between skilled and unskilled; consequently, the earnings gap between native-born (who had been favored with the skilled jobs in mills) and immigrant narrowed. The feminization of teaching, firmly established by midcentury, afforded some women job security and status. Substantial numbers of women entered the male-dominated printing trade; typesetting was a skill in demand that paid well.[21] But skilled jobs that provided women with a decent standard of living were the exception rather than the rule.

A gender separation of work by tasks and trade emerged early within industrial capitalism. This had the effect of defining women's traditional skills, sewing and service occupations, as unskilled work. It also tracked women into the lowest paying jobs within industries that employed both sexes. Even in trades where women and men did the same work, women were paid only a portion of what men made. This dual labor market was based upon prevailing assumptions that men earned the family wage and working women were unmarried, lived with their parents, and either supplemented the household income or earned money for luxuries. But this view ignored the realities of scores of women who were primary wage earners—single women who supported themselves or their families—and women's vital contribution to the family economy among the working class.[22]

The prostitutes in these surveys during the 1850s and 1860s had been employed in traditional female occupations. Over 75 percent of Sanger's respondents listed a former occupation, a significant percentage given the rough estimates of women's labor force participation in this era—between 10 and 15 percent of women working outside the home and family farm. These women tended to be employed in the unskilled occupations. Both the New York and Philadelphia prostitutes followed the standard trades of nineteenth-century working women. Only three women out of Sanger's two thousand prostitutes were in white-collar professions. All three of these were teachers; an additional eight were still attending school. Domestic service was the major occupation, with 49 percent, followed by the garment trades, with 21 percent (see table 4.3). One-quarter of the women claimed to be still living with their parents and not employed.[23] Among prostitutes in Philadelphia, the occupations for native-born and immigrants were almost identical.

As noted earlier, domestic service, the most common occupation for women throughout the nineteenth century, had features that made prostitution a seductive alternative. On the surface, domestic employment had some advantages over most other female jobs. Domestics were guaranteed shelter and food and their wages were comparable to those of other unskilled working women. Weekly wages averaged between three and four dollars, not much less than that earned by many unskilled factory

TABLE 4.3

Occupations of New York Prostitutes at the Blackwell's Island Prison, 1855–58

Trade	Percentage	N
Domestic	48.6	972
Garment-Related	20.6	412
General Trades[a]	4.6	92
Living with Parents	25.0	499
Miscellaneous[b]	1.3	25
Total	100.0[c]	2,000

[a]Including cigar packers, factory workers, shoe binders, and so on.
[b]Anomalous types of employment and white collar jobs: nurses, schoolteachers, students, and so on.
[c]Figures do not total 100 percent due to rounding.
SOURCE: William W. Sanger, *The History of Prostitution: Its Extent, Causes, and Effects Throughout the World* (1858; reprint, New York, 1974), p. 254.

workers, who also had to pay for rent and food. Most important, domestic service was not seasonal, in contrast to so many other trades. Although a servant might suddenly be fired because of her employer's financial losses or as a result of a fight with her mistress, there was always enough demand for qualified help for her to get another job.[24]

What made service an undesirable work situation for many women was the long hours, isolation, and lack of freedom and control over their lives. Social reformer Lucy Salmon's investigation of service in the late nineteenth century recorded the universal distaste for service among working women. Respondents to her survey revealed a general attitude toward service as demeaning and degrading work, which most of the women felt was pervasive in American society.[25] According to Carol Lasser, by midcentury Yankee farm girls no longer went into service.[26] Similarly, Alice Kessler-Harris documents the superiority factory workers felt toward domestics, even though the latter were often better paid. A New York newspaper in 1881 reported that factory operatives believed "they take a higher place in the social scale than is accorded them when they do housework." As one study of Toronto prostitution at the turn of the century argues, the move from service to prostitution was one step down for a woman already at the bottom on the occupational ladder.[27]

The low status attached to domestic service might also have been the reason behind the contradictory responses of prostitutes at the Philadelphia hospital. Asked what their trade was, only 15 out of 135 women said that they were domestics; yet, in response to a question on what employment they had had before or while they practiced prostitution, 75 replied that they had worked at service.

One of the first professional statisticians, Carroll Wright, conducted a survey of prostitutes in Boston houses of ill fame, in 1884, more than twenty-five years after Sanger's study. Like Sanger, he found that prostitutes came from low-status, low-paying jobs. Having interviewed 170 women in brothels, Wright noted that 60 of them had come directly from service-related employment: housework or restaurant/hotel work.[28] Domestic servants were the dominant group in every study of prostitution in America, Britain, and France in the nineteenth century. The vice reports of early twentieth-century investigators also show that service was the main occupation of women before they became prostitutes, although domestic work represented a much smaller proportion of the female labor market by then.[29]

Wright's survey showed that a very high proportion of the prostitutes—82 percent—had been employed in some occupation. But in tracing the former occupations of prostitutes, he also revealed that frequent job changes were common. Most women had pursued two or three jobs before becoming prostitutes. Considering the average age of prostitutes, this meant several changes in types of employment before they reached their mid-twenties. The vast majority had performed housework at some point in their careers. One woman started out as a nurse, switched to waitressing, and then was a houseworker. Another, more on the fringes of the work force, began as a coal picker, took up begging, and then became a dressmaker.[30] This unusual documentation of prostitutes' job histories tells of the instability of their work lives and their lack of integration in the work force. They comprised a transient labor force, but their experiences were not that different from those of most working women, who continually faced seasonal unemployment or lacked the skills to ensure them a place in a trade or profession.

Economic incentives must be seen as underlying the complex social and psychological forces in prostitution—a convergence of expectations, options, and circumstances. According to Sanger, prostitutes could earn in one night what working women earned in up to several weeks. Studies done in the second decade of the present century show striking findings. Whereas women earned between forty-six and eighty dollars a week as prostitutes, their wages in former occupations had averaged five or six dollars weekly.[31] Other major studies of prostitutes in the twentieth century confirm the association of occupation and wages with prostitution. One of the most provocative is Mary Conyngton's 1911 report on the relationship between female criminality and occupation. Predictably, she found that domestic servants comprised the main group in the female criminal population and that other low-skilled and low-paying jobs were also overrepresented. Women in nontraditional female jobs, or holding newly created jobs in the service sector and retail sales, were the smallest group.[32]

Two physicians, Jau Don Ball and Thomas Hayward, conducted another survey of San Francisco prostitutes between 1915 and 1917; they found a broader occupational cross-section among the women they interviewed. In contrast to Conyngton's survey of prostitutes in private and public reformatories—who tended to be from the lowest class of prostitutes—they probably reached the upper levels of the prostitute economy. The Berkeley Chief of Police escorted them to 66 houses of prostitution, and they gathered data on the former occupations of 262 prostitutes.

While the majority of the women they interviewed had come from blue-collar jobs—60 percent had done domestic and factory work—a third listed stenographer, telephone operator, or sales clerk as their former occupation.[33]

Conyngton considered the element of ambition the strongest deterrent against a woman choosing an immoral life. She believed that saleswomen had the possibility of working their way up the occupational ladder to managerial positions with high wages and responsibilities.[34] Though she romanticized the opportunities sales- and service-sector jobs offered working women, she nevertheless understood the structural underpinnings of prostitution and insisted that higher wages and better employment opportunities would remove the economic incentives.

Conyngton pinpointed the play of expectations and options that enticed women into prostitution, an insight that few social investigators in the nineteenth and early twentieth centuries acknowledged. Yet one can find evidence even in the first wave of female industrial workers in the United States that wage-earning women derived a sense of competency and worth from work outside the home. Letters of Lowell mill workers in the 1830s and 1840s expressed a sense of pride and personal independence stemming from their earning capacity.[35]

Motivation

Nineteenth-century women confronted an extremely constricted labor market and wage system that assumed they were marginal or temporary workers. Prostitution may have appeared as a rational choice, especially for those most disadvantaged in society—immigrants and blacks. This is not to say that prostitutes weighed the costs and benefits of entering the trade, or that they even had an accurate picture of the risks, rigors, or psychological effects of the life choice. Yet this perspective is perhaps more realistic than the view of social investigators and reformers who portrayed prostitutes as totally passive actors, driven by starvation or kidnapped by procurers.

Throughout the Victorian era, discussion of the causes of prostitution centered on the voluntary-or-involuntary question. Both Sanger and Duchatelet in their studies emphasized the lack of volition in a woman's entry into prostitution. Sanger employed categories such as *"abandoned* by paramours" or *"banished* from home" (emphasis added). Duchatelet characterized one group of prostitutes as "products of extreme misery or sheer destitution."[36]

In his study Sanger asked two thousand prostitutes what caused them to enter prostitution. More than one-third cited having a personal inclination to prostitution, wanting an easy life, or being too idle to work. "Inclination" was the second most frequent answer, only one percentage point lower than "destitution." Refusing to accept the idea that women might be inclined to prostitution, Sanger insisted that these respondents were really motivated by other forces: liquor, seduction, or persuasion by other prostitutes. He discounted inclination because he interpreted it as sexual desire. But "inclination" as a reason may have captured a search for adventure or independence, a desire for a life of ease and financial security, or merely the practical outcome of weighing options.[37]

Economic hardship was undeniably the crucial factor in the lives of many women who became prostitutes in American and European cities. In both Sanger's and Duchatelet's surveys, the majority of prostitutes gave destitution as their reason for entering the trade. Sanger recounted many histories of seamstresses unable to eke out a living during unemployment or slack periods. One prostitute he quoted "took to the streets because she had no work, no money and no home." The captain of a New York police station to which another prostitute was brought claimed that the girl had struggled hard with the world before she became a prostitute, sleeping in stationhouses at night, living on bread and water during the day.[38]

As these examples illustrate, there were desperate women who had to prostitute themselves or starve. However, the belief that only starving women prostituted themselves missed the range of situations and experiences of women who claimed that economic necessity was the cause of their entering prostitution. An account from British journalist Henry Mayhew's *London Labour and the London Poor,* published in 1862, sheds some light on a prostitute's perceptions of her options. One woman— after having been seduced, kept by her lover for several months, and then abandoned—spent more than ten years in the "gay ladies life" because she had nothing else:

I don't leave this sort of life because I'm in a manner used to it, and what could I do if I did? I've no character. I've never been used to do anything, and I don't see what employment I stand a chance of getting. Then if I had to sit hours and hours all day long and part of the night too, sewing or anything like that, I should get tired. It would worrit [sic] me so never having been accustomed, you see, I couldn't stand it.[39]

What Mayhew described as this woman's philosophy of sinning was in reality a hard pragmatism, a way of making the best of what she saw as a no-win situation. In other words, her choice was reasonable in an irrational social universe: one in which social and economic conditions forced some women to earn a livelihood but fostered an ideology that denied them decent wages; one that censured only women in illicit sexuality but insisted that they were the weaker parties unable to protect themselves against male sexual advances; and one that idealized motherhood but did not provide social services for single women who had to raise children.

Although moral reformers insisted that seduction was the primary cause of prostitution, few prostitutes cited that reason. Only 15 percent of Sanger's interviewees listed seduction as the cause of prostitution. Among the Paris prostitutes, seduction was given as a cause by 14 percent.[40] Statistics that compare the age of a woman's first sexual experience with the age she began prostitution suggest that loss of chastity did not lead directly to prostitution. In fact, on the average, the age of first sexual contact came one or two years before the first prostitution experience.[41] Still, nonmarital sexual relations often had consequences that led a woman to turn to prostitution. Premarital pregnancy was the most obvious example. Nearly half of the New York prostitutes at Blackwell's Island claimed to have children; a third of the prostitutes were single mothers. Similarly, among registered prostitutes in nineteenth-century Paris and Stockholm, about a third had children outside of wedlock.[42] In an era without social services for single mothers, prostitution was one of the few occupations to provide women with enough resources to board children with either relatives or other families.

Although women who engaged in nonmarital sexual relations or who had illegitimate offspring did not necessarily become prostitutes, studies of prostitutes suggest a pattern of drift from sexual encounters to noncommercial casual sex to full-time prostitution. One can find evidence for this pattern in the Stockholm police registers, which noted the names of young women who had been warned by police about their involvement in casual sex or the fast life. Some, according to Johansson's research, took the warning seriously, but many others soon made their way into the registers as prostitutes. Even today, in an era of greater tolerance for premarital sexual activity, two extensive research projects on juvenile prostitutes (in Seattle and in San Francisco) assert that a reputation for being promiscuous contributed to identification with a deviant lifestyle, and subsequent entrance into prostitution.[43]

In Sanger's nineteenth-century study, in the vice commission surveys of the second decade of this century, and in present-day research, bad relations with parents, family abuse, and incest have been shown to be primary causes in a prostitute's assessment of her motivations. Still, the critical fact remains that women in these situations have few options that enable them to leave home and earn a living, other than going on the street. Young men in the nineteenth century could find unskilled work and cheap boardinghouses when they faced an intolerable home situation. Even today, young male runaways are in better position to live on their own than are young females in the same situation.

Opportunity

In many instances, some circumstance or event precipitated a woman's entry into prostitution—for example, loss of employment, premarital pregnancy, or parents' driving her out of the house. But a main link in the chain of events that led into prostitution is opportunity—the contact with a madam, a pimp, a prostitute, or a person with other connections to sex commerce. Nineteenth-century novels and moral reform journals were obsessed with the procurer who sought out women traveling alone on trains and boats. Some impressionistic evidence casts doubt on how frequently such meetings, if they occurred, led to prostitution. Recruitment into prostitution most often came through neighborhood contacts, relatives, or friends. Sanger recognized this phenomenon as "bad company," which he claimed 16 percent of the women in his study gave as the cause of their entering prostitution.[44] Vice commission surveys and probation records in the early twentieth century had more specific references, such as "persuaded by girl friends" or "met bad associates at work."

The visibility of prostitution in certain neighborhoods in itself increased the probability that a woman might take up the trade. Opportunity lurked at every street corner where a prostitute solicited; it called out from every known brothel. Prostitutes often lived in the same tenements or next door to working class families, and children sat on stoops watching customers go with women to their rooms.[45] The open vice districts that existed in certain cities until World War I—Storeyville in New Orleans, the Barbary Coast in San Francisco, the tenderloin areas in Chicago and New York—were magnets for women who were attracted to prostitution but lacked contacts in the trade. Even in cities with a less institutionalized sex commerce, runaways could easily locate the brothel district.

Current studies of prostitution have focused on the importance of a key contact already in the trade as a catalyst in the process.[46] Eleanor Miller, in a recent study of Milwaukee streetwalkers, maintains that the interrelationship between family and neighborhood deviant networks may account for the high proportion of black women among prostitutes today. According to Miller, being closely connected with large numbers of people through living under one roof in extended families and having multiple caretakers that include both neighbors and friends increases the chances that a poor girl will be influenced by someone already in a deviant network.[47] What we know of tenement life in the late nineteenth and early twentieth centuries suggests that the same principle of family and neighborhood networks may have been operating then.

Rather than trying to isolate single causes of prostitution, as nearly every past and present investigation of prostitution does, it is important to see prostitution as a process in which expectations, options, and opportunity all play a role. This general framework is just as relevant for prostitution in the twentieth century as it was for the nineteenth, although the importance of each component shifts over time with the greater commercialization of prostitution and the changing roles of women.

In the early twentieth century, as more women entered the work force and new clerical and sales jobs became available to women, disappointed expectations became a more important motivation for prostitution. Not immigrants but their children now swelled the ranks of prostitution. Unlike their parents, who compared themselves to countrymen back home, the new generation adopted the American myth of mobility and high expectations. Therefore they experienced their poverty and lack of opportunity more acutely than had their parents. Many more prostitutes in studies of the early twentieth century stated such reasons as wanting money, being tired of drudgery, wishing for pleasure (theater, clothes, and good food), and craving excitement or a good time. The growth of advertising and new styles of conspicuous consumption during this period helped to intensify feelings of relative deprivation. Also, at the turn of the century, changes in the economy of prostitution, such as the expansion of the trade and increasing numbers of middlemen, resulted in the more efficient recruitment of women into sex commerce.

Certain characteristics of prostitution in industrial societies remain unchanged because the majority of women are still stuck in low-paying, unskilled jobs. Prostitution continues to lure those women with no chance of realizing their expectations other than through selling their sexual services. The quintessential fact about prostitution is that it is the ever-present alternative for women. For those at the bottom of the social ladder, the possibility is more realistic and the forces pushing in that direction stronger.

Futures

Since American police did not register prostitutes or keep track of their comings and goings, as European police did in regulated systems, we know very little about the subsequent lives of prostitutes. Sometimes private reformatories for prostitutes kept manuscript records of their former inmates; these records are of interest but may not be widely applicable because those who chose to submit to the strict discipline inside often had the fewest options outside. The Boston Penitent Females' Refuge, for example, listed the outcomes of 136 former residents in the asylum over a thirty-year period, from 1825 to 1855. Two-thirds of these women reentered respectable situations: they returned to their families, became domestic servants, or married (see table 4.4).

Duchatelet was able to trace the outcomes of French ex-prostitutes because they had to report their whereabouts and status for several years before their names could be removed from the official registers. The reintegration of French prostitutes, who were officially labeled, suggests that even the most public women did not find the road back to respectable society blocked with insurmountable barriers. Most important, few prostitutes remained on the registers very long. Duchatelet claimed that about seven hundred of the one thousand women were erased from the records every year. Only 5 percent of the women who left prostitution chose an

TABLE 4.4

Futures of Ex-Inmates of the Boston Penitent Females' Refuge, 1824–55

Outcomes	Percentage	N
Remained in service	8.8	12
Married respectably	35.3	48
Returned to family	1.5	2
Died	8.8	12
Returned to vice, almshouse, or House of Correction	35.3	48
Other	10.3	14
Total	100.0	136

SOURCE: Registers of the Boston Penitent Females' Refuge, 1824–55.

illicit course, as mistresses or brothelkeepers. Most of the women returned to the occupations they had previously had: half took up trades such as millinery, seamstressing, or washing clothes; one-fourth became domestic servants. A small percentage became shopkeepers, a fact that offers some evidence that prostitutes could indeed rise on the occupational ladder. Although the record lists only a small percentage of the women as married, many more may have wed in subsequent years (see table 4.5).

Gunilla Johansson, tracing the outcomes of women in the regulated Swedish system, found similar patterns. From one register in the 1880s, she calculated that 23 percent of the women left the trade in a year or less. After five years, about half the women were still prostitutes. Of those who left during the first five years, 30 percent had found a job, gotten married, or were living with relatives; 10 percent had died; and 36 percent had merely disappeared from the registers. Many of this last group may have started practicing prostitution in another city—for example, in Abo, Finland, or St. Petersburg, Russia, two cities that attracted prostitutes

TABLE 4.5

Futures of Parisian Prostitutes Removed from the Register

Outcomes	Percentage	N
Returned to respectable employment	33.0	1,572
Rescued by family, husbands, or Magdalen Homes	17.6	840
Retired from Paris/Retired with a competence	29.0	1,380
Married	2.5	121
Became mistresses or brothelkeepers	8.8	420
Died	9.0	428
Total	100.0[a]	4,761

[a]Figures do not total 100 percent due to rounding.
SOURCE: All figures calculated from Alexandre Jean-Baptiste Parent-Duchatelet, *De la prostitution dans la ville de Paris* (Paris, 1837), p. 16.

from Nordic countries. But others may have sought anonymity in other towns and cities and did not want police to be able trace their whereabouts.[48]

Despite the scarcity of data on womens' futures after prostitution, these examples offer some persuasive evidence that to be a prostitute did not condemn a woman to a life of shame and degradation. Even the most public prostitutes, such as Duchatelet's registered women, usually moved back into respectable lives. In cities without regulation, where most prostitution was seasonal, part-time, or a short-term solution, women must have easily slid back into former trades, returned to hometowns, or found husbands. This was probably more often the case for women who did not have a criminal record or unsavory reputation.

A surprising number of prostitutes in American cities actually held respectable jobs while plying their trade off-hours. Nearly three-fourths of women in the Philadelphia city register were either practicing a trade or employed as domestics during the period when they resorted to prostitution. Reformers and law enforcers referred to this type of prostitution as *clandestine,* but the term is misleading because it implies that prostitutes were either public or private, professional or nonprofessional. But in a society without an official register of public prostitutes, the lines demarcating public and private forms of sexual exchanges were not clearly defined. The domestic who met men on her day off and traded sex for dinners or small gifts may have turned to prostitution as a full-time trade during periods of unemployment or financial pressure. Kept women who lived with one man or a series of men often moved into brothels when the relationship collapsed.

A series of sketches of Boston prostitutes published in 1850 depicted women who moved in and out of work, marriage, and prostitution. For example, Kate LeCompte, a notorious Boston prostitute, had a checkered career. She was seduced by a libertine and kept by a merchant. After her paramour left her, she joined the public order of prostitutes at an infamous house run by Susan Bryant. At one point, she did a brief stint in a New York brothel. When she returned to Boston, Kate descended to the middle ranks of prostitution. But she never became a common streetwalker. In fact, she opened her own house and even accumulated enough capital to establish a respectable boardinghouse for seamen. That venture failed (or became boring) and Kate again took on the role of brothelkeeper.[49]

Another account from this source presents a clearer picture of the lack of fixed boundaries between respectable and unrespectable spheres. Helen

Gurney, known as Little Hel, was a capmaker before she slipped into prostitution. In the beginning she was mistress to a clerk and to his employer. Afterward she married respectably, but soon she tired of conjugal ties and took up prostitution in a house in Boston's vice district. From there, she ran away with a circus tightrope walker. Then she went back to her husband. When last heard from, she had returned to her old haunts among the city's brothels. The overriding conclusion one can draw from these sketches, as well as from statistical sources, is that prostitution was an unstable and transitory situation for most women in it.[50]

Hundreds of novels written during the Victorian era portrayed the tragic fate of the prostitute. Religious reformers and physicians on both sides of the Atlantic consistently asserted that even the most elegant courtesan sank to the gutter and rarely survived more than five years after commencing her career.

British physician William Acton was one of the few who challenged the notion of both the harlot's downward progress and her early death. In fact, he went to the other extreme and argued that prostitutes were healthier and happier than most working class women. He portrayed prostitutes as shrewd, calculating, and endowed with strong survival skills. They rarely remained in the profession for more than a few years, according to Acton, because they soon grasped the horrors and dangers of continuing in the streets, and they sought alternatives. The better class often met and married men above their station. Others, who had accumulated savings in their trade, opened shops, established lodging houses, or became keepers of brothels.[51]

Acton's rosy picture of a prostitute's life was not based on systematic interviewing; he argued from logic and not empirical evidence. Also, he had a hidden agenda, since he sought to gain support for the campaign to regulate prostitution in Britain. Nevertheless, Acton was one of the few among his contemporaries who admitted that prostitution was a transitory phase for nearly all women who practiced it and that prostitutes' futures varied depending on their class backgrounds and experiences in the trade.

As is the case today, there was a prostitution hierarchy in Victorian cities. Acton, writing about London, listed three types of prostitutes—kept women, the common prostitute, and the "subsidiary" (part-time or seasonal) prostitute—and within these groups he noted several subclasses. Sanger presented an elaborate description of New York prostitution, which included four grades of brothels and several classes of houses of assignation. At the top were elegant brothels with lavish displays of luxury, a sense of decorum, and high prices; nearly three-fourths of the prostitutes working in these houses were native-born, and, according to Sanger, some were educated. At the bottom were squalid basements partitioned into bedrooms; prostitutes who worked in them were dirty and often diseased women, and patrons were rowdies and thieves. Both Sanger and Acton agreed that women were tracked according to their social backgrounds. Acton alone recognized that social class determined not only a woman's situation in the prostitution system but also her life chances after leaving it.

Among public prostitutes, there probably was some movement downward in the prostitution class system, especially for women who became diseased or who began drinking or taking drugs. Still, the popular image of the polished courtesan sinking to the gutters of prostitution seemed to be based on the conventions of the Victorian novel rather than on prostitutes' actual lives. The manuscript records of prostitutes implicitly refute this stereotype. Consider the ages of prostitutes—mainly twenty-five and under—and the short duration of their careers, and it is hard to imagine that they could have been so rapidly transformed into the most down-and-out whores.

On the other hand, the image of the prostitute as someone who accumulates savings from her trade, wisely invests her capital, and obtains a small fortune was not very realistic either. We know of some famous successful madams at the turn of the century, including the Everleigh sisters, who operated gilded palaces of vice in Chicago, and Nell Kimball, the famous "queen" of Storeyville. They were the successful entrepreneurs of the demimonde, and they even published their memoirs.[52]

What little we know of typical prostitutes' futures suggests that few women achieved upward economic mobility through prostitution. The nineteenth-century police registers tell us that women in regulated prostitution were most likely to reenter traditional working class occupations. According to Johansson, the fees Swedish prostitutes had to pay for medical examinations, the percentages madams took for room and board, and the expenses for dress and cosmetics did not leave very much money for savings. Prostitutes in the high-class brothels in nineteenth-century American cities were paid high prices for their sexual services. But madams usually took 50 percent of a prostitute's receipts, and expenses were high. In addition, prostitutes in many of these cities had to take a cut from their earnings for police protection. Research on nineteenth-century St. Paul documents that career paths within prostitution were limited. Only four out of sixty-one brothel prostitutes listed in official records became madams, a revealing statistic in a city where prostitution was aboveboard—unofficially licensed.[53]

Rising through the ranks became less and less feasible by the turn of the century, when pimps began to manage women's labor; it then became more difficult to operate independently. Early on, Chinese and Japanese prostitutes were controlled by a pimp system. They entered prostitution with the fewest options (many had been brought to the United States illegally as "brides," by a middleman in sex commerce). They also had the most brutal experiences in the trade and the highest mortality rates.[54] Prostitution in the twentieth century became more organized and rationalized, and pimps became an integral part of the prostitution economy as a whole. These managers limited women's autonomy in the trade and restricted their future. How long a woman remained in prostitution was related to a host of factors: whether prostitution provided supplemental or total income; whether a woman was a public prostitute, that is, practiced openly or had an official label through police registration or arrest; at what age a woman started; and what the chances for marriage or employment were.

The outcast or the fallen woman, the images Victorians gave to prostitutes, implied a fixed status or caste. They totally misrepresented the social reality of prostitution: that it was short term; that women moved between prostitution and other employments; and that a vast majority of women practiced the trade occasionally, seasonally, or off hours from regular jobs. The theories of female sexual deviance that emerged in the latter half of the nineteenth century and the programs for rehabilitating fallen women assumed that to prostitute oneself defied a woman's nature, and was a sign of pathology. The backgrounds, life chances, and experiences of women who used their sex for a livelihood or supplemental income provide the strongest arguments against that view of the prostitute. Rather than being an aberration of woman's role—the overriding premise in the scientific discourse—prostitution was a natural outgrowth of women's social dependencies and weak economic position.

5

Within and Without
Prison Walls

Francis Lieber, one of the leading criminologists in nineteenth-century America, expressed a widely held view of the female offender as more depraved than the male. Supposedly, after one departure from virtue, she fell rapidly and soon became a hardened criminal. "A woman once renouncing honesty and virtue passes over to the most hideous of crimes which women commit, with greater ease than a man from his first offense to the blackest crimes committed by his sex."[1] Behind the "greater fall" thesis was a fixed idea that sexual deviance was the source of all female criminality. According to the theory, a woman who crossed the great divide between chastity and unchastity had no way back, not only because of society's condemnation but also because she had upset the delicate mechanism that governed her nature. Whereas men's moral actions were believed to be governed by reason, women's were thought to spring from their intuitive faculty. This meant that a man who committed a crime still retained his "reasoning faculty and judgment," but a women in the same situation lost all power to regulate her conduct; her whole moral ground was shaken.[2]

Popular writers like Sydney Southworth described the distance between woman on the pedestal and woman on the streets and made the connection between female sexual appetite and depravity: "A women is of more delicate organization than a man, finer strung, of more refined essence, so she can be lower, more degraded and viler, when she sinks. As love is the highest, purest, divinest element in the universe of the soul, so lust its opposite is deepest, blackest, most loathsome."[3] William Acton, in his study of prostitution published in 1857, used similar metaphors to describe how totally transformed a woman became once she began prostituting herself:

She is a woman with half the woman gone, and that half containing all that elevates her nature, leaving her a mere instrument of impurity; degraded and fallen she extracts from the sin of others the means of living, corrupt and dependent on corruption, and therefore interested directly in the increase in immorality—a social pest carrying contamination and foulness of every quarter.[4]

Apparent statistical support for the fallen-woman thesis was available. As early as 1829, Joseph Tuckerman, a Boston missionary, provided figures showing that women were more often repeaters in prison than were men. He found that 271 men were involved in 775 male commitments in Boston's house of correction, whereas 215 women were responsible for 793 sentences. According to Tuckerman, prostitutes were the group that inflated women's recommitment rates, and he coined the phrase "habitually lascivious" to refer to chastity criminals, whom he considered to be the least reformable.[5] Annual reports from the institution over the following decades support Tuckerman's findings. The bulk of the three-, four-, and five-time losers were women. But this pattern reflected the types of crimes women committed, which resulted in shorter prison terms; hence they were out on the streets sooner.

The fallen-woman ideology itself was not based on empirical evidence. Rather, it exemplified what Michel Foucault has called the "systematic blindness" in nineteenth-century sexual discourse: "It is as if a fundamental resistance blocked the development of a rationally formed discourse concerning human sex, its correlations and effects."[6] This resistance was strongest in regard to female sexuality. The Victorian commentary on women who violated sexual codes had a logic of its own, disconnected from reality. It assumed that women and men had distinct biological and moral natures and that sexual passion was a sign of pathology in the female sex. Moreover, it also categorized the female personality as either thoroughly depraved or thoroughly virtuous.

This dual vision of woman, embodied in the fallen-woman paradigm, expressed a basic paradox in the Victorian construction of female sexuality. How could one explain the fact that women were endowed with greater moral sense, while being less in control of their morality? What transformed the innocent prey of seducers and procurers into the predator of the streets? On the one hand, women's passionlessness appeared to be inbred (they were endowed with less sexual drive than men); on the other, it seemed to be a consequence of advanced moral development and refined sensibility, which inhibited them from animal lust.[7]

Bram Stoker's novel *Dracula,* which appeared in 1897, sought to resolve this paradox of female sexuality through literary allegory. In the novel, the awakening of female passion comes from an evil source outside the woman. However, once initiated she becomes a slave to the erotic and a destroyer of others. Because of their emotional nature and passivity, women appear extremely susceptible to Dracula's power. He, the emissary of darkness, is attracted by their innocence and purity.[8] Popular novels as well as scientific treatises described the fallen woman in images that were not very different from Stoker's female vampires, and prostitutes were often called vampires in Victorian literature. So dramatic was the metamorphosis of the fallen woman that one could seemingly detect visible marks of depravity on her face—a drooping mouth, a fiendish glint in the eyes, or discoloration of the skin.

Interrogations and investigations of female delinquents sought to ferret out the heresy of sexual knowlege, in an era when sexual ignorance (called modesty) was held as an ideal for women. Sexual status came to be part of the female criminal profile from the mid-nineteenth century onward, and juvenile offenders well into the twentieth century were subject to degrading physical examinations to determine whether they were virgins. A female offender's sexual history was the criterion for determining the extent of her criminal tendencies and, ultimately, her reformability, no matter what her alleged crime.

What is striking about the treatment of female chastity offenders is the extent to which institutional solutions were prescribed. Throughout the nineteenth century, incarcerating the criminal and the insane was standard. But the kinds of delinquent women placed in institutions, and the degree to which confinement was employed, were exceptional. Whether one ascribed the cause of a woman's fall to environmental, hereditary, or other factors, the outcomes were the same. Whether women or men were their keepers, female sexual delinquents tended to wind up in institutions more often than men who committed what the penal code defined as minor crimes.

Throughout the nineteenth century, definitions of deviance became more and more gender-specific. Enoch Wines and Theodore Dwight, criminolgists who in 1867 published an extensive survey of American prisons, made sexual behavior the basis for classifying female juvenile delinquents, though it was considered irrelevant for male delinquents. They divided boy criminals into three classes: (1) those who had just entered a course of pilfering, (2) those who had more confirmed habits of stealing and lying, and (3) those who had become habitual thieves and who had forfeited all means of obtaining a livelihood. Female offenders consisted of only two groups: (1) those who had formed habits of pilfering and idleness, and (2) those who had addicted themselves to unchaste practices. What distinguished the hard-core female juvenile was not the depth of her involvement with criminal acts, but whether her crimes were sexual or not.[9]

Scientific experts played a key role in shaping both the discourse on and the treatment of chastity criminals. Evolutionary theorists indirectly influenced the institutional response to female sexual delinquents. By arguing that female purity represented an advance in human civilization and, conversely, that the sensual and promiscuous woman was a reversion to a primitive type, they widened the fissure between normal (natural) and abnormal (unnatural) women implied in the fallen-woman paradigm. In contrast to earlier notions of crime as a product of a sinful nature, which are, in theory, class- and gender-neutral, the analysis of female sexual crime as pathology embraced the class and gender bias within Darwinian social theories. A woman's fall meant not only a fall from grace but also a descent into a lower, more savage order of beings. That licentiousness and "coarse sexuality" were most prominent among working class women was logical, according to Social Darwinist thought. It assumed that the lower classes were lower orders on the evolutionary scale.[10]

As authors of books about sexuality and as advisers to patients on personal sexual matters, physicians had a profound impact on the treatment of prostitutes in institutional settings. Some American doctors became involved in prostitution policy debates, though not to the same extent as European medical professionals who were administrators of a regulated policy. Nevertheless, American physicians, through their public discussion of female sexuality, set the boundaries between deviant and normal responses and helped to forge the links between sexual misconduct and pathology. According to the dominant medical theory, women's reproductive organs and sexual functions were the central forces that determined her physical and psychic well-being. Yet women seemed to exhibit no sexual appetite. In the medical literature, a woman's sexual feelings were tied to her maternal instincts and procreative functions.[11]

For middle class women the ideology of passionlessness was a source of power to control sexual relations within marriage. But this ideology was a source of oppression for working class women who violated chastity codes and came under the purview of the state. They were labeled as sexual deviants and often put into public and private "reform" institutions.[12]

Some women doctors, among the first wave of female physicians, began challenging the constructions of male and female sexual natures by distinguishing passion from appetite, mental love from physical love, and love/touch from intercourse. From this perspective, they argued, women were more passionate than men. By elevating sexual relations to the highest spiritual function, they tended to reinforce the differences between pure and impure women and between middle class and working class sexual behavior. These physicians attacked medical defenders of the sexual double standard who claimed that men endangered their health by repressing sexual drives. Still, they assumed that sexual promiscuity was more deviant in women and that women who fell from virtue experienced an "immeasurable depth of degradation."[13]

Scientific explanations of gender differences anchored the notions of male and female social roles in a framework of immutable natural laws. This had a profound effect on definitions of deviance and the consequent development of rehabilitation programs. A gender-specific discourse on deviance clearly influenced the treatment of women chastity offenders. First, it presumed a generalized female deviance based on sexual inclination rather than specific acts of misconduct. Thus the potential prostitute as well the actual one were often sentenced to the same institutions. Second, it produced special laws and institutions for rehabilitating female deviants. Once these differences were institutionalized and women chastity offenders were treated as special cases in the criminal justice system, the penalties became more severe and supervision more sweeping.

Changes in the system were gradual. Throughout the first half of the nineteenth century, the length of imprisonment for a chastity offender was fixed by statutory codes on vagrancy crimes; where a woman was sent depended on space available in existing institutions. Whenever correctional facilities became overcrowded, law enforcers chose to imprison those who posed the greatest threat to property and persons. Chastity criminals had low priority and were placed in workhouses or jails with the least supervision, the weakest discipline, the loosest system of classification, and the least regimented work routines. It was difficult to apply the central tenets of prison discipline—separation by sex, class of offender, and age—to women criminals, particularly the juvenile sex offender. How many sexual experiences, with whom, and where, made a girl a hardened offender? On purely practical grounds, the small numbers of women criminals and the uniformity in the types of crimes they committed made it hard to justify the expense of separate female institutions for adults and juveniles and for felons and misdemeanants.

Prison Discipline and Female Criminality

The main features of women's imprisonment in the first half of the nineteenth century can be summarized in three statements: women were sentenced for minor crimes, they had high commitment rates, and they were incarcerated for short terms. Women made up between 12 and 14 percent of the total prison population, a figure that remained remarkably constant throughout the nineteenth and most of the twentieth centuries. The average sentence length for women convicts was less than a third that of men. However, this apparent sexual difference is, to a large extent, due to the types of offenses. Women were rarely prosecuted for felonies or other serious crimes; when they were, they often received lighter sentences than men. For chastity offenses, the opposite was true; women were confined more often and given higher sentences than men (see tables 5.1 and 5.2).

Most women in penal institutions were convicted of crimes against morals and order. Common drunkards represented half of the female commitments in the Boston House of Correction between 1835 and 1860. Women convicted of nightwalking and lewdness made up about 20 percent of the female prison population. The proportion of chastity offenders fluctuated but was never less than 10 percent or more than 40 percent (see table 5.3). By midcentury, only one-third of the chastity offenders were committed to the county prison; the rest were sent to a section of the workhouse with minimum security and supervision.

TABLE 5.1

Outcomes for Males and Females in Lower Courts, 1816–50, Annual Averages

	Prostitution Offenses		Assault and Battery		Drunkenness		Misdemeanor Property	
	Males	Females	Males	Females	Males	Females	Males	Females
Fine (N)	118	129	236	31	95	19	11	3
Confinement (N)	64	102	156	18	1,418	219	221	122
Imprisonment (%)	35	44	40	37	94	92	95	98

SOURCE: Boston Municipal Court, 1822–50. Data for crimes other than prostitution offenses gathered by Theodore Ferdinand, *Boston's Lower Criminal Courts, 1814–50,* unpublished manuscript.

TABLE 5.2

Average Sentences (in Months) of Offenders in Lower Courts, 1816–50

	Larceny	Prostitution/ Brothelkeeping	Public Drunkenness	Vagrancy
Males	4.4	3.0	2.8	2.8
Females	2.8	3.8	3.1	3.1

SOURCE: Boston Municipal Court, 1822–50. Data for crimes other than prostitution offenses gathered by Theodore Ferdinand, *Boston's Lower Criminal Courts, 1814–50,* unpublished manuscript.

TABLE 5.3

Males and Females in the House of Correction, 1833–60

	Lewdness/ Nightwalking		Brothelkeeping		All Offenses	
	Males	Females	Males	Females	Males	Females
1833	4	18	—	—	151	93
1837	7	69	—	2	409	247
1839	5	60	5	7	329	272
1840	13	91	4	1	363	298
1843	4	95	6	9	321	226
1845	2	20	9	6	418	191
1846	1	20	4	3	503	198
1847	—	47	11	7	432	268
1850	—	34	10	10	501	268
1852	—	31	7	2	334	135
1855	—	54	6	6	421	198
1860	—	24	10	5	664	183

SOURCE: *Reports of the Inspectors of the House of Correction,* Boston City Documents, 1833–1860. Derived from aggregate statistics for biannual reports.

In the pulpit and press, prostitutes may have been charged with destroying families, spreading disease, and corrupting youth. But in the eyes of the court, they were public nuisances and disorderly persons. The nightwalker was treated much the same way as all minor offenders. Over 90 percent of the women convicted of nightwalking and lewdness received prison sentences averaging between three and six months. Issues in these cases were rarely in dispute, guilty verdicts certain, and commitment to a penal facility nearly automatic. Other minor crimes, such as drunkenness and vagrancy, had similarly high rates of incarceration and sentences averaging two to three months. This is not to suggest that in the early nineteenth century officials took prostitution lightly. Few nineteenth-century law enforcers would have classified prostitution as a "victimless crime," a fairly commonplace description today. But the laws and punishments did not fit the rhetoric of danger and pollution ascribed to the prostitute.[14]

Nevertheless, within the penal system extreme prejudice existed against the female offender, particularly the prostitute. Women were shut into attics and basements and denied exercise for fear that they would make sexual contact with male prisoners. Prison administrators considered them hopeless cases and more troublesome than male convicts. Defending his frequent use of corporal punishment against female inmates, the master of the Boston House of Correction chided inspectors for their naiveté in thinking women prisoners more tractable than men. He testified that he would rather have five hundred men in his institution than one hundred women.[15]

Even young female delinquents, most notably those said to be lasciviously inclined, were considered beyond redemption. The first girl placed in the Boston reformatory for juveniles, in 1826, had been taken from a brothel. She was accepted only after repeated applications by the court. Resistant to the idea, the institution's directors insisted that she be kept away from other inmates at all times. In the years that followed the majority of girls sent to the reformatory were on the road to ruin—classified as stubborn, dissolute, or wayward—and not necessarily prostitutes. So paranoid were the directors of the reformatory that these lascivious girls would somehow make contact with the boys—even though it was impossible since thick walls separated the sexes—a decision was made in 1840 to expel or apprentice all female inmates.[16]

The reformatory's directors argued that girls committed different types of crimes than boys, for different reasons, and were less likely to be reformed. Generally, a boy sent to the institution for stealing, drunkenness, or stubbornness could be made to see the enormity of his offense because he had consciously acted defiantly. Although it did not necessarily follow that he would repent of his crime, he could at least be prevented from repeating it. A lascivious girl, on the other hand, could not be made to realize how much her indulgence destroyed her social and moral well-being, for she had acted from "natural appetite" and was "feeble in reason."[17]

Police who found a young girl on the streets may have been reluctant to charge her, knowing she might be sent to the house of correction or to a workhouse. Judges having to sentence a young prostitute faced a difficult choice: they could fine her, which in effect was putting her in a crowded jail since few could pay the fines; commit her to a house of correction with the most hardened female criminals; or send her to the workhouse, where there was no supervision.[18] One other option existed: to persuade a young prostitute or her family to have her enter a Magdalen home. Although these private institutions took only a small percentage of female sexual delinquents, they are worth examining because the girls' and the women's reformatories founded in the late nineteenth century had many of the same characteristics and similar philosophies of rehabilitation. All began with the assertion of gender difference and the need for female-centered institutions.

TWO HOMES

In England during the 1750s, philanthropists founded the first Magdalen home for outcast women. Such institutions were to provide "females plunged into ruin" a place of refuge and a conduit back to respectability.[19] These homes for the fallen nevertheless anticipated the type of penitentiaries and asylums that would be constructed over the next decades. The walls built to seclude and protect women from the censure and cruelty of the outside world functioned to keep those inside imprisoned.

Patterned after the British Magdalen homes, the Penitent Females' Refuge, one of the earliest and most long-lived penitent homes in the United States, was founded by the City Missionary Society in Boston in 1822. At first it was meant to be a temporary shelter for fallen women who expressed a desire to turn away from a wicked life. Residents were to remain only a few months, until a family could be located who would agree to employ a penitent as a domestic. However, after two years with few successes, the directors of the society realized that it was naive to expect such "long and inveterate habits of vice to be so easily retrained and eradicated."[20]

The society built a larger facility, added a female auxiliary board to govern the institution, and required all inmates to agree to accept a mandatory two-year term in the refuge. (A one- or two-year commitment was usual in homes of this type.) In the strict legal definition of the term, the Penitent Females' Refuge was not a prison. Women were not sentenced there by court order or forced to remain by official decree. However, in the administrative sense, it functioned that way, and the institution partially filled the need for a female juvenile reformatory in the years before one opened. It is impossible to determine how closely bound the refuge was to the criminal justice system, since informal practices and judicial discretion are not recorded in the early court files. The registers of the refuge offer some proof that the court used the institution and suggest that "voluntary" commitments were not so voluntary. Between 1822 and 1850, about one in four of the inmates in the society's records were sent from the workhouse, from the house of correction, or through the courts. A significant portion came at the request of interested parties—family and friends—but the largest number was directed to the refuge by missionaries and private reform groups. The three city missionaries who brought the majority of women to the refuge were often found in court trying to prevent a youthful offender from being thrust into the jaws of the house of correction.[21]

Only about one in six women had made application themselves. They tended to be older and foreign born and during their term were the least likely to be dismissed for bad conduct or to escape (see Table 5.4). (Less than half of the inmates actually remained a full term at the refuge; while in theory any inmate could leave the institution after giving the directors fourteen days' notice, more women left the institution by escaping than by any other means.) Given that they accepted the long term of incarceration, women who came to the refuge on their own appear to have had the fewest options on the outside and probably needed food and shelter.

Although the directors repeatedly denied that the Penitent Females' Refuge was punitive, in nearly every respect they adopted the structure and style of a penitentiary. They aptly coined the phrase "wisely ordered household" to describe their institution. The term not only connoted discipline and regularity but also suggested a homelike setting. Compared

TABLE 5.4

How Native-Born and Foreign-Born Inmates Came to the Penitent Females' Refuge, 1821–55

	Percentage of Native-Born Inmates	Percentage of Foreign-Born Inmates	Total	
			Percentage	N
Own Application	15.7	21.9	17.4	55
Missionaries/PFR Agents	45.8	49.3	47.3	150
Family/Friends	18.9	8.2	16.7	53
Courts/Police	5.2	2.7	4.7	15
Almshouse/Prison	14.5	17.8	13.9	44
Total	100.0[a]	100.0[a]	100.0	317

[a]Figures do not total 100 percent due to rounding.
SOURCE: Penitent Females' Refuge Inmate Register, 1822–55, New England Home for Little Wanderers Archives, Boston, Massachusetts.

with the regimentation of the prisons built in the same period, the refuge must have appeared more humane. Indeed, physical conditions were more agreeable than at Boston's house of correction or city jail; women were clothed and fed better and had more comfortable accommodations. Emphasizing the difference between the refuge and the local prison, female managers of the society declared at their first board meeting that inmates in their institution would eat white bread, to be prepared at the refuge, instead of brown bread, the coarser fare of the prison or almshouse.[22]

Penitents in private refuges were often young. The average age of women in the Boston refuge was nineteen, slightly higher than several of the British homes, but lower, for example, than in the Philadelphia Magdalen home.[23] Generally, private refuges did not admit pregnant or diseased women, and some had a policy of not readmitting escapees.

A range of private institutions existed in Scotland and England for fallen women. Some took only victims of seduction; others concentrated on juveniles. Certain refuges openly acknowledged a class system. For example, the Glasgow Lock Hospital contained a ward for lower class women and another for "fine girls of the fashionable class." British reformer William Blackmore opened a temporary home in the 1850s for women of the "better class." Blackmore claimed that there needed to be refuges for well-bred women with finer sensibilities.[24]

American Magdalen homes differed from their British counterparts in that women who had been involved in various types of sexual misconduct were put together. The Penitent Females' Refuge housed women sentenced for prostitution as well as stubborn or wayward young women who were brought there by relatives. Catholic foreign-born women lived alongside native-born Protestants; young girls mixed with older women. Underlying this policy was a belief that unchastity was itself a great leveler and that the religious instruction, domestic training, and regimen of these "moral hospitals" were the best treatment for women who had strayed from the path of virtue, no matter how far or by what age.

The life of an inmate at a Magdalen home was regimented. For example, at the Penitent Females' Refuge, she had to rise at five o'clock (summer hours) or six o'clock (winter hours). Before breakfast, a half hour was set aside for prayer and devotion. For the remainder of the day she would be employed in one of many tasks: weaving, sewing, ironing, laundering, or household chores. After a day's work and the evening meal, she was required to attend prayers at eight thirty before retiring. Steady work, prayer, and seclusion were the society's antidote to a wayward and undisciplined female character.[25]

The society contrasted their method of "resolute affection" with the harsh treatment of offenders in prison. Though the refuge did not place its inmates in cell blocks or discipline them with the lash or solitary confinement, the institution assumed the main characteristics of the well-ordered asylum: separation from other inmates, rules of silence, and prayer and work schedules formed the basis of the rehabilitation program.

Other refuges that sprang up over the following decades were built on the same model. The House of the Good Shepherd, a Catholic institution, was one of the most common. Nearly every large city had a branch run by nuns. Like the well-ordered household of the Penitent Females' Refuge, inmates were required to stay one to two years, trained in domestic tasks, and tucked away in quiet retreats far from family and community. Courts committed young women to these homes as an alternative to jail, prison, or the workhouse. In certain states where no girls' juvenile reformatory existed, Magdalen homes served that function for the courts well into the first decades of the twentieth century.

The exception to the penitentiary model of the Magdalen home was the temporary shelter, which offered women a place to stay for a short period until they found work or returned home to families. The Temporary Home for Fallen Women, run by the New England Female Moral Reform Society, exemplified this type. The average stay at the shelter was between two days and a week, although pregnant women often spent several weeks in the home before and after their confinement. Unlike the managers of most refuges, the home's managers accepted pregnant women and did not turn away women who had slid back into prostitution. They continually took back women who had resolved to abandon a sinful life but had fallen again; their records noted seven-time repeaters.

Founded in 1844, the home was the antithesis of the well-ordered asylum. During an average day, one might find one woman nursing her baby, another about to give birth, an alcoholic suffering from delirium tremens, and a prostitute who had just escaped from a brothel. Whereas the Penitent Females' Refuge had a stable group of ten to twenty women a year, the Temporary Home had a floating population of between one hundred and four hundred a year.[26] No one was required to perform household chores, and the society hired a woman to clean the home, justifying the expense on the grounds that residents stayed only a short time and were often physically unable to attend to domestic work. The only task women were asked to do was to sew their own wardrobes. This was a valuable project since few women left brothels with suitable clothing. Sewing at the home, therefore, was aimed not at improving character but at equipping women for a respectable life.

A complex mix of radical evangelism, anti-institutionalism, and solidarity with women whom they believed to have been exploited by men lay behind the nonpunitive character of the home. Though the society's central concern was awakening in their charges religious feelings, which they considered the only real protection against temptation, fallen women came to the home for the social services they received there. As the society's minutes attest, managers were aware of this but continued to admit all women who applied.[27]

The managers of the home, in the first part of the nineteenth century, performed a range of social services for women who had violated chastity codes—from the prostitute to the unwed mother. Most important, they provided shelter, a halfway house back to respectable employment or to a woman's home and family. Present-day accounts of ex-prostitutes reveal how isolated women in prostitution become from other contacts and networks. This was probably just as true a century ago. Agents from the home, who visited brothels and talked to prostitutes inside, may have helped women to leave prostitution without having to endure a long period of institutional confinement.

The managers clearly sought to enforce sexual codes and social controls over delinquent women. They were often involved in helping parents locate runaway daughters. One such case involved an elderly women from the countryside in search of her wayward daughter. The mother blamed her husband for leading the girl astray (perhaps by incest). All she knew was that her daughter was living in Boston among the vicious and degraded. Hearing this, agents from the home went to an area with the lowest class of brothels, where they found the girl in one of the roughest houses. The daughter, upon hearing her mother's voice, tried to evade her, but after the mother pleaded for hours the girl left with her and returned home.[28] But the managers also offered protection to women who wanted to leave prostitution. One of their most helpful functions was to put pressure on brothelkeepers to return a prostitute's wardrobe; the keeper often claimed that the clothes were kept as payment for a prostitute's debts to the house.

The populations of the Temporary Home and the Penitent Females' Refuge were similar. In both, ages ranged between fifteen and twenty-five years; and both had women in various stages of delinquency (many of the women had been in the house of correction or jail). They differed in one significant respect: nearly all women in the Temporary Home were Protestant and had rural backgrounds. The society's managers expressed solidarity and sympathy for fallen women, even prostitutes, as long as they were Protestant, native-born women. As the prostitute population become more and more dominated by immigrant and Catholic groups, the society changed its open policy and in the 1880s became a home for unwed mothers.

The society's managers denied that unchaste women were pariahs who had to be isolated from society. Nevertheless, they maintained the lines between respectable and unrespectable. In addition to the Temporary Home, they also ran a boardinghouse for single women. Women who applied for admission were subject to interrogations about their purity. If managers detected a blemish on their character, they were directed to the home for fallen women. Alternatively, when a black woman of intact character came to the home, the managers offered her a room in their respectable boardinghouse. Although the society's members acknowledged the mitigating circumstances that produced the fallen woman and insisted she was a victim of male exploitation, they could not violate the codes of purity that defined Victorian womanhood. In this way they helped to perpetuate the fallen-woman thesis by treating women with a range of unconventional behaviors as a class. Still, their social service approach was forward-looking and enlightened compared with the approach of most other institutions for fallen women in the nineteenth century. Evidence that the society was out of step with the main currents in rehabilitating delinquents can be found in the State Board of Charities surveys of institutions. The state welfare bureaucracy viewed the Temporary Home as a marginal institution, and it had low priority for state subsidies. The private institution that received the most state support was the Dedham Female Asylum for Discharged Female Prisoners. It was an institution that required inmates who had already served a term in prison to spend two more years in confinement.[29]

FEMALE REFORMATORIES

Private refuges were the antecedents of the special institutions for juvenile and adult female offenders founded in the second half of the nineteenth century. Like the private refuges, they were built in pastoral settings with a family style organization and were controlled and staffed by women managers. Advocates of these institutions did not dispute the fact that women offenders appeared hardened and depraved, but insisted that they had become that way because of the treatment they had received in male-dominated institutions.

Women most active in prison reform represented both continuity and discontinuity with the earlier tradition of female benevolence. They were motivated by a belief in a common sisterhood, and they used gender identity as a rationale for taking charge of women's prisons and reformatories. Yet their experiences set them apart from earlier female reformers. They were a new breed of pragmatic managers who had served their apprenticeships in chapters of the sanitary commissions that emerged in northern cities to support the Civil War effort. They had raised money, nursed the wounded, and organized charity for soldiers' families. Carroll Smith-Rosenberg has characterized this generation of female reformers as "new bourgeois matrons," who did not question the main tenets of the ideology of domesticity but viewed themselves as "the conscience and housekeepers of America."[30]

In contrast to the more radical ideology of moral reformers a generation earlier, women prison reformers did not challenge the workings of a class and gender justice that sentenced only women to institutions for sexual unchastity. While they portrayed the chastity offender as a victim of circumstances and male exploitation, women prison reformers ultimately believed that the fallen woman needed to be institutionalized because she posed a threat to social stability. Nevertheless, they repudiated the idea that criminality was a product of nature not nuture. Instead they insisted that a woman's fall was the result of a disjuncture in her development, a loss of female moral influence and domesticity.

Advocates of separate female institutions maintained that the military style and regimen of male reformatories could not reach women. Furthermore, they documented hundreds of cases of sexual abuse of women in mixed prisons. Their rationale for confinement was that it would awaken dormant domestic natures and maternal instincts. Within a prison setting, female administrators introduced softening influences—farm animals, flower gardens, and cultural events. Prison reform journals carried accounts of the most hardened female criminals being "melted to tears" by rabbits and deer.[31]

Underlying the reformatory ideology for girls' industrial schools and adult women's prisons was an affirmation of gender differences, both in the analysis of causes of female criminality and in the remedies sought. The essential difference between male and female deviance was that men and boys were assumed to be rational actors, willful lawbreakers, whereas delinquent women or girls appeared to be malleable personalities, child-like and emotionally unstable, who succumbed to the influence of bad associates or were driven into crime from a home life of violence and drunkenness.

This concept of female psychology meant that females charged with violating sexual codes faced incarceration regardless of the seriousness of their crime or their degree of criminality. In the case of juvenile delinquents, the industrial schools concentrated on the predelinquent girl, and protective custody meant three to four years in an institution. Girls in reform schools tended to be confined longer than boys. For example, the age of majority at Lancaster Industrial School for Girls, in Massachusetts, the first female juvenile institution, was seventeen, two to three years older than the age boys were released from the state reformatory for boys.[32]

Arguing for reformatories for delinquent girls, editors of the *Prisoner's Friend* cited the New York City police chief's disclosures on juvenile depravity. He presented a portrait of young female vagrants without a single attribute of innocent childhood. "Their persevering advances, and the lewd billingsgate of their voices, involuntarily gives rise to the question, 'What fearful fruit will the seeds of sin, thus early sown, bring forth in womanhood?' " Implicit in descriptions of female delinquency was a sense of urgency to intervene early. Unlike the petty thieves who formed bad habits and practices, the police chief claimed, these "embryo courtezans" became "addicted" to immoral practices.[33]

Prevention became the catchword in female corrections. The vast majority of girls committed to the Lancaster School had no formal complaint or legal proceeding against them; they were committed voluntarily by a parent. They were charged most often with stubbornness or waywardness, and in effect their sentence was a precautionary measure that isolated them from moral danger during the years in which they were believed to be most vulnerable to sexual advances. Girls who peddled apples, picked rags, or roamed the streets and were truant from school could now be supervised. If police or missionaries suspected sexual misconduct, they could pressure parents to commit a girl to a reformatory.

Women's prisons, begun in the 1870s, sought the youngest and least experienced in crime. The inmates committed there in the early decades tended to be young, white, and native born. The majority of offenders were women sentenced for crimes against order and morality. About one-quarter of the women at Framingham reformatory in Massachusetts were chastity offenders, a higher proportion than among women in local jails and houses of correction. Women with diverse criminal backgrounds—from murderers to alcoholics—were in the institution. This was also true for sexual offenders; some were prostitutes and others were women openly cohabiting with men outside of marriage, though in a monogamous relationship. Here again the assumption of generalized female sexual deviance within the ideology of the fallen woman shaped the institutional response.[34]

The growth of reformatories for female delinquents created more space for those who probably would not otherwise have found their way to correctional institutions. Female reformatories created places for women convicted of fornication or lewdness, though not involved in commercial sex, who, in the past, might never have been charged or sentenced to institutions. Having been once inside prison walls, these women would be caught in the revolving door of reformatory institutions.

Such was the case of one young woman charged with fornication and sentenced to the Framingham reformatory. She had been an inmate at the Lancaster school and, upon leaving, had taken a job at a hospital and begun a nurse's training course. During that time, she started seeing a married man, whom she had known since she was twelve years old. Although those interviewing the woman at the institution implied that the man was also guilty for taking advantage of her, he was probably not charged or sentenced since he was middle class (a real estate broker) and had a family to support.[35]

Another consequence of gender-specific penal institutions was longer terms of imprisonment for sexual offenses. Reform-minded prison administrators continually sought maximum terms for offenses. In effect this meant that often the youngest and least criminal, who tended to be sent to these institutions, wound up serving long sentences for minor offenses. On the average, women in Framingham charged with chastity crimes spent over a year in the institution. Those sent to local houses of correction or workhouses for similar offenses had a three- to six-month term. In defense of their policy of long confinement for minor offenders, directors of women's reformatories insisted that there was no greater unkindness than to commit women delinquents for short terms and send them back to lives of vice and crime:

At every point the brevity of even the longest sentences is found to be a barrier to the best operation of the elevating influences; and when the education of a life-time or evil precept, association and experience are to be overcome, together with inherited predisposition to lives of vice and crime, the need of extended opportunities for applying reformatory training will be realized. It frequently happens that the term of imprisonment expires at the very time when a continuation of good influences promised the best results.[36]

Since the rationale behind female reformatories was treatment and not punishment, longer prison terms for minor offenses did not appear discriminatory to their sisters' keepers. Nor did it appear contradictory that female delinquents were trained in domestic arts, fine needlework, and other domestic housekeeping tasks that provided few job opportunities outside prison walls. In both adult and juvenile reformatories, training and discipline were aimed at enveloping the wayward personality in a blanket of domesticity. Many prison administrators realized that limited employment opportunities were a source of criminality. Still, they saw their task as one of resocializing girls and women into the proper female roles of mother, helpmate for a husband, and moral custodian for society.[37]

Domestic influence and domestic training, the cornerstones of female penal institutions of the nineteenth century, reinforced the social, economic, and psychological dependency that brought the majority of women there in the first place. All prison settings demand obedience and regimen and create institutional personalities, but the kinds of dependencies fostered in female reformatories were intimately linked to female gender roles. Inmates released from them faced double jeopardy in the job market. As women, they could find few jobs that guaranteed a living wage, and they lacked training to compete for low-skill jobs open to women. As former prison inmates trained for domestic service, their criminal background made them undesirable as servants to live with respectable families.

Ironically, the one environment that mirrored the reformatory experience on the outside was the brothel. There inmates (and they were called inmates in nineteenth-century prostitution literature) had shelter, food, and daily routines. Like the reformatory, the brothel was a women's institution administered by a woman. The madam in a brothel had many of the same functions as the matron in a prison. She mediated conflicts between women in the house; she punished the disobedient; and she provided her charges with training in female roles, advice about pleasing men, and information about fulfilling male role expectations. The shrewdest madams and prostitutes exploited the ideology of purity and passivity in female roles and scripted fantasies for men based upon betrayed innocence.[38]

Madams and matrons played similar roles in the lives of women who broke sexual conventions. Both created institutional settings that offered protection and nurtured female dependency. Though female prison reformers would have been horrified at the comparison, the brothel and the female reformatory had a curious symbiotic relationship. Inmates from juvenile reformatories often found their way into brothels, then wound up in adult reformatories after their arrest, and returned to brothels again after their release.

A substantial number of the women who served terms at reformatories were not rearrested, especially in the early decades of these institutions, when they took in younger, less delinquent women. Still, a term in a public or private institution often turned predelinquents into criminals, sexually promiscuous girls into professional prostitutes. Maimie Pinzer, a Jewish prostitute at the turn of the century, characterized her arrest and sentencing as the turning point in her prostitution career. Her original misstep was staying out with a man for a night; for this her family lodged a complaint against her. Maimie was sentenced to a Magdalen home and spent the next year there alongside girls older and more experienced in the exchange of sexual services.[39]

An account of a prostitute in 1985 describes a similar process. After numerous foster care situations, a young black runaway and truant was sentenced to an institution in Oregon for delinquent girls. There she met some young women, who, like herself, had been committed for status offenses; others had been convicted of criminal offenses. These women had been involved in prostitution, shoplifting, and forgery. "My education was all in Oregon. I met people that did it all, you know; I heard talkin and I knew, if I had to, I could do it too."[40] In both cases, these contacts gave girls on the road to ruin a map. Another important element in the process was the institutional label, which stigmatized reformatory inmates and isolated them from family, school, and neighborhood.

A nineteenth-century reformer, Samuel Gridley Howe, perceived early on the dangers in the female reformatory model. Howe, once an avid supporter of the penitentiary, lost enthusiasm for institutions as a panacea for reforming the criminal. He was so opposed to the idea of institutionalizing delinquent girls that in 1855 he published a minority report attacking the founding of Lancaster Industrial School for Girls. "Large congregate establishments are not the proper homes for wayward girls" but breeding places for crime, according to Howe. His solution was to place delinquent girls with virtuous families, and by doing so, diffuse the polluted strains in society. He also noted the mark that would be left on an ex-inmate's character. Once a girl was placed in an institution, he claimed, she would become known as a house of reformation girl and the label would stick for the rest of her life: "The girls would be become known as a class apart—as unfortunate if not a criminal class. But much worse than all this—they would learn to consider themselves as such."[41]

By the end of the century, Howe's predictions were borne out, and the informal arrangements he proposed began to be used. The women sentenced to reformatories tended to have a long delinquent history or to come from families with members already in institutions.[42] Changes in the institutional commitment patterns reflected a broader tendency toward filtering out the youngest or first-time offenders. The vast majority continued to be arrested for status offenses. How was one to classify or sift out the least deviant? The debate among corrections experts at midcentury revolved around purity and impurity. Was a girl chaste who worked as a domestic in a brothel, though she did not serve customers? Or was she already fallen, though still "technically pure"? Sexual status was still the basis for grading female deviance; however, by the turn of the twentieth century, women involved in casual sex, promiscuity, or commercial sex were classified differently from women who made just one misstep.

Institutions such as the New England Home for the Fallen and the

Florence Crittenden homes throughout the country became places strictly for unwed mothers. In other private and public institutions for delinquents, the same diversity in types of criminal offenders existed. However, they tended to be most often urban immigrant rebels against sexual codes.[43] Individual traits and attitudes rather than criminal behaviors became the basis for grading female deviance.

Individual Justice

Class and gender had always influenced the day-to-day workings of the criminal justice system, but new legal definitions formalized women's special deviant status and traits. Although they were not aimed at women per se, the main features of discretionary justice—indeterminate sentencing, and probation—had an enormous impact on women, particularly chastity offenders, in the criminal justice system.

Throughout the latter half of the nineteenth century, short prison terms became the rallying point for prison reformers. These people claimed that whereas in three to six months a convict could make the acquaintance of experienced criminals, a short sentence did not encompass enough time to alter depraved habits or cut off contacts in vice on the outside. The system, according to Franklin Sanborn, first secretary of institutions and agencies in Massachusetts, produced a class of habitual offenders—mainly drunkards, vagrants, and prostitutes—who were rearrested days after their release from the house of correction.[44]

The attack on fixed, short sentences was not directly aimed at women criminals, but it was highly relevant to female crime patterns, particularly prostitution-type offenses. Prostitutes were classic examples of the habitual offender; they committed minor crimes, had short prison terms, and had high recidivism. Habitual offender laws became the means by which the criminal justice system could remove perpetual criminals from the streets as well as the dockets. Significantly, these laws were first applied to prostitutes. In 1855 Massachusetts passed the first habitual offender law for nightwalkers; it carried a five-year term in the house of correction after the third conviction. A Michigan statute, passed several years later, went even further in setting a minimum sentence of three years for all common prostitutes (though it provided inspectors with the power to discharge or conditionally release offenders upon good behavior).[45]

Habitual offender laws were the antecedents to indeterminate sentencing, put into effect several decades later, which allowed judges and prison administrators wide latitude in deciding what kinds of individuals needed long-term incarceration, whether they be prostitutes, drunkards, or persons who had committed serious crimes. By the early twentieth century the open-ended sentence had been incorporated into nearly every women's institution.

Habitual offender laws and indeterminate sentencing represented more than reforms intended to clear the dockets and cut costs. They reflected the growing influence of theories that defined criminal behavior as a product of inherited traits. These theories argued that criminals transmitted characteristics of indolence, immorality, and criminal tendencies to the next generation. The emphasis on criminal types dovetailed with the earlier fallen-woman thesis, for it offered a scientific basis for some of the assumptions regarding female deviance. According to the theory of criminal types, sexual promiscuity was characteristic of a defective and degenerate female type. The rationale for long-term imprisonment for sexual delinquency now rested on the belief that such weak personalities needed to be confined and protected since they lacked the moral sense to determine right from wrong.[46]

By the end of the nineteenth century, courts tended toward more lenient treatment for many minor offenses, including drunkenness and liquor license violations. In Massachusetts urban courts, for example, a smaller proportion of these offenders found their way into jails and prisons than had in earlier decades—usually because they could not pay small fines. The reverse was true for prostitution offenses in the same court. Nightwalkers had the highest percentage of guilty outcomes and commitments to penal institutions.

Undoubtedly a filtering-out process had already taken place in the many steps before a court appearance. Police did not arrest many first-time offenders. City missionaries intercepted young prostitutes after a brothel raid and brought them to private refuges. Prosecutors charged the novice in prostitution with a lesser crime, disorderly conduct or fornication. Still, the pattern of sentencing sexual delinquents appeared so firmly entrenched that in the first decades of the twentieth century, when noninstitutional approaches were being advocated, it was taken for granted that chastity offenders should be confined.

Meanwhile, during the period when open-ended sentencing was gaining momentum, another type of prison reform, probation, was also becoming accepted. Some cities began assigning probation officers to local police departments in the 1880s, but the roots of probation can be traced back to the mid-nineteenth century, to John Augustus—who was called the father of probation. Augustus, who advocated alternatives to imprisonment for minor crimes, voiced his strongest opposition to putting young female chastity offenders into institutions. Ironically, when probation became an official part of the criminal justice system, these were the group of minor offenders least likely to benefit from the reform.

A shoemaker who abandoned his trade to become a full-time reformer, Augustus conducted a one-man probation agency in Boston courts. Beginning in the 1840s, and for over a decade, Augustus was a fixture in both municipal and trial courts. His own book about his work and a scroll now housed in the Harvard Law School Library document the thousands of persons for whom he posted bail; 39 percent were women, a higher proportion than passed through Boston courts. Lacking any bureaucracy to help administer his bailing program, Augustus's methods were simple. He chose candidates likely to reform. If they did not relapse or return to evil associates between the time of arrest and trial, he petitioned the judge to assess them one cent and costs.[47]

Just how Augustus singled out his reformables is difficult to determine. In his memoirs, he wrote that he employed the "most scrupulous investigations" of the personal history of defendants before he became their bondsman. Yet the volume of defendants processed through urban courts in itself casts doubt on this claim. Also, such an approach seems out of character. Accounts of his case work suggest that intuition and firsthand impressions were his guides. He could be moved by a downcast eye or glint of remorse; a blush on a cheek or an air of innocence influenced his decision to intervene in a case. The nearest he came to screening most cases was in the brief interview he conducted in the prisoner's box minutes before the defendant was charged. Though not grounded in any legal or scientific theory, Augustus's informal probation most likely tracked the youngest and the least experienced in crime out of the penal system. He was attacked in the press as soft on crime, but he was supported by judges with heavy caseloads and prisons filled to capacity.[48]

The alternatives to prison Augustus advocated were incorporated into the criminal justice system by the first decades of the twentieth century: placement in foster homes, social work counseling, and probation. The last became the most highly developed and integral part of the administration of justice. Probation departments were attached to the courts, and each defendant's background was "scrupulously investigated" in a manner that Augustus could never have imagined. In the case of the female offender, her demeanor, her family background, her institutional past, and, most important, her sexual history determined whether she was to be a candidate for supervision outside or inside prison walls. In effect, individualized justice built into the judicial bureaucracy the class and gender bias that had always operated informally.

The emphasis on the individual and not the crime, implicit in Progressive penology in this century, clearly widened the powers of public and private agents to control female sexuality. In most states, probation officers attached to courts became extensive bureaucracies to trace the backgrounds of defendants and their families. Elaborate files on each person processed through the courts provided a data base that circulated between counties and even states. New technology in the form of fingerprinting made it impossible for defendants to hide a previous record with a false name or to protect their families from investigation. After learning of a defendant's hometown or previous residence, investigators would often write to a probation department there and obtain information about previous arrests or time spent in other reformatories. It became more difficult for individuals with a criminal record to seek refuge in the anonymity of a new town. Prostitutes, whose lives were very mobile, must have felt this acutely.[49]

An example of this extensive bureaucratic networking system appeared in the case of a young black woman arrested for fornication in Boston in 1923. The Boston probation investigator wrote to the New York probation officers and asked them to track down the girl's parents to determine whether they were respectable and would be willing to pay her fare home. After several visits to former addresses of the girl's family, a New York probation officer wrote back that he had been unable to locate any of her relatives. Nevertheless, he did pass on vital information about the defendant's previous record, and the New York Bedford Hills Reformatory forwarded her inmate history to Boston. The woman, who had appeared as a first offender in the Boston courts, now turned out to have had an illegitimate child at fifteen, to have been arrested as a common prostitute several years later, and to have been rearrested for a violation of parole.[50]

Probation did not necessarily divert from prison women who might have been sentenced there in the past. Nor did the growth of the probation system decrease the numbers of female sexual delinquents in institutions. Probation mainly enabled the state to supervise greater numbers of delinquent women for longer periods of time. The chastity offender in the probation records was usually the nonprofessional, the woman who met men after work, the casual pickup who traded sexual services for dinners or entertainment. Two girls from Keene, New Hampshire, were typical. They had been employed in the shoe factory there and were tired of living at home, so they ran away to Boston. Within three weeks they were arrested and charged with disorderly conduct. The officer testified that he had seen them coming back to their rooms with different men several nights. The judge sentenced them to six months in the House of the Good Shepherd.[51]

Another case involved a promiscuous girl who was arrested with her lover in a boardinghouse. During the investigation, it was learned that she had borne the co-defendant a child; the co-defendant had paid two hundred dollars to keep the baby in St. Mary's Infant Asylum. Witnesses in the case testified that the defendant's behavior was bad and her parents lacked control over her. The judge urged her parents to commit her to the House of the Good Shepherd, which they refused to do. She was then sentenced to the women's reformatory, and she appealed.[52]

From one perspective, this type of discretionary justice was a response to the growing resistance of parents to the confinement of sexually active daughters to public or private reformatory institutions. In the past the majority of commitments to these institutions had been initiated by parents and relatives. Working class families did not necessarily internalize Victorian sexual mores, but a daughter who began staying out with men or giving away sexual favors indiscriminately to the corner boys could bring shame to other household members. However, immigrant parents, often suspicious of state interference and needing a daughter's contribution to the family economy, were less and less willing to cooperate with social agencies, judges, and probation officers. Probation consequently became a vehicle for forcing defendants or their parents to accept confinement in a private refuge. This was called inside probation, and often the defendant was required to sign an agreement that she was willing to stay in the institution.

Probation also enabled the courts to monitor the behavior of chastity offenders for long periods. Most courts allowed judges to extend probation up to three years. Though this kind of supervision did not represent the same abridgement of rights and freedoms as did confinement in a penal institution, still it allowed frequent intrusions into a woman's home and work life. Probation officers often would call employers if they could not contact a client or interview neighbors to see whether a client had been bringing men home. Violation of probation also had tough consequences if a woman was rearrested. She could be charged with two crimes, including the probation offense, and receive a stiffer sentence.[53]

Many public and private agencies were able to use the system of discretionary justice to extend their control of working class sexual mores. One supervisor of the Society for the Prevention of Cruelty to Children claimed that in neglect cases, where a girl had had sex with a father, brother, or lodger, for example, the society always tried to secure a complaint against the girl for fornication and not against the man for abuse. This approach gave the society more power to commit a girl to a reformatory if she proved unmanageable.[54]

In the newly created juvenile courts, which recommended treatment based on the individual's social and psychological profile, girls tended to be put in juvenile reformatories more frequently than boys. Eric Schneider found that in Boston's juvenile court, 36 percent of the girls were sent to institutions, compared with 13 percent of the boys. Whereas girls guilty of shoplifting were most often placed on probation, those convicted of sexual offenses were committed to institutions, particularly if it had been shown that the girl engaged in frequent and casual sex.[55] Of the women convicted of sex offenses in New York Women's Court in the first decades of the twentieth century, between 60 and 70 percent found their way into institutions. Similarly, in Philadelphia Women's Court, about two-thirds of sex offenders charged were sent to a prison, private refuge, or hospital.[56]

In specialized courts and probation departments, judgments involving female sexual delinquency continued to use the rationale of women's vulnerability and receptivity to sexual dangers to justify confinement for the predelinquent and longer terms for the young prostitute. The same view of female weakness and sexual victimization had shaped the homes for fallen women, which had mandatory two- or three-year terms, and the separate institutions and reformatories for female offenders. Prison reformers claimed that women's special qualities and characters required that they be cared for in gender-specific institutions. Outside prison walls, reformers saw a host of sexual dangers awaiting young women who lacked parental supervision and moral training. When reformers became managers and keepers of fallen women, they continued to reproduce the structures of psychological and social dependency that underlay prostitution and kept in motion the vicious circle of women in search of keepers and keepers in search of women.

The fallen-woman metaphor appeared anachronistic to the twentieth-century scientific experts; yet many of the suppositions within the fallen-woman ideology persisted. One was that sexual deviance was the at the center of female criminal behavior. Another was that a woman's sexual and social history, not the specific criminal act, should influence the treatment she received in the criminal courts and social agencies. In the twentieth century, the advocates of environmental explanations of prostitution debated the proponents of hereditarian theories. Nevertheless, both positions took for granted women's passivity in sexual matters, and the motivations ascribed to prostitutes continued to assume a lack of agency; sexual slavery and mental deficiency expressed this teleology.

PART III

A National Crusade and Its Aftermath, 1900–1930

6

The War on Prostitution

THE FIRST TWO DECADES of the twentieth century, known as the Progressive Era, were a time of reform ferment and activism. All kinds of social ills become targets for investigation and intervention: sweatshops, slum housing, child labor, juvenile delinquency, corruption in city government and police departments, intemperance, and prostitution. These were not newly discovered social problems; what set this period apart were the assumptions, strategies, and expectations of a broad coalition of activists. A pervasive optimism underlay the reform impulse, which took for granted that the social engineering of society could be accomplished through efficiency and key placement of experts. The spirit, captured in Herbert Croly's manifesto of the Progressive Era mentality, *The Promise of American Life,* reflected the idealism of a new generation of middle class, college-educated women and men trained in the new social sciences. Immigrant working class communities became their social laboratories, and they organized projects and services to reshape community life, work life, and leisure. At the heart of Progressive reform activity were two overriding assumptions: that the state had to take a more active role in regulating the social welfare of its citizens, and that private and public spheres of activity could not be disentangled. Prostitution was an issue that underscored the interrelationship between home life and street life; between the wages of sin and the low wages of women workers; between the double sexual standard and the transmission of venereal disease to infants; between immigrant political ward bosses and the immigrant vice networks. The social response to prostitution revealed the competing ideologies within Progressive reform activity over social justice and social control. Moreover, the outcome of the antiprostitution crusade showed that the Progressives made up not one movement, but many movements with competing agendas.[1]

Together these currents set in motion the most intensive campaign ever waged against the prostitution trade in American cities. In 1921 Howard Woolston wrote: "It was not until the early years of the twentieth century that the whole country awoke to the disgrace of a system of commercialized vice which, unknown to the vast majority of our citizens, had grown up in our midst." In the first two decades of the century, prostitution, referred to as the social evil, became a household word. Muckraking journalists exposed the web of corruption between police, politicians, and vice magnates. Novelists and even filmmakers sensationalized the traffic in women in lurid tales of abduction, rape, and sexual slavery. Twenty-seven cities established vice commissions, and several massive volumes described every facet of commercialized sex in the American city. One estimate, probably not an exaggeration, has set the published material on prostitution at one billion pages during this period.[2]

Historical studies, with few exceptions, have portrayed the campaign as a response to social and psychological anxieties. They trace the sources for antiprostitution to all kinds of social stresses—fears over immigration, urbanization, industrialization, commercialization. Mark Connelly presents the most coherent and subtle analysis of the argument; he concludes that antiprostitution was the last gasp of a dying moral and social order, of a civilizing morality, where "all moral values were absolute and timeless, masculine and feminine roles were sharply defined and demarcated, sexuality was seen as a potentially destructive force, and life, in general, was conceived in terms of duty, service, and self denial."[3]

To view antiprostitution as a psychological clearinghouse for a host of social disorders is to discount the economic and social problems reformers were addressing: low wages paid to women, local government and police corruption from sex commerce, and the spread of venereal disease (in an age when no safe cure existed). Such a view, moreover, ignores the general ideological current in the campaign, a belief that the state should create a net to catch those fallen outside its protection and should suppress rather than manage the business of prostitution—keep it in certain districts and license its practitioners. The American campaign had its counterparts in other European countries during the same era; Germany, Holland, Sweden, Finland—all had antiprostitution drives with the main goal of dismantling the regulation system. Some of the same reform impulses sparked these campaigns; reformers called on the state to find remedies for women's poverty and social dependency rather than support a system that exploited them. In Finland and Sweden, the successful campaigns against state-licensed prostitution were linked to broad political movements for social democracy and women's suffrage. In 1907 Finland ended regulated prostitution, and in the same year a new parliamentary system was established that gave workers and all women political participation. Swedish Social Democrats, in a coalition government formed in 1918, ended the system of licensed brothels, claiming that it subjected a class of poor women to unfair treatment.[4]

To analyze the social forces and ideological underpinnings of antiprostitution in the first decades of the twentieth century is not to deny the symbolic content of the crusade, particularly its obsession with the white slave trade, an image that conjured up a highly organized syndicated traffic in women for prostitution. Rather, this approach assumes that a sex commerce that had become increasingly institutionalized by the turn of the century was in fact antagonistic to the reform agenda of the Progressive Era, although reformers did not recognize the contradictions they faced.

A Changing Prostitution Economy

Certain facets of prostitution appeared to have become more threatening by the first decades of the twentieth century. The economy of prostitution had become more organized and rationalized; an individual or group might own several houses; pimps sometimes managed several prostitutes; and owners often bought shares in each other's businesses. Moreover, a greater division of labor was evolving in sex commerce: there were proprietors, pimps, madams, runners, collectors (who paid off police), doctors, clothing dealers, and professional bondsmen. It was a commercial enterprise that yielded enormous profits and had many middlemen. It was a business managed by immigrants who had ties to urban machines and police departments. Some women still worked as independents, but it was more difficult to evade police without an institutional base or the protection of a pimp.[5] White slavery was a symbolic figure that expressed these fearful aspects of prostitution. Another figure was the vice trust, used in the assumption that sex commerce had evolved into a central monopoly and was even more dangerous than the other corporate trusts under attack in this period.

Sexual slavery had been one of the central concerns of female moral reformers of the early nineteenth century, but they never characterized the practice as an organized regional, national, or international traffic. British reformer and journalist William Stead's documented exposé in 1885, "The Maiden Tribute of Babylon," was one of earliest and most celebrated cases to make this connection. In the series of articles Stead described how he purchased a thirteen-year-old from her parents for one pound and handed her over to a procurer who intended to have her sent to a brothel on the Continent. For his part in the drama, Stead was imprisoned for three months.[6]

White slavery was a highly charged metaphor in the Progressive Era: not only did it capture a belief that all women were potential victims of sexual enslavement; it had as its protagonists an underworld of European immigrants operating an international traffic in women's bodies. (To call the traffic in women *white* slavery was a misrepresentation, for there also existed an established trade in Asian and African women to the United States and Europe.)

During the Progressive Era, typical white slave narratives described men with hypodermic needles waiting to drug and abduct their prey in darkened movie theaters or subways. These fantastic accounts sent shock waves through the American public. Charges that an international syndicate was trafficking in women mobilized the U.S. Immigration Service to send hundreds of agents into cities as underground investigators. The sensational narratives also led to the passage of the landmark Mann-Elkins Act, a federal law that prohibited the importation of any girl or woman for immoral purposes or prostitution between countries or across state lines.

However, as investigators gathered more and more data about the vice trade, it became evident that the majority of prostitutes in the United States had not been trapped unknowingly in houses of bondage. The U.S. Supreme Court in 1914 formalized this view, ruling that "woman cannot be considered victims if they take interstate journeys voluntarily." Vice commission statistics on prostitutes revealed that the majority of prostitutes were native-born daughters of immigrants. Supporting this view,

Helen Bullis, an immigration officer at Ellis Island, testified that procurers and pimps in the United States did not need to take the risk of bringing alien women into the country, for there was an ample supply here already. The exception was the traffic in Asian women—nonwhite sexual slavery—which had been operating for decades before the white slave hysteria.[7] According to Sue Gronewold's study of women in prerevolutionary China, selling daughters into prostitution was one of many strategies poor peasants used to rid themselves of unwanted daughters, who might also be sold as brides or as adopted children to be servants in households. The traffic of Asian women in the United States therefore says as much about poverty and patriarchy in Chinese society as it does about organized prostitution in the United States.[8]

The fear of white slavery did reflect certain real changes within the American prostitution economy. One was that opportunities for recruitment into the vice trade had increased. Another was that the level of coercion by managers in the trade had also increased. Red-light districts were open employment centers for runaways, amateur prostitutes wanting to turn professional, and women facing economic pressures or family conflicts. In addition, more women by this time were living on their own in boardinghouses, beyond parental supervision. Changing patterns of leisure in working class communities provided another conduit for prostitution; women were spending more of their leisure time seeking entertainment outside the home in dance halls and amusement parks.[9] Finally, and what made up perhaps the most important influence, more middlemen and businesses had become linked to the prostitution economy.

The rise of the pimp system was documented in nearly every study of prostitution during this period. Whereas in the past prostitutes had had bully boys or lovers who often exploited them, by the turn of the century more and more prostitutes' labor and wages were actively managed by pimps, who in some cases arranged clients or installed women in particular brothels. Moreover, instead of managing the affairs of one woman—an arrangement one recent sociological study calls "house pimping"—a new breed of entrepreneurial pimps emerged who tended to control a string of women.[10]

In the most extensive study of European prostitution during this period, Abraham Flexner noted that the pimps or dealers in prostitutes were gaining control of the trade and that even the European morals police could not keep them out. Nell Kimball, a madam who operated brothels in New Orleans and San Francisco—cities with open prostitution districts—noted that most of her girls had pimps who mooched off them. Features of the American prostitution scene may have encouraged the dominant position of the pimp. The absence of a regulation system with sanitary control made it easier to break a girl into the trade, since she did not have to enter the system formally. At the same time, the policy of quasi-toleration operating in most American cities meant that police could arrest a streetwalker or conduct a raid at any time, which gave the pimp an important role as protector and police payoff man, as well as business manager. Whether writing about European cities where prostitution was legalized or about informal systems of control—the situation in most American cities—few commentators failed to mention the growing importance of the *soutenir* or pimp.[11]

George Kneeland, in his 1913 survey of New York prostitution, commented on the varied roles the pimp was now playing: as a prostitute's business agent, go-between with the police, and companion, the only person she believed cared for her. In analyzing the "psychology of the pimp," Kneeland understood the combination of dependency and control in this relationship. Pimps took amateurs or clandestine prostitutes and made them into professionals; they showed the women how and where to hustle. He claimed that some men beat their women on the principle that it was the only way to make them fear and love them. "This may seem a paradox; but . . . a spark of affection lives at the heart of this ghastly relation."[12]

Maude Miner, in her 1916 study, used the phrase "breaking-in system" to characterize the ways in which a pimp employed a combination of affection, threats, brute force, and protection. She perceived that physical force alone did not account for a woman's sexual slavery; the power of the pimp rested on his ability to gain control over a woman's mind and will. In this context the notion of white slavery covered all forms of sexual exploitation where coercion existed, whether mental or physical.[13]

To call this kind of dependency sexual slavery was to simplify a complex economic, social, and psychological relationship. Surveying the seventy-seven white slavery cases in Chicago courts in the following decade, sociologist Walter Reckless stressed the extent to which images of white slavery distorted the dynamics in pimping and pandering. It was, in Reckless's words, "a survival of this lingering patriarchal pattern of family life and male human nature transferred in perverted expression to a modern urban situation where it took the form of exploitation."[14]

Reformers like Kneeland and Miner were aware that a more organized prostitution trade in big cities would increase the coercive sides of the system. The network of underworld gangs and police protection in immigrant communities could easily track a prostitute who decided to become an independent operator. Clearly there were pressures for women to stay in prostitution when so many middlemen had an interest in keeping them on the streets. The power of the pimp turned a prostitute into a unique kind of exploited laborer. White slavery as a metaphor captured a prostitute's growing dependence on a manager/pimp and her loss of the freedom to move in and out of prostitution—to work part time or seasonally.

Whereas experts sitting on vice commissions imagined a highly organized prostitution empire in the hands of few vice moguls—the vice trust—the corporate analogy did not really fit the ways in which the underworld operated. Kneeland, who orchestrated both the Chicago and the New York investigations, believed that sex commerce was under the control of a few powerful magnates, who formed partnerships, sold shares, and netted millions in profits. In actuality, however, the societies of pimps and managers were informal associations that provided contacts, passed on trade secrets, and collected money for police payoffs; they constituted what a study of present-day prostitution calls deviant street networks.[15] One such group Kneeland referred to in his report, the Independent Benevolent Association, served as a social club for its members, who met on the East Side of New York at a local cafe owned by a former pimp. Other operators in the prostitution business, lacking a formal name and less organized than the New York association, met informally at certain hotels and cafes. In San Francisco it was the European Palace and Regent Cafe, and the dominant group was French; in Boston, Italian pimps had their headquarters at two dive restaurants. These groups had similar functions: protection, political contacts, and social meetings.[16]

The vast majority of big city "exploiters" in prostitution were foreign born. One study of urban crime in Chicago in the 1920s did not show one native-born member of prostitution, gambling, or numbers rackets. The keepers or managers of prostitutes tended to be the most recent arrivals in American cities. This is not surprising; prostitution is one of the few business that requires little capital, offers quick returns, and involves few risks for those who are not doing the actual selling. In the mid-nineteenth century, the Irish managed the houses of prostitution; by the early twentieth century, new immigrants from southern and eastern Europe began taking over the vice rackets. Black migrants coming from the rural South to northern cities in the 1930s found some of their few employment opportunities in the sex trade during the depression, and they later became the dominant group managing prostitution.[17]

The vice rackets were not European imports, as the media and many commission experts charged. Instead they sprouted from the poverty in immigrant neighborhoods and the dreams of a better life. The Horatio Algers of the immigrant underworld were men like Max and Louis Soviner, pushcart peddlers who came to New York from Russia in 1892. They turned to the oldest profession, beginning as procurers, then working as watchboys for brothels, and finally making the big time as owners of houses. These successful men were living proof that American streets were paved with gold.[18]

Commercialized vice was moving not in the direction of a monolithic combine but toward a range of institutions with a host of entrepreneurs taking advantage of the good market conditions. There were not only traditional brothels, hotels, and tenement prostitution, but also new forms—massage parlors and call girls. There were moneymakers like Mortke Goldberg, who owned several houses in New York, and small-fries, who ran the affairs of one or two prostitutes. The organization and institutions varied according to the social, political, and cultural landscape. How big a city was, who ran the local government, and whether a segregated zone existed all shaped the prostitution economy.

At the turn of the century, a combination of social and economic forces produced rapid expansion in the prostitution market. Districts where prostitution was tolerated allowed networks for prostitution businesses and recruitment to flourish. During that period European single men emigrated in vast numbers, an influx that increased the demand for prostitutes. At the same time, more women were in the labor force and living on their own in cities and consequently had greater opportunities to become prostitutes. Finally, new immigrants who found traditional enterprises closed to them turned their skills to illegal ones and thus stimulated supply and demand.

The actual statistics on arrests of prostitutes, keepers, and procurers suggest that a remarkable number of persons were living off vice in the cities. For example, in Chicago between 1908 and 1928, the average number of cases of recruiters, keepers, and pimps reaches into the thousands. One estimate set the number of full-time prostitutes at five thousand in that city. During 1912, before the major crackdowns on vice in

New York, Kneeland's investigators reported close to four thousand prostitutes just in brothels and tenements—not including hotel, rooming-house, or massage-parlor prostitution. Records from the San Francisco municipal clinic for prostitutes noted that doctors performed 60,736 examinations between March 1911 and December 1912, an average of 116 women per day.[19]

What appeared most disturbing to reformers was not the increasing numbers of prostitutes or the visibility of sex commerce, but the tendency toward institutionalized and state-sanctioned prostitution. When the first New York committee investigating vice made its pioneering investigation of urban prostitution in 1902, it listed thirty-two cities where police admitted that a "system of regulation" was in effect, and thirty-three cities where special areas in which prostitution was permitted had been established. Police and courts in many American cities had a de facto regulation system of prostitution through fines, segregated zones, and venereal medical certificates, regulation in all but name and statutory code. It seemed that the American cities were only a small step away from a formal system of state control.[20]

Regulating Prostitution

Until Nevada legalized prostitution in the 1970s, only one city in the United States, St. Louis, had ever adopted a formal regulation system. It came about through a revision in the city charter which gave the city the power to prohibit, restrain, and regulate bawdyhouses. The addition of the word *regulate* formed the basis for the broad powers of the "social evil ordinance." It called for the licensing of brothels, the medical inspection of prostitutes, and enforcement for noncompliance by the city's board of health. It resembled the continental system but medical officers (physicians) rather than policemen were responsible for enforcement.[21]

The St. Louis experiment was short-lived, from 1870 to 1874, and aroused a storm of protest. The fight against regulation there attracted reformers from all sections of the United States as well as from England. Indeed, the arguments of clergymen, feminists, and civil libertarians that St. Louis was the first step toward a national system of regulation were not wholly without merit. In fact, during the 1870s several state and municipal governments pressed for similar legislation. In New York three attempts were made and came close to passage. The state legislature in 1871 voted through a regulation bill, but it received a pocket veto from the governor. In Philadelphia, Cincinnati, Chicago, and San Francisco, social evil ordinances had strong support and were defeated only after intensive petition campaigns by reform groups.[22]

After the defeat of the St. Louis social evil ordinance, American police and politicians interested in controlling prostitution through a system of licensed brothels and medical inspection carefully avoided formalizing such a system. But in many cities public officials used existing statutes and legal traditions of police powers to implement similar kinds of control by segregating prostitutes in districts, requiring women to have medical examinations, and licensing brothels through routine fines. Storeyville, the famous red-light district in New Orleans, came into being through the skillful legal wording of alderman Sidney Storey's ordinance, which made it unlawful for lewd women to occupy any house outside specified limits, while at the same time maintained that nothing in the law authorized such women to practice their trade in any part of the city. In effect, the law did not legally sanction prostitution but prescribed where it could be practiced.[23]

The Houston experience illustrates perfectly cities' ambivalence toward prostitution regulation. Texas state law meant to repress prostitution. A revision of the Texas Disorderly House statute in 1907 gave any citizen— personally injured or not—the power to bring action against a bawdy-house through injunction; thus a person offended by a brothel could in one stroke close it down. Paradoxically, the state law also had a provision that gave municipalities the right to establish vice districts that could not be touched by citizen initiatives. By allowing communities extraordinary latitude in developing a policy toward prostitution, the Texas law recognized the lack of consensus between and within municipalities.[24]

In Houston, certain residents opposed to the open practice of prostitution brought suits against the brothels housed in a traditional vice area. Shortly thereafter, the brothels dispersed and several moved to quiet, respectable neighborhoods. Several brothels located themselves next to the local school, and residents mounted a campaign to create a "reservation" for vice. Although the mayor urged citizens to use their power of injunction, they pressed for a change in the city charter to set up a separate district for brothels. The ordinance for the "colonization of prostitution" was passed in 1907 and a new vice district was located on the outskirts of town, in an undeveloped area. It remained there until the World War I, when the federal government demanded that the city eliminate the district or lose a valuable army base. As the Houston case reveals, policies to repress vice or to regulate it can stem from the same impulses: an attempt to contain moral and physical contagion and, more generally, a desire to keep prostitution out of sight.

The experience of the San Francisco Municipal Clinic is a striking example of the contradictory responses to prostitution. There, the same reform-minded groups that, in other cities, joined forces with those seeking to abolish licensed prostitution stood behind a system of inspection and licensing of prostitutes, which promised to be effective, efficient, and corruption-free. Dr. Julius Rosenstirn, the chief supporter of the clinic, belonged to a host of civic and good-government associations. Believing that prostitution could never be eradicated nor the sex drive suppressed, he urged the city to adopt an inspection system with a team of medical experts. In 1911 Rosenstirn's reforms were adopted, in effect legalizing prostitution in the city. All prostitutes were examined twice a week in a clinic under the auspices of the board of health. They were then given a card certifying that they could practice prostitution or denied their license to practice until they took treatment. Failure to register or comply with medical inspection procedures led to police intervention, and if a woman remained recalcitrant, she was arrested. Businessmen, physicians, and even clergy were on the board of the clinic at the outset. But as more and more revelations of corruption and underworld ties were revealed, the reform groups dropped out. Neil Shumsky's detailed account of the clinic persuasively argues that from its inception the vice interests and corrupt politicians saw the scheme as a way of keeping the eradicators at bay and retaining control of prostitution.[25]

The San Francisco episode underscored how entrenched prostitution interests were in city government; even appointees to the local board of health could be controlled. Vice commission reports hammered away at these links. But the lesson of San Francisco supported the more general claim of antiprostitution activists, that the evil effects of prostitution could not be segregated from the everyday life of city residents or the society at large.

Reformers and Their Agendas

Much of the first wave of the campaign against commercialized vice in the United States was directed at the red-light district and the legal, medical, and urban institutions that controlled the prostitution system in American cities. Reformers devoted enormous energy and resources to showing the "moral and sanitary" weakness of European regulation. The coalition of clergy, temperance, and women's groups in the National Purity Alliance had been responsible for subverting drives for regulatory legislation in the nineteenth century and continued to attack any tendency toward institutionalized prostitution. Feminists saw that institutionalization would establish a permanent class of degraded women and thus perpetuate the belief in women's inferior social status. Physicians in the social hygiene movement, who were the last group to join the bandwagon, realized that state inspection could never control venereal disease.

The antiprostitution movement was a loose coalition of diverse groups with varied reform agendas, political ideologies, and sexual politics. They organized around a single issue and strategy—suppression of prostitution—and opposed regulating or licensing vice; however, they had different motivations, different political and social ideologies, and different visions of what their campaign could accomplish. One could divide the groups along the general lines of those who defined prostitution narrowly and those who defined it broadly. For example, prostitution was a single-issue campaign for municipal reformers who wanted to get rid of the corrupt politicians and ward bosses profiting from the vice trade and for physicians who wanted to limit the spread of venereal disease.

Other groups analyzed prostitution as a symptom of deeper social ills and antiprostitution as a means to adopting a long-term reform agenda. Social purity advocates sought to uplift the nation's morality and return to Christian values; they linked antiprostitution to a range of moral and educational goals to protect home and family. For feminists, a prostitution-free society was an essential step toward women's emancipation. Social justice motivated many antiprostitution reformers whose social welfare objectives included the amelioration of poverty, poor housing conditions, and unemployment.[26]

Like those of earlier times and of today, women's groups in the Progressive Era were instrumental in mobilizing support for antiprostitution. They mounted petition drives and pressured state and local governments to pass laws against promoters of vice and slavery. Women's voices were clearly heard in areas where they had obtained the vote. In California, for example, women used the ballot to put through "abatement laws," which allowed any citizen to bring a civil suit against a brothel, and which constituted a key strategy for dismantling red-light districts.[27]

Women's impact on the antiprostitution campaign was a result of two opposing trends in the feminist movement. One was the growth of separate women's organizations and federations; the other was the integration of women into mainstream legal, medical, and educational institutions. Women's political culture evolved through local and national associations that promoted temperance, social purity, and suffrage throughout the nineteenth century. Many grass-roots women's associations were reluctant to address prostitution as too indelicate a subject, though they lobbied for issues indirectly related to prostitution, such as raising the age of consent. However, by the 1890s suppression of prostitution became an open part of the reform agenda in mass organizations such as the Women's Christian Temperance Union.[28]

Women in social work professions, in prison and probation departments, and in settlement houses gained a foothold into the social welfare bureaucracy; they were thus able to launch a series of public debates over prostitution policy. For example, Martha Falconer, who had been active in Chicago's Woman's Club, later served as a probation officer in the Juvenile Court. Maude Miner also entered the criminal justice system as a New York probation administrator.

A range of otherwise competing feminist groups linked antiprostitution to the emancipation of women. The compulsory inspection and registration of prostitutes touched a nerve in the feminist pulse as one of the most blatant examples of women's second-class status. Men created institutions that legitimized women's sexual degradation, which they maintained was physically necessary for themselves. They then treated the women they ruined as outcasts and pariahs. Antoinette Blackwell, sister of Elizabeth and the first ordained female minister in the United States clearly made the connection between prostitution politics and sexual politics. She attacked the regulation scheme as "a shield manufactured and uplifted exclusively for men. . . . It ignores the interests and rights of their women associates as completely as some vivisectionists ignore the sentiment claims of animals."[29]

When Blackwell spoke of "women's point of view" toward prostitution, she referred to a general consensus within the women's movement on the question of "equal moral obligation" between the sexes. While feminists did not necessarily speak in one voice in antiprostitution, they did place prostitution and the double sexual standard in the larger framework of men's domination of political, economic, and social institutions. For the women's movement, the red-light district and de facto regulation of prostitution underscored how imperative female suffrage was; prostitution became the symbol of a corrupt male polity that sanctioned sexual exploitation and permitted vice syndicates, politicians, and police to profit from the sale of women's bodies.[30]

Through their organizations and institutions, feminists had developed their own political culture and networks, which they could mobilize in small-scale or local campaigns. But they lacked any real institutional power base—in political parties or unions. To mount an attack on prostitution, they had to convert powerful men to their cause. The medical profession, which many feminists perceived as the embodiment of the male point of view, had to be won over to the antiprostitution side.

Doctors had been the strongest advocates for implementing regulation systems in Europe and the United States. In 1873 the international medical congress at Vienna actually passed resolutions urging all nations to establish a compulsory system of supervision in all large seaport cities. Many of the studies of prostitutes were conducted by physicians involved in the day-to-day administration of compulsory inspection, and one argument for regulation was that it facilitated the collection of statistical data on prostitutes.[31]

During the nineteenth century, some prominent American physicians viewed the European regulation system as a positive public health measure and sought to persuade their colleagues of this. But American physicians generally steered clear both of actively supporting a regulation policy and of engaging in campaigns for suppression. Their professional status was much more precarious than that of their colleagues in Europe. Having to treat prostitutes for venereal disease would have meant a loss of prestige for any American doctor.[32]

When, in their own journals, physicians debated the pros and cons of suppression versus regulation, they treated the issue within the narrow framework of effective disease control. Doctors writing about prostitution often began their articles with disclaimers that their purpose was not to consider the ethical sides of the issue or the validity of the necessity of the prostitute. Whether doctors took a regulationist or antiregulationist stand, the issue was the same: How effective is the system for controlling the spread of disease?[33] Within the medical community, the prostitution debate became a war of statistics. By the turn of the century, the evidence supported those opposed to sanitary control.

Prince Morrow was the physician most responsible for forcing the medical community to confront the ethical issues in the prostitution debates. Through his contacts with European venerologists, Morrow had became familiar with research on the transmission of both syphilis and gonorrhea to innocent wives and children, and new evidence on the extent to which venereal disease was a major cause of sterility in women. He coined the phrase "social disease" to dramatize the extent to which venereal disease menaced family life and posed the greatest threat to the perpetuation of the race itself. For Morrow the devastating consequences of venereal disease undercut any arguments for sanitary controls—which could never assure protection—and most important, called into question the longstanding tradition of doctor-patient secrecy.[34] He launched in 1905 the Society for Social and Moral Prophylaxis, which was mainly composed of physicians, although open to all persons who sought to educate the public about venereal disease. That society evolved into the American Social Hygiene Association, which ultimately came to set the agenda on prostitution policy during World War I and the years after.

The medical establishment, when it rallied behind the campaign against prostitution in the United States, gave prestige and legitimacy to the movement. But physicians' participation also helped to undermine the broader goals of sexual equality that feminists sought. For the majority of physicians, the policy of suppression was solely intended to limit venereal disease.

More than any other figure, Abraham Flexner, a physician who studied prostitution internationally, closed the curtain on the regulation debates in America. Flexner had been recruited by John D. Rockefeller to investigate how successful registration systems in Europe were in controlling venereal disease. After researching prostitution in twenty-seven European cities, Flexner concluded that licensing failed in its main objective of limiting clandestine prostitution and venereal disease. He described the haphazard way examinations were performed and offered evidence that as many as three-quarters of women in the trade were ignored by the morals police in the Continental system.[35]

Flexner was the ideal candidate for such a project. His study of medical education in America, known as the Flexner Report (also commissioned by Rockefeller), established his credentials within the medical profession and among Progressive reformers. His research wove together scientific, moral, and social justice arguments—the various threads in the antiprostitution campaign. Alongside his attack on the medical dangers in regulated prostitution, Flexner addressed its social consequences, arguing that regulation encouraged some of the worst abuses in the prostitution system: corruption of police, exploitation of women by middlemen, and the use of espionage by the state on its citizens.[36]

Flexner's study expressed the mood and impulse that lay behind much of the reform ferment during the early years of the Progressive campaign against social evils. He condemned regulation because it was undemocratic, unscientific, inefficient, and pessimistic. Furthermore, he believed that the state should be a "positive force," an engine of reform, not a passive actor. To argue for necessary evils would have gone against the grain of this generation of reformers.[37]

By the time Flexner's study was published in 1914, activists in the campaign had dropped their defensive posture. They had witnessed the passage of scores of state and federal laws against the business of prostitution and the creation of new agencies to enforce them: vice squads, women police officers, and probation officers. At the same time, hundreds of vice commission studies were amassing data that reformers naively believed would solve the problem of prostitution. Debates centered no longer on the suppression or regulation of prostitution but rather on the reduction or elimination of vice.

Scientific Knowledge and Solutions

Jane Addams ended her study of prostitution with a vision of a future society where sexual exploitation no longer existed:

> In that vast and checkered undertaking of its own moralization to which the human race is committed, it must constantly free itself from the survivals and savage infections of the primitive life from which it started. Now one and then another of the ancient wrongs and uncouth customs which have been so long familiar as to seem inevitable, rise to the moral consciousness of a passing generation; first for uneasy contemplation and then for gallant correction.[38]

For Addams and other reformers in this era, prostitution appeared anachronistic, a prehensile tail that would wither away as society evolved into
its next stage of moral development. They had the same millennialist
fervor as the evangelicals who had mounted crusades against vice over a
half-century earlier. Both groups believed society could be perfected, but
rather than relying on spiritual armor and conversion, the architects of
the antiprostitution drive in the twentieth century would employ statistical analysis and scientific theories. Experts would become scientific
managers in both the public and private spheres, and the state would play
a central role in social engineering.

An essential component in the campaign was the collection of data.
Vice commission reports and reform journals included statistics on every
facet of prostitution: the number of houses and classes of brothels, the
average cost, the social and mental backgrounds of prostitutes. The sheer
amount of data testified to a study's scientific seriousness. Reformers
believed that scientific investigations of prostitution would yield a solution, as laboratory experiments isolated bacteria and produced cures for
disease. However, hidden agendas, unconscious motivations, and assumptions about sexual and social relationships permeated the social laboratory
in prostitution studies. Take, for example, the Boston Women's Educational and Industrial Union study of prostitution in the early years of the
antiprostitution campaign. The women who sponsored the study—
women most likely sympathetic to the prostitute—developed a question-
naire on the social backgrounds of prostitutes: their nativity, marital
status, housing, wages, and occupations. All the questions were very
straightforward, except for the final one on "reasons for entering the
business." There, reformers' social perceptions were visible, since they
ascribed such causes as degeneracy (to 49 percent), weakness of character,
or laziness.[39] The organization had a long history of addressing the
economic needs of working women and supporting women's unioniza-
tion. Many of the vice commission studies included similar categories of
mental deficiency as the cause of women's entry into prostitution. Perhaps
the most revealing fact about the scientific study of prostitution is that
patrons were left out. Gathering statistics on patrons was more difficult,
especially since they were rarely arrested or put into institutions (much
of the prostitution data was from these kinds of official sources). Still,
there were researchers who went into the field and interviewed prostitutes,
but did not dig into men's motivations for seeking out prostitutes.

A pervasive belief in the antiprostitution campaign was that "the facts" were disembodied from social perspectives and would lead to enlightened, sane, and scientific reforms. John D. Rockefeller created the Bureau of Social Hygiene as a research "laboratory" for the dispassionate scientific study of prostitution, an antidote to the hysteria surrounding white slavery.[40]

For reformers, scientific knowledge signaled an advance in the evolution of man that could provide answers leading to the mastery of mind, body, and social relationships. Scientific methods appeared as a powerful argument against those who insisted that prostitution was a necessary evil. In the words of the Massachusetts Vice Commission:

It had been held that prostitution always has existed and always will exist, and that all remedies will be ineffective and of no avail, because it represents a variation of the most fundamental human instinct. . . . Modern methods of scientific study of first causes and the logical removal of these causes have prevented, alleviated or cured many physical and social ills of mankind which were considered necessary and inevitable.[41]

Scientific knowledge would provide the fuel for the moral engines in the antiprostitution drive, according to Maude Miner, and her study of prostitution begins with a paean to science:

A new scientific and humanitarian spirit sharply challenges the necessity of this ancient evil. It holds that since nothing that is necessary is evil, nothing that is evil can be necessary. The traditional methods of dealing with vice totter and fall before this new spirit.[42]

Results of the War

With hindsight we know that prostitution neither fell nor tottered under the weight of statistical studies, police raids, and the general fervor around organized vice. It is difficult to assess even the impact of closing down red-light districts. The laws and general strategy of repression seem to have had remarkably little effect on the prostitution economy.

Antiprostitution could boast of an impressive number of laws passed against pimps, procurers, landlords, and even patrons in the years after the vice reports. The major pieces of legislation were aimed at the traffickers in, and businesses of, prostitution. Uniformly, between 1910 and 1920, states enacted tougher laws that targeted all kinds of institutions believed to be associated with vice traffic: dance halls and massage institutes were licensed; businessmen receiving benefits from prostitution became liable, particularly tenement owners who tolerated prostitution in their buildings. Most important, legal codes defining prostitution were widened to include those who rented rooms for immoral purposes and all others who aided, abetted, or "participated" in activities of prostitutes.[43]

Red-light districts in hundreds of cities were shut down by 1920. A journalist, George Anderson, compared Chicago's levee area to a ghost town after the crackdown on sex commerce:

> The hall of revelry was barred and in blackness; not a single light or a woman in sight. The disorderly saloon was in like desolation with only one dim gleam in a room of the deserted hotel above. Around the blocks we were met everywhere by bar and bolts, by boarded windows and the signs of real estate agents.[44]

Turning out the red lights and dismantling the districts merely dispersed the trade and produced a new set of institutions in the prostitution economy. Reckless's study of Chicago's vice districts revealed that the number of prostitution establishments had decreased somewhat, from 1,020 in 1910 to 731 in 1931; that the trade was less visible in the 1920s; and that the most notorious clubs and brothels were gone. But organized crime was able to keep its tight hold on the business of vice and to wait out a reform mayor's campaigns against them by playing a cat-and-mouse game of moving from one property to another. The big-time operators were never caught in the net of antiprostitution laws.[45]

Reckless concluded that the major reason that prostitution in its syndicated form endured was the continued power of the ward bosses who delivered the votes. "Hinky Dink" Kenna and "Bathhouse" John Coughlin, two notorious Chicago ward bosses, restored the revoked licenses of their friends and protected them from grand jury action. In 1923, when the grand jury presented seventy-five indictments against keepers of disorderly houses, some of the most notorious establishments were not listed, even though testimony had been given against them. Chicago represented the most blatant case of organized crime's tight hold on city government, but in other cities ward bosses were also beholden to underworld crime.[46]

Reformers' demands to supress vice conflicted with the vested interests of police and politicians. Prostitution payoffs passed from the district cop to the highest levels of city government; Shumsky's studies of San Francisco suggest that the mayor was a shareholder in one of the largest vice operations. The policy of repression was at odds with fundamental attitudes and expectations of urban police, judges, and ward bosses. Surveys revealed that the majority of urban police favored some form of regulation. The system gave them wide powers to define the spatial boundaries of prostitution, monitor the managers, and punish the prostitute who did not obey the rules. Unlike reformers, they did not see organized prostitution as a serious problem, nor did they consider sexual exploitation or the spread of venereal disease to be law enforcement issues. Immigration officers noted that police were often quite willing to comb the vice district for alien prostitutes but had no interest in disrupting the established houses or women on the right streets—and sometimes even warned them of pending immigration investigations. Municipal police looked upon the brothel district and vice racketeers as an effective means of keeping prostitution from spreading to middle class neighborhoods, where voters had more clout. Woolston noted in his study that eighteen out of twenty police chiefs interviewed said they favored a policy of regulation. Only after media pressure and public outcry did police begin to dismantle the red-light districts.[47]

To understand the persistence of organized prostitution, one must dig deeper than machine politics, corrupt police, or indifferent public officials to reach the politics of class and gender. When the laws threatened to dislodge the double sexual standard, they were blatantly ignored; when juries encountered a business that supported prostitution, they were loathe to convict. Although reform groups, particularly women activists, bitterly attacked the double standard in the policing of prostitution, few states enacted laws penalizing the customer. Two states, Indiana and Iowa, had their statutes against patrons overturned by the state supreme courts, which ruled that men could not be guilty of prostitution. Even laws such as those against fornication or idle and disorderly conduct, which could be applied to both prostitute and customer, seldom were. Instead they were used to prosecute women who had rarely been arrested in the past, mainly prostitutes lodged in hotels and tenement rooms. Maude Miner, who worked as a probation officer for New York's district courts, described business as usual in prostitution raids:

I have frequently seen ten or twenty women arraigned in court as inmates of a disorderly house and heard the judge ask the arresting officer if all in the house were taken. The usual answer was that the men were allowed to go and the doors were open for them to depart before the women were under arrest.[48]

The New York Committee of Fourteen was composed of prominent civic reformers who set out to investigate economic, legal, and social aspects of sex commerce; they stated that laws against prostitution could be applied to both men and women. In their report, they maintained that the 1915 solicitation law was to include both men and women who attempted to entice a person into lewdness in a public thoroughfare. But they conceded that magistrates and police did not enforce the law equally because public opinion was not ready to support actions against the men who paid for sex commerce.[49]

The Massachusetts Vice Commission concluded that, in the treatment of customer and prostitute, "there seems to be a lack of even justice," an understatement considering that during their investigation, out of 223 men arrested for fornication only 5 were given prison terms. Women reformers active in antiprostitution were bitter that the burden of punishment fell on the prostitute. They put a great deal of energy into getting women into municipal police forces, imagining that female officers might "entrap" the masher just as male officers were decoys for prostitutes' soliciting. It didn't happen that way.

The managers of prostitutes and the owners of vice establishments were rarely convicted, even though one might think that widely read sadistic and brutal white slave narratives would have prejudiced any jury against a defendant charged with living off the profits of prostitutes. Legal procedures worked in a defendant's favor. To convict a pimp required a prostitute's testimony against him. Whether owing to emotional attachment or to fear of reprisal, few women were willing to testify. The New York Committee of Fourteen complained that when a jury trial was granted in a case of pimping, procuring, or keeping a brothel, the defendant always was treated more leniently than if the case were tried before a judge in an urban municipal court.[50]

The Massachusetts Vice Commission bemoaned the difficulty of getting convictions for the merchandisers of sex commerce in that state. Conviction usually led to appeal, which resulted in probation, a suspended sentence, or some other alternative to imprisonment. In 1913, the year of the commission's investigation, only four keepers out of sixty-five convicted received prison sentences. Hotel owners and saloonkeepers with a prostitution trade were rarely prosecuted. Property owners were not seen as a vicious criminal element, and their "vested property interests" were almost never taken away from them, even when it was clear that they had full knowledge that their properties supported a brisk prostitution trade. One study revealed that law authorities often had an unwritten agreement in which pseudo-respectable hotels and the better class of prostitutes and patrons would not be molested by police.[51]

The body of laws and administrative procedures that were supposed to close off sex commerce in the United States had the greatest impact on prostitutes, particularly women who solicited in the streets or sold their services in low-class houses, the most visible and vulnerable prostitutes. During the height of the antiprostitution campaign, urban night courts were instituted. Hailed as landmarks in court reform, they were specialized for processing large numbers of women picked up for prostitution. In New York and Philadelphia all the personnel and facilities were under one roof: these courts had lockups, resident doctors to diagnose venereal disease, and psychiatrists to determine a woman's mental capacity. Judges were permanently assigned to these courts and consequently became experts in the field. Unlike her keeper or pimp, who was tried in district court and could be found guilty only if the arresting officer's testimony was corroborated, the prostitute was subject to less stringent rules of evidence. These women's courts were models of efficiency. Cities with these specialized courts tended to convict more prostitutes and send greater numbers to institutions.[52]

In the years before World War I, probably the most controversial new police power used against the prostitute was entrapment. One early test of its constitutionality came in New York, but the practice was upheld. The Committee of Fourteen admitted its unpopularity and found themselves having to defend the tactic in their annual reports. Another controversial law allowed courts to impose an indeterminate sentence for prostitutes who were convicted of a third offense and introduced fingerprinting as the basis for convicting recidivists. That law also withstood legal challenges. New York was a pioneer in the use of fingerprinting, and prostitutes were the first criminal types to be sentenced under this foolproof scientific way of identifying a recidivist.

New statutes and law enforcement strategies greatly increased the risk of imprisonment for prostitutes who were two- or three-time losers. In New York a specific statute prevented a judge from imposing a fine. The end of the fining system was supposed to eliminate a woman's dependence on her trade and to ensure her rehabilitation. But most women did not find their way into reformatories; they had a brief stint in the county jail or house of correction. In 1930, when social scientist Willoughby Waterman evaluated the effects of the antiprostitution campaign in New York City, he highlighted the discrimination against prostitutes in the courts. Comparing the treatment of prostitutes with that of pimps or procurers, who were most often charged with vagrancy, he found that women had a much higher conviction rate. Most striking was the number of commitments to prison. Over a ten-year period, 1,782 persons were sentenced to institutions for chastity offenses; only 67 of them were men. As had been true in the past, prostitutes were the easiest targets in antiprostitution campaigns.[53]

The Legacy of the War

Both scholars and activists in prostitution politics today have used the results of the antivice crusade of the Progressive Era to argue that all attempts to attack the institutions of sex commerce are doomed to failure.[54] However, the strategies and outcomes of the campaign arose from particular groups with particular agendas operating in a particular social and political milieu. A campaign against organized prostitution in Sweden in the 1970s offers some contrary evidence that different ideologies, reform agendas, and political alliances can have some effect on the prostitution market. Antiprostitution in Sweden had many of the same characteristics as the earlier Progressive crusade in the United States. Most important, sex commerce in Sweden appeared to be taking on a more organized and institutionalized structure, with more links to a criminal subculture than it had had in the past. Like the American campaign, the Swedish campaign occurred during a period of optimism about the state's ability to eliminate social problems. And, feminists were again the dominant pressure group.[55]

In contrast to the law enforcement agencies during the American Progressive crusade, Swedish law enforcers vigorously prosecuted the predators and even some of the businessmen who profited from prostitution. Not only pimps but also owners of legitimate businesses, and even one newspaper editor, were convicted under profiteering statutes. No one perceived the measures against the profiteers in sex commerce as a threat to free enterprise; no one defended the right of advertisers in the prostitution business on the grounds of free speech. But in no way are the differences between the two campaigns more apparent than in the treatment of the prostitute. In contrast to the United States, criminal penalties do not exist for prostitutes or patrons in Sweden, and the antiprostitution campaign generated social work remedies rather than legal ones. In the three major cities, municipalities set up programs, support groups, and social services for prostitutes. The campaign has been largely successful in meeting its goals; although street prostitution still exists in Sweden, syndicates and pimping rings have lost their position in the prostitution economy.[56]

The Swedish response to organized prostitution was based on a different set of assumptions and ideologies from the American response. Reformers attacked the notion of an institutionalized and permanent prostitution culture within the framework of social democracy. They wove together class and gender issues and characterized prostitution as upper class men's exploitation of working class women. Women's groups, the most vocal in the campaign, were integrated into mainstream political parties and exerted pressure on lawmakers. Though the Swedish campaign took place in a different period and social context, it offers some evidence that feminists can use political power to raise consciousness about prostitution issues, guide the discourse, and influence the public policy adopted.

Naively, the reformers in the American Progressive antiprostitution campaign believed that merely by gathering evidence and enacting stringent laws, they could force a new prostitution policy to emerge without changing the institutions and power alliances that had interpreted and administered the old system. Once a policy of repression was adopted, all the ideological underpinnings that had produced the class and gender bias in the law and its enforcement somehow were supposed to collapse.

For American feminists, who saw antiprostitution as a measure to increase gender equality, there were hard lessons to be learned. The sexual double standard lay firmly implanted in the legal institutions and everyday lives of women. The expansion of state power to suppress prostitution led to increased penalties against prostitutes. That feminists did not anticipate such a result is surprising. After all, they found physicians' proposals to implement a sanitary control policy for prostitutes and their customers absurd, realizing that men would not tolerate a venereal disease examination system that applied to them.[57] Yet feminists did not extend their reasoning based on gender bias when it came to policies of arrest and prosecution of prostitution's customers.

Antiprostitution revealed both strengths and weaknesses within the feminist movement. Feminist groups could mobilize thousands of women to lobby and petition, but they could not shape the policies and institutions that emerged from the reform impulse. The dilemma, which still plagues American feminism today, is how to translate the separate political culture and voices of women into mainstream institutional sources of political power.

Historian Kathryn Sklar, in a recent study, uses the Hull House settlement community in Chicago during the 1890s as an example of how women's separate institutions enabled them to implement and sustain reforms against child labor and the sweatshop system. Through the Hull House network of reform groups, a cross-class coalition of women got behind the campaign. Florence Kelley, a major activist in the Chicago feminist alliance, drafted the legislation and ultimately became main administrator of the reform, in the capacity of chief factory inspector for the state.[58] But protective legislation against sweatshops, child labor, and workdays longer than eight hours for women did not pose the threat to existing gender and class relations that laws against sex commerce did. Protective legislation had the effect of reinforcing class and gender systems, that is, institutionalizing a dual labor market, which may be why they were so readily accepted.[59]

Prosecuting customers of prostitutes, hotel managers, and landlords for prostitution offenses would have required a radical transformation of values toward gender, class, and the role of the state to regulate the economic and social life of its people, ideas the majority of reformers in antiprostitution could not grasp or, for the most part, countenance. Walter Lippmann, one of the most outspoken critics of the national vice crusade in the Progressive Era, seized on this contradiction between reformers' goals and their immediate methods. He accused them of "whacking the mosquito while ignoring the marsh."[60]

Lippmann's metaphor is an apt one since much of the crusade's outcome was cosmetic. Closing down the red-light district removed an eyesore from the urban landscape but did little to stifle the robustness of sex commerce. And from the perspective of reformers who sought social justice for the prostitute, the campaign had negative results. Getting rid of the prostitution zone and brothel system actually increased the dominance of the pimp in sex commerce and in the daily life of the prostitute. The brothel, which did not necessarily foster sisterhood, still offered prostitutes some protection against the abuses of pimps and customers. Equally important, the brothel grapevine informed prostitutes about the trade in other parts of town and other cities and probably gave them more independence from pimp managers.

The campaign set in motion a backlash against women who violated sexual codes. The campaign also sent a message to law enforcers that while the public might not tolerate open vice districts, the cry for a crackdown on vice could be satisfied by rounding up cartloads of prostitutes and pushing up the crime statistics. Frank Norris, a novelist and editor of *Pearson's Magazine,* alluded to this strategy. He ran a series of articles in 1917 that attacked the police and courts for railroading prostitutes in courts. Articles in the *New Republic* in 1930 specifically charged that innocent women were being framed by police.[61]

Lippmann rightly assessed the danger inherent in the sexually repressive stance of vice commissions. But he did not grasp a facet of prostitution that they understood. Not only did prostitution represent an expression of the sex impulse; it was also a commodity in a market, an erotic package. Lippmann and other prewar radicals deeply involved in the political and social revolutions of the Greenwich Village scene romanticized the prostitute as a figure rejecting bourgeois morality and rebelling against the injustices of capitalism. They also believed that libertarian attitudes toward sex would undermine the demand for prostitutes, an assumption that was to be proven false by continual expansion in the prostitution and pornography industries, despite the greater availability of sex partners and eroticism in films and books in our own day.

At the time of the Progressive Era vice commission studies in the United States, Agnes Maude Royden, an English feminist, warned her compatriots against panic legislation and easy answers to prostitution. The sexual exchange in prostitution, according to Royden, called for a reconsideration of the "whole economic position of women, and much that we have accepted as part of the very fabric of society must be challenged."[62] Without this perspective, the reform impulse could increase rather than lessen the evil. Royden's prophecy was borne out by the outcome of the American crusade.

7

Public Enemy Number One

WHEN WORLD WAR I was declared, the prostitute was cast as the enemy on the home front. The white slave victim, a pervasive image in journals and popular novels of the prewar years, disappeared. War propaganda presented the prostitute as someone predatory and diseased, who "could do more harm than any German fleet of airplanes" to the men fighting the war. As has been shown in earlier chapters, prostitutes' rights were violated in the street sweeps and extensive raids against sex commerce that characterized the antiprostitution campaign that preceded the war. However, the war years were the first time a national, concerted policy sanctioned the total abrogation of civil rights for women on the streets. A witch hunt of prostitutes and sexually promiscuous women began, but without the public trials and moral catharsis of witch hunts in Puritan times.[1]

Wartime produces all kinds of pressures toward consensus and conformity. Political parties, ethnic groups, and regional factions are called upon to close ranks and support the war effort. The universe becomes divided into us and them, patriot and subversive, good and evil. Women have been asked to play special roles in wars, and symbols of motherhood and home and hearth take on an added significance during periods of national stress. In the Civil War, women became nurses, and on the home front they raised money, visited war widows, and sewed clothing and bandages. But another class of women left the domestic sphere to offer sex for hire or to commit petty crimes. Their behavior appeared more threatening at a time when husbands and fathers were fighting and dying.

Throughout the Civil War, and even during the years after, a larger proportion of women were sentenced to penal institutions, and historians who speak of the Civil War crime wave are referring to a period when women's minor crimes and deviant behaviors were punished more severely.[2]

During World War I, the threat posed by prostitutes and sexually promiscuous women took on another dimension as a result of intense anxiety about venereal disease. (To understand the fears concerning venereal disease in this period, we have only to look at the panic over AIDS in our own era.) Though new discoveries about the pathology and transmission of venereal disease had occurred in the first decades of the century—isolating the bacteria and documenting their passage to new-born infants—knowledge was imprecise, and more important, no effective or safe cure existed. Even before the war, discussions of venereal disease reached near hysteria. The public was cautioned against infection from drinking fountains, factory toilets, public baths; the disease appeared to be lurking everywhere. Medical writings and war propaganda portrayed the prostitute as the most prolific source of the contagion. Prince Morrow had estimated that as many as eighty out of every one hundred men in New York City had been infected at one time or another with venereal disease. These are incredible figures, and they probably exaggerated the scope of the problem. Nevertheless, military records, which are considered to be reliable, suggest that the disease was fairly widespread among men.[3]

Women were recruited to combat the venereal disease threat in this period of national crisis. Their activism in local women's federations, settlement work, and all types of community service organizations enabled them to mobilize for the domestic war effort. They initiated volunteer hostess clubs that offered wholesome entertainment near training camps; they acted as chaperones for servicemen and single women at public dances. Women activists also became responsible for directly implementing the domestic war policies aimed at controlling venereal disease. These women became law enforcers attached to the government bureaucracy, administering a policy that violated basic civil rights and was highly discriminatory against women. Ultimately they had to chose between the rights of women and the protection of soldiers.

World War I unleashed a series a campaigns against public enemies and attacks on First Amendment rights; socialists, pacifists, and other persons who denounced the war effort were arrested. Nevertheless, there was a critical difference in the perceived threat of the promiscuous woman. Rather than being based on her beliefs or statements, suspicion against her was a reflection of her gender and class. The chain of circumstantial evidence took for granted that any woman on the streets alone after dark, who did not look respectable, was probably a prostitute and therefore a disease carrier.

During World War I, any woman walking unescorted near a military base ran the risk of being labeled a "suspected prostitute." At the very least this meant a humiliating night in a detention center and examination by a health official, who was in many instances a male doctor. But for thousands of women it resulted in a prison term or long-term commitment in a juvenile reformatory. For some it even meant permanent custodial care in a home for the feebleminded. Federal legislation, which mandated the quarantine and isolation of civilian venereal disease carriers, represented one of the most blatant examples of sex discrimination in the history of American justice. The basic assumption of all federal, state, and local legislation concerning venereal disease control was that the infection was spread from women to men. The policy of quarantine, though gender-neutral on the surface, was directed at the women who traded, sold, or gave away their sexual services. A diseased prostitute did not provide law enforcers with a list of civilian customers who would be forced to undergo examinations. For the soldier who contracted venereal disease, there were serious consequences if he did not report to a health station, but no penalties at all if he checked into an army clinic within twenty-four hours of contact.[4]

In effect, the policing of prostitution in the war years became an administrative matter under the auspices of local health boards. Women did not have to be charged with a crime in order to be forced to undergo an examination for venereal disease. They could be held without bail until the results were known. If found diseased, they could be held until cured, in some cases without any formal charge. A person under suspicion, usually a woman, was presumed guilty unless the venereal disease examination showed a negative result. A positive result was tantamount to a conviction for a chastity offense; the hearing was a mere formality. One district attorney actually admitted in the course of a trial that judges offered leniency if a woman voluntarily submitted to the examination: a case would be dismissed if the test was negative. However, if a woman agreed to take the examination and it came back positive—as was true in this instance—she lost her right to a fair hearing. To challenge a health officer's basis for suspicion was not a good strategy either. A woman who was subsequently found guilty on a vagrancy or prostitution charge might be forced to undergo an examination anyway. Then she would be more likely to receive the full brunt of the law, detention in a hospital and/or a prison term.[5]

Much the same reasoning operated in the administrative regulation of prostitution. The system was organized to control public prostitution, not to determine the guilt or innocence of individual prostitutes. Consequently, the question of a prostitute's loss of rights lay outside a bureaucratic framework of rules, as did the class and gender bias of policies that ignored the men who bought her services or the upper class prostitutes who bartered sex more discreetly. In the American wartime campaign against prostitutes, the same narrow administrative policy operated. It affirmed that a positive venereal disease test was a scientific fact that warranted a loss of rights. That the test was nearly always applied to women of the lower classes was not an issue.

The tradition of civil rights and legal protections in the United States led many persons to test the constitutionality of such an abridgement of rights. The laws were challenged in the courts only on the basis on habeas corpus, the right to a fair hearing. Little attention was paid to one of the most sensitive and volatile sides of the law, the right to privacy. In 1890 the U.S. Supreme Court had ruled in favor of a woman who refused to be examined by a doctor hired by the Union Pacific Railroad to assess the extent of damages she received in a railway accident. The right to privacy derived from the Ninth Amendment was interpreted as a woman's right to protect her modesty and control her body. Right to privacy was not a part of the legal strategy to overturn the quarantine laws, most likely because of the implicit assumption that promiscuous women forfeited this right; they were considered immodest, and their bodies were consequently viewed as public property.[6]

From the late nineteenth century on, American feminists had taken the offensive against the "sanitary control" of prostitution. They rallied behind Josephine Butler in her crusade against the Contagious Diseases Acts in England and kept regulationists in America from gaining support among state lawmakers. The most organized opposition came from purity reformers who perceived medical examinations as a double symbol of women's degraded status. First, they saw it as a flagrant example of the sexual double standard; the prostitute was assumed to be responsible for moral impurity, whereas her customer was not subject to the same treatment. Second, they considered the examination itself a sexual assault on women, referring to it as "speculum rape." (Not until the 1940s did internal exams become common for women without medical complications.) Purity reformers thus viewed a doctor's invasion of the prostitute's body as merely an extension of the general power of men to abuse women sexually in the marriage bed and in the brothel. A woman's right to control men's access to her person was an emotionally charged issue among women in the feminist movement, from the most conservative to the most radical.[7]

When the New York legislature in 1910 passed the Page Bill, which required any woman convicted of a prostitution offense to be examined for venereal disease, a storm of protest arose. The Page Bill was a broad, sweeping court reform law, and its framers considered venereal examination of prostitutes a minor clause in a far-reaching piece of legislation. No real opposition was raised at the time of the legislative hearings on the bill, and the reform-minded *Survey* magazine reported its passage as a "marked step forward in the administration of justice." Letters of protest followed over the next several months in the *Survey* from feminist activists, including Anna Garland Spencer and Florence Kelley.[8]

Spencer considered the bill a dangerous assault on women's rights; examinations and fingerprinting fixed women's status and ignored the fact that there were two parties in every act of prostitution. Although the law stated that all persons convicted of vagrancy would undergo venereal disease examinations, it was clear that only women would be forced to submit to them: Spencer claimed this bias was obvious since the provision cited that such persons were to be examined by a female physician and that throughout this section of the bill, feminine pronouns were used for the convicted person. Florence Kelley, social reformer and founder of the Women's Trade Union League, offered a modest proposal as an addition to the Page Bill: "Why not let all convicted criminals be treated for all the communicable diseases they have, then the principle involved in the law would be threshed out: whether it is legitimate to bring the health of the prisoners into the length of sentence. What a revolution if every jail had a sanatorium annex!"[9]

Not surprisingly, many women were agitated by the implications of the Page Bill, and all kinds of groups, inside and outside New York, passed resolutions and sent letters against it: women's federated clubs, municipal leagues, and nurses' councils defined their position as "the women's point of view"—a distinction that was partially valid. Consider the rebuttal of the male editors of the *Survey* to the barrage of letters by women attacking their support of the bill. Responding to the charge that the law ignored the culpability of the male patron, the editors insisted that prostitution was not an offense of two parties and cited the most recent court decision on the matter; the next issue carried the letter of an angry woman, who referred to the insensitivity of "the high-handed man" who had written the *Survey* editorial.[10]

Opponents and proponents were divided not along sex lines (Prince Morrow, for one, was an outspoken critic) but rather according to their beliefs about the broader goals of the campaign against prostitution. Within the controversy surrounding the Page Bill lay the divisions between those who defined the antiprostitution campaign narrowly as a single issue of commercialized vice suppression or of venereal disease control and those who had broader goals of eliminating the sexual double standard.

A New York state court ruled that the provision in the Page Bill requiring medical inspection of convicted prostitutes was unconstitutional. But the issues that had been raised were to have tremendous significance during the war years, when venereal disease threatened the efficacy of American soldiers. The prewar debates surrounding the bill revealed how tenuous the coalition against prostitution was. Furthermore, they underscored the incompatibility of sanitary control and social justice ends in the campaign against prostitution.

Despite the fact that the government policy of venereal disease control during World War I went much farther than the Page Bill—it allowed mandatory examination of *suspected* prostitutes—public opposition to it did not materialize. In fact, the strongest condemnations came from British activists who had successfully repealed the Contagious Diseases Acts there. Katherine Bushnell, an American physician and Women's Christian Temperance Union missionary, was the exception. She dared to attack publicly wartime measures to protect soldiers from venereal disease as a violation of a woman's right to protection "from the vile masturbating hand of a doctor."[11]

Appeals for patriotism and sacrifice muffled all kinds of dissent and campaigns for reform during the war years. The mainstream women's movement put the suffrage amendment on hold so as not to endanger the war effort. In light of the times, it is understandable that few persons openly denounced government policies that were justified as necessary to keep our boys fit to fight. What is difficult to comprehend is that so many women actively supported a policy that singled out women as the guilty parties in the spread of venereal disease.

Reformers and the War Effort

Many of the leaders in Progressive reform movements for social and sexual equality were directly involved in enforcing the federal government's policy against suspected prostitutes and disease carriers. They were recruited to form the federal Committee for the Protection of Women and Girls, which had an elaborate bureaucratic structure with a national governing board, regional directors, and local agents in every large city or town near a training camp. The board and regional directors of this protection agency read like a register of social feminists in America. Maude Miner, a key activist in the antiprostitution movement and formerly in charge of the New York Juvenile Probation department, was recruited as director of the agency. Other high-ranking officials were Julia Lathrop from Hull House and the Children's Bureau; Jesse Binford and Jane Rippen, who were also settlement house workers; and Ethel Dummer, founder and trustee of the Chicago school of philanthropy, which underwrote the Chicago Psychopathic Institute for Juvenile Offenders.

The beginning of the war effort seemed to presage a moral revolution that would produce a single standard of morality. The enlistment of women in the federal agency meant that women would have a key role in shaping the morals of the nation. They believed that the federal government had the means to transform sexual mores, to reshape male behavior, and they were committed to those ends. An example of the enormous power of the federal government to enforce moral conformity was the wiping out of one of the most institutionalized red-light districts. The closing of Storeyville in New Orleans represented the supreme victory. Before the war, Storeyville had seemed impenetrable to reform. But when the secretary of war threatened to use military force to close the district, city authorities took action.[12]

The women who were asked to take charge of this government agency must have envisioned a tremendous opportunity to influence policy as well as to enhance their professional status. The lure of administrative power and enormous budgets may have been too strong, despite misgivings once it was clear that the policy would be applied mainly against women. In addition to the operating budget of the Committee for the Protection of Women and Girls, $250,000 was allotted by the president for the construction of detention homes. These were placed under the direction of Martha Falconer, one of the early reformers in the field of women's penal institutions. At last women would be their sisters' keepers and take charge of all the institutions for their treatment and rehabilitation. Katharine Bement Davis, former administrator of Bedford Hills Reformatory in New York and Commissioner of Corrections for New York State, was given a special assignment on sex education, which aimed to instruct both sexes in a pure view of sexual relations.

The active support by these women of an agency that led the way for an invasion of rights and liberties aimed only at their sex cannot be dismissed as naive optimism or blind ambition. Within the ideology of protection—and the word was in the name of this agency and of many others that had previously dealt with actual or potential sex delinquents—lay the basis for authoritarian and repressive policies toward women. All the contradictions in the feminist response to prostitution were embodied in its ideology, practical applications, and hidden motivations. Even those reformers most sympathetic to the prostitute could not free themselves from the class and gender biases expressed by the word *protection*. It assumed that the lower classes had an inferior sense of morality, and it implied that the central responsibility for nonmarital sexual relations was to be borne by women. (Feminists believed this, even as they insisted that men were more culpable for prostitution.) Protection was the keyword that linked prewar antiprostitution strategies with wartime policies.

THE PITFALLS OF PROTECTION

Among antiprostitution reformers, *protection* and *prevention* were used interchangeably. Both encompassed a wide range of measures that were supposed to anticipate moral danger or, as reformers put it, to erect barriers in dangerous zones. *Danger* itself was the word used most often to describe the journey of women alone, away from parental and community control. Protection implied an outlook about women's powerlessness in all spheres of life—in domestic relations, work, and leisure. Furthermore, it assumed that working class and poor women in particular were in double jeopardy because they had greater opportunities for temptation and fewer protectors.

According to proponents, the most successful protective remedies were those that did not appear coercive. Ideally, protective agents were supposed to be big sisters keeping a watchful eye on those in precarious moral situations. Social workers and probation officers, or other helping professionals, particularly if they were women, may have functioned that way. But their official status and police powers made them suspect among tenement dwellers. Family and neighbors often withheld information from probation officers seeking missing clients, and in some cases deliberately sent them on false chases.

Believing that preventive work would be best accomplished by insiders, Maude Miner formed the New York Girls' Protective League in 1910. Her experience with this association made her a logical choice to be at the helm of the War Department agency formed eight years later. The leagues were something like the social clubs for working girls at settlement houses, but there was a difference. Members of the protective leagues were policing their own working class neighborhoods and extending the safety net into areas few reformers had access to: factories, tenement houses, movie theaters, and all kinds of places of recreation. Though they had no official status, agents of the league could have a girl arrested or put under surveillance because of Miner's position as chief probation agent in the New York court.

The league's agents played various roles—spies, ombudsmen, advocates. For example, league members made complaints against the many employers who sexually harassed their workers. At the same time they might use their power to have an immoral girl removed from the workplace. Miner also urged working girls in the league to report violators of protective work laws, such as employers who allowed girls under the age of sixteen to work after five o'clock.[13] The double edge of protection was most apparent in these cases, where protective strategies actually deprived women of means of support and therefore could have had the perverse effect of forcing them into prostitution. Protection continued to be the Achilles' heel of the feminist response to prostitution, because it defined women as emotionally weak and childlike and justified punitive measures as for their own good.

Through their approach of protection, feminist reformers reconciled their ideology of women's passivity and victimization in sexual encounters with their practical knowledge—as social workers, probation officers, or volunteer rescue workers—of sexual delinquency. On some level, though never acknowledged, they were aware of the new generation's female sexual precociousness—that there was greater sexual curiosity, more opportunities for sexual experience, and general peer group acceptance of sexual adventures. However, when confronted with the facts, they sought explanations that were less threatening. White slavery was their naive interpretation of the sadomasochistic relationship between pimp and prostitute; they analyzed the sexual aggressiveness of girls seeking the companionship of soldiers and sailors in terms of the hypnotic spell of the uniform. To accept the notion that women actively sought sex with men in a casual way or sold their sexual services like any other commodity in the market undercut the rationale for the women's movement. That would suggest that women, seeking political power to refashion the moral fabric of society, were not a class different in nature and values from men.

Protective strategies allowed feminists to turn away from this Gorgon. If faced directly, such knowledge of a female sexual nature would have been paralyzing. Ethel Dummer actually analyzed the attack of tuberculosis that prevented her from continuing a leadership role in the war work as a "sign of her obliging unconscious": "Was it wish fulfillment that sidetracked me from actively visiting the camps or did some hidden wisdom postpone action until sympathy and imagination showed clearly what should be done?" Hers was the paradigmatic case of the conflicts among feminists who were raised with Victorian moral standards and came of age in an era of changing sexual norms.

Among antiprostitution reformers, Dummer was at the radical end of the spectrum of social feminism. She met many of the key sexual theorists of her day: Havelock Ellis, Ellen Key, and Edward Carpenter. She championed liberal Scandinavian laws supporting single mothers, and placed the prostitution debates in the broad context of women's economic and psychological dependence on men. Despite her theoretical sophistication and sympathy for the prostitute, she initially supported repressive policies when faced with promiscuous casual sexuality among young women.[14]

Dummer, and other sexually liberal feminists in this era, went beyond the traditional view of sex as solely a means of reproduction. They saw the sex act in spiritual terms, as an expression of psychic and social relations. Dummer applied the term oversexualization to both men and women, but it did not refer to the number of acts. Rather, it referred to an individual's obsession with the erotic and the denial of the emotions in intimate relations.[15] For feminists like Dummer, expectations of sexual intimacy made casual sex appear uglier and more deviant. They recog-

174

nized women's sexual passion, but they could not distinguish between sexual pleasures and sexual dangers or between normal and abnormal sexual interests.

The feminists' divided consciousness had unintended and painful consequences. Women who had championed women's rights and a single standard of morality now supported legislation and policies that punished only women for sexual misconduct; the end result was a more entrenched double standard of morality and a more deeply imbedded stigma for prostitutes.

ENFORCING THE LAW

Fear of women's sexual natures underlay many of the policies that the War Department initiated. At the outset of the war, Raymond Fosdick, in charge of the department to make military camps morally safe and free of venereal disease, received complaints from the commanding officers about the girl problem. Reports from camp cities, such as Decatur, Illinois, put pressure on Fosdick as head of the Committee on Training Camp Activities. In that town over half the girls of the high school's senior class were reported to have become pregnant after the construction of the aviation base. Fosdick responded with the idea of a special branch of protective officers:

I feel that we ought to have a special committee to assume responsibility for the negative side of the work—the protective side—keeping girls off the streets, putting them in touch with their homes and friends and by such means as suggest themselves to experienced women officers striving to prevent an increase in delinquency.[16]

The negative side of the work Fosdick was referring to became more and more repressive toward promiscuous women. At first the agency was compared with other informal protective societies, such as the YWCA or Travelers' Aid groups, but within eight months of its founding the Committee for the Protection for Women and Girls was placed under the War Department's Division of Law Enforcement. Soon after this happened, Maude Miner resigned as director of the agency and gave her reasons in a private letter: she bluntly stated that what was sought by the War Department was not really the protection of girls, but rather the protection of the soldier.[17]

The emphasis of the agency changed after the passage of the Chamberlain-Kahn Act in July 1918, which gave local boards of health the authority to force any person thought to be a carrier of venereal disease to be detained and to undergo a compulsory examination. If a woman had a venereal disease, she was to be committed to a hospital ward for venereal disease patients or to some other institution to be treated until cured. Although administrators in the program insisted that these were health measures and not punishments, the barbed-wire fences and guards told another story. All manner of restrictions on women's freedom in public places followed in the wake of the federal legislation. In certain camp cities, nine o'clock curfews were imposed on women. Some communities enacted laws that required a woman accompanying a soldier or sailor either to be related to him or to carry a letter of permission from her parents.

The facts and figures were bold statements of the sweeping powers of the state to take action against women of "careless chastity." The War Department claimed that 18,000 women were quarantined in federally supported institutions; of these, 15,000 were said to be diseased. However, these statistics are only the tip of the iceberg and ignore the thousands of women who had to submit to a humiliating physical examination and were incarcerated in local jails and workhouses. Outcomes of cases brought by protective agents were described in official manuals as "types of services," but in fact, the majority were types of punishments. One report noted that 30,000 women were "helped" by the authorities in various ways.[18] Dummer claimed that only half the women detained were infected with venereal disease.

The statistics gathered by the War Department on 15,010 women who were *detained* as suspected venereal disease carriers during the war years in themselves suggest that suspicion did not have to be based on any act of solicitation. There was no formal complaint against them, and 45 percent of these cases were dismissed without any record of arrest. The majority of these women do not appear to have been prostitutes, either by the court's definition or by common usage. Only about a third were charged as prostitutes. The others were brought in under vague categories of suspicious conduct, incorrigibility, or infection by venereal disease.

These women were for the most part amateurs, often trading sex for dinners and gifts; they were given the incongruous label "charity prostitutes" during the war years. Of the total number, 4,803 were noted as commercial prostitutes; the others were classified as promiscuous women and "one man only"; 1,800 women were said to have no "sex irregularity." Only 285 were living in houses of prostitution; half were living with parents, husbands, or other relatives. Compared with other statistics on women in institutions for prostitution, these women were slightly younger and did not have a long history of arrests (44 percent had no record). Similar to the women who were sentenced as prostitutes in the prewar years, they were working class, underemployed, and had had their first sexual experiences between sixteen and seventeen years of age.[19]

Some typical cases from the official reports reveal the degree to which class background determined the treatment and outcome of women apprehended by protective agents. One young girl came to the attention of an agent through persons in her rooming house. She had come to New York to marry a soldier, but he had put it off and left her stranded after he was sent to France. Her test showed that she had gonorrhea and was pregnant. The agent assigned to her case contacted her parents, who were told of her condition and advised of the urgency for medical treatment. They wired her money, and she returned home to their care. Another case was of a sixteen-year-old girl found at a beach with a sailor. After the first violation, she was sent home. But when she was again found on the same beach with another sailor, a field agent brought her home. According to the agent, the girl's mother seemed unconcerned about her behavior, and the agent thus concluded that both mother and daughter were mentally defective. The girl was given a psychological test that determined her mental age as six years. She was committed to an institution for the mentally defective.[20]

Special agents were often women involved in organizations such as the YWCA, WCTU, or groups formed during the war—the women's patriotic leagues. Field workers combed the beaches and parks for delinquent women. In Massachusetts, a trained social worker, Helen Pigeon, hid in the bushes of the Boston Common, waiting for women who came with servicemen late at night. Protective agents were able to secure more lighting in public places and to force dance hall managers to provide chaperones.[21]

It is clear from these accounts and data that the war legislation allowed private agents a degree of control that they had not had previously when dealing with sexual delinquents. No crime had to be committed; no proof was necessary for a charge of immorality to be made. For the juvenile offender the situation was most critical because she could be sent to a reformatory for several years on an indeterminate sentence. This had always been true, but in these years there were many more agents hired to locate these wayward girls. There were also hundreds of new facilities where they could be sent. This was especially the case in southern states, which had few reformatories for girls before the government subsidies.[22]

From the outset, the authoritarian current within the federal protective agency was strong. Jane Rippen, a regional director of the agency, interpreted the data from the first one thousand case records of women detainees as a call for stringent measures. She viewed with alarm the early sex experiences of this group and suggested that the federal law enforcement division bar girls between the ages of twelve and eighteen from public dances. These adolescents were, according to Rippen, at the "gravest danger point . . . of unstable emotional control."[23]

The protective agents took on the role of military strategists preparing for a war against immorality and somehow rationalized the coercive means for protective ends. Rippen, when questioned about the unfair burden placed on women by the war policy, answered that although she found the compulsory examination dangerous because of the possibilities for blackmail, she did not in theory see anything wrong with the curfews. Without a trace of irony, Martha Falconer, who was in charge of coordinating the detention houses for women, referred to these institutions as human reclamation centers.[24]

Underlying the *in loco parentis* rationale of protective agents in the war campaign were the same class prejudices as had existed in the prewar protective strategies. However, these attitudes did not dominate the discussion of what was called a social evil. During the war years experts tended to emphasize inherited traits, not environmental causes, of sexual delinquency. Batteries of intelligence tests and psychological examinations of interned women offered proof that these women needed protection because they were emotionally unstable, feebleminded, or had defective personalities.

With the exception of Maude Miner and Ethel Dummer, who early in the game sensed the dangers in the government program, most of the officers in the protective agency supported the government's policy. Some, at first, even hailed the Chamberlain-Kahn Act as a milestone in controlling disease. Not the lack of procedural guarantees nor the denial of women's civil liberties but the failure to implement the law properly caused them to become disillusioned. The women believed not that the government had overstepped its bounds in detaining sexual delinquents but rather that it had not carried through on its promises to provide facilities for housing and reforming wayward girls.

The money approved for building female reformatories was discontinued after a ruling denied the federal government the right to use funds for institutions under state control. Hence, offenders were often detained in local jails or makeshift facilities: a town hall, an empty school building, and in one case the top floor of the YWCA. Hospitals were the places with the least oversight, and numerous cases of abuse came to the attention of women in the protective agency. Jessie Binford, regional director for the Midwest, concluded: "Our hospitals are the most demoralizing places and sometimes I think that it would have been much better not to have started at all until we were really ready for this work."

Women directly involved in the daily enforcement of the law tried to mitigate some of the worst effects—at some risk to their own position. A volunteer from the Boston Society for the Protection of Young Girls spent two nights in the Lowell town hall with women picked up near Fort Devans, rather than have them sent to the city jail. Her superior characterized her as high-strung, upset if results did not come immediately. A female doctor, also wanting to protect innocent women from a night in jail, pressured authorities to allow her to examine women as soon as possible. She was replaced by a male physician.[25]

In 1918 feminists active in the campaign held a conference in Atlantic City to air their grievances. Perhaps most painful to the women enlisted in the protective agency was the realization that they had very little power within the federal bureaucracy. In the day-to-day administration of the detention program, health officers and military police made all the decisions. They were interested not in rehabilitating delinquents but in keeping women off the streets and away from soldiers.[26]

The Military and Medical Mind

War Department officials used the language of efficiency and scientific management to justify the policy of quarantine for immoral, diseased women. The main slogan of the venereal disease prevention campaign was "fit to fight." But the War Department's policy goals were not merely instrumental—to maintain an efficient army. Fosdick and most of the architects of venereal disease policy who had been recruited from the ranks of the social hygiene movement could never countenance licensed prostitution, the European solution to the soldier's needs. In contrast to World War II policy, there was no mass distribution of condoms, though doctors were aware at the time of their usefulness in disease prevention. Instead, war policy makers sought to offset prevailing negative attitudes toward male virginity through training camp discipline that presented continence as manly and Spartan. War posters with portraits of the dutiful and loyal war wife, mother, and girlfriend also put across the message: "Go back to them physically fit and morally clean."[27]

Allan Brandt, in his study of the response to venereal disease during the war, rightly concludes that the central rallying point of those involved in the domestic war effort was an attack on unrestrained sexuality, and venereal disease was its most visible symbol. But it is important to emphasize that the campaign to control sexual immorality was aimed primarily at women. War propaganda reaffirmed the traditional dichotomy between good and bad women, between women in need of protection and women who were dangerous predators. On the one side, soldiers were told in training camps that they were fighting for the safety of their mothers, sisters, and girlfriends—so vulnerable to the sexual aggression of a conquering enemy. On the other side, government pamphlets accused the prostitute of being an enemy agent sent from Germany to debilitate American forces.[28]

Underlying the strategies to control disease were several key assumptions: that the disease was always transmitted from prostitute to customer and not the other way around; that working class women who defied sexual codes were potential prostitutes; and that male sexuality was explosive and could not be controlled. The war policy around venereal disease makes clear the impossibility of divorcing microbes from morality and from gender and class issues in cases of sexually transmitted disease.

All kinds of policies in addition to those regarding venereal disease control placed the responsibility for illicit sexuality emphatically on women and not on men. One federal decree denied an enlisted man's wife accused of sexual immorality her family allotment. At the same time, federal legislation was passed giving soldiers and sailors total immunity from paternity suits.[29] The laws, policies, and images of women during these years reaffirmed male prerogatives in the domestic sphere and sexual arena and marked the eclipse of movements to end the sexual double standard.

Dummer and other feminists had envisioned the mandatory sex education in training camps as a step toward ending the sexual double standard and men's sexual exploitation of women. But the lectures to servicemen were not sex education but sex aversion—venereal disease horror films. The numbers of men who checked into treatment centers revealed the ineffectiveness of the propaganda.[30]

Dummer identified the sexual politics of War Department bureaucrats as expressions of the "military and medical mind." She perceived them as a class of men acting in men's interests, with different goals and priorities than the women reformers in the campaign. For Dummer, the male bureaucratic approach was narrow and utilitarian; it equated sex education with prophylaxis against venereal disease and measured success in terms of cost effectiveness. Thomas Storey, executive secretary of the War Department's Interdepartmental Social Hygiene Board, epitomized this mentality. Evaluating the government's venereal disease program, he estimated that the program of venereal disease control had prevented over 3,892,860 exposures to venereal infection during a period of twenty-seven months, at a cost to the government of less than eleven cents for each prevented exposure.[31]

Dummer came to suspect not only these male experts but scientific investigation itself as a force for social reform. At first she believed that case histories of quarantined women would elicit greater sympathy for delinquent women and therefore provide some justification for the policy of quarantine. But the sociological and psychological data did not lead to the enlightened view of the prostitute that she expected. Instead, analysts seized on the low IQ scores of these women and diagnosed them as feebleminded. In fact, the label so dominated the discussions of experts that Dummer found herself having to provide some alternative scientific explanation. Was it not possible that these delinquent girls and women had become so traumatized from early sexual experiences and from society's condemnation that their condition was comparable to the shell shock of soldiers?

Dummer presented her hypothesis to her scientific mentors, including distinguished psychiatrists Adolf Meyer and William Healy, but they did not take her seriously. Writing to Adolf Meyer, Dummer insisted that science should be an adviser, not a dictator. To understand the complexities of prostitution, she insisted, lawmakers had to consult persons who had come in contact with the day-to-day problems and realities in social work cases and divorce courts. But her viewpoint was clearly outside the mainstream, and she was painfully aware of the necessity of working within the existing framework of scientific authority and expert testimony. During the war years, she tried to persuade criminologists and doctors to publish articles in academic journals as a means of opening the debate against the War Department policies against women. Lewis Michelson, a lawyer and director of the San Francisco Social Hygiene Bureau, responded by saying that he did not have the knowledge or time to write an article for the *Journal of Criminology*. Others, such as Paul Kellogg, sloughed off her suggestion that the *Survey* open its pages to a discussion of the young prostitute. No one wanted to become involved in a debate over prostitutes' rights during the war years.[32]

Dummer succeeded in organizing a panel at the annual meeting of the American Sociological Society with papers from social psychologists, penal experts, and psychiatrists. However, this tactic actually worked against her long-term goals of a single sexual standard. Once the issues were recast in a framework of individual pathology, the perspective on prostitution as a general societal problem was lost.

The National Conference on Venereal Disease held in Washington, D.C., in the autumn of 1920 demonstrated the extent to which medical men shaped the debates around prostitution and excluded feminists from the inner circle of experts. Dummer, Miner, and Binford (former members of the protective agency) came to the conference to offer a resolution against the Chamberlain-Kahn Act, calling for voluntary clinics to replace compulsory examination. They attacked the government policy on several fronts: it deprived women of their personal liberties, discriminated against women and girls, and was ineffective because it did not protect society from venereal disease. But, in Dummer's own words, the conference debates were staged, and no dissident voices could halt the "steam roller" in favor of law enforcement. Their resolution never reached the floor of this august body because all dissenting opinion was channeled through special committee meetings chaired by medical experts.[33]

Although prostitutes during the next great war were arrested in vast numbers and singled out as a dangerous group, the campaign differed in degree and context. By the time World War II came about, more facts were known about the transmission of venereal disease, although the miracle cure penicillin did not became available until the middle of the war. Perhaps most important, sexual norms and views of female sexuality had changed between the two wars. In the next war, it became more evident that amateur "good-time Charlottes" were having sex with soldiers and that the venereal disease threat was more complicated than once thought.[34] The kind of mass hysteria around prostitution and the full-scale war against the woman who violated chastity codes would never be repeated again. But the legacy of the World War I years would have an enormous impact on the response to prostitution over the following decades.

In 1918 the armistice was declared, but from the perspective of feminists engaged in the antiprostitution campaign, the war at home had been lost. Dead and buried were the broader goals of social and sexual equality that they had envisioned would result from the campaign begun in the prewar years. Even after the Chamberlain-Kahn Act expired (1923) and the federal agency administering the quarantine program was dismantled, the effects remained. Preventive detention had made it clear that women bore the responsibility in illicit sexual encounters. But over the long term, the war policy would have its greatest impact on the scientific discourse on prostitution. Sex commerce, which had been the central focus of the vice commission reports in the prewar years, embraced a range of economic, social, and political questions surrounding prostitution. After the war the discussion narrowed and shifted back to the prostitute—her inherited traits, criminal tendencies, and psychological disorders—and would continue this way for the next forty years.

8

The Unadjusted Girl

AT THE CONCLUSION of his 1923 study of female delinquency, the sociologist W. I. Thomas asserted that the evolution of morals, customs, and norms required new perceptions and approaches to female delinquency. No longer relevant were the old categories of the completely good and completely bad; instead, he saw many gradations and variations: charity girl, occasional prostitute, demivirgin, and equivocal flapper. Thomas envisioned a new set of norms and definitions that would replace the old and that would in turn be replaced by others as they lost social significance. His book, *The Unadjusted Girl,* was completed at the height of the Roaring Twenties, when popular writers spoke of the new woman and John Held's flapper drawings captured her brash, seductive style. However, Thomas's assumption that the emergence of the new woman would inevitably lead to radical change in sexual mores was not borne out. Nor did the acceptance of seductiveness in films or on the dance floor lead to a more tolerant view of the prostitute.[1] In fact, once the idea that women had sexual needs gained acceptance, there arose a new urgency to draw the line between normal sexual expression and deviant sexual response.

The Unadjusted Girl was one of many studies about female delinquency in a period when sexual norms and behavior were changing. Psychiatrists and other physicians, social scientists, and feminists grappled with the question of female sexual responsiveness. What was the difference in the sex relationship between prostitute and patron, between lover and lover, and between wife and husband? In the past, feminists had seen little difference, which is why they identified with the prostitute and cast her in the role of slave and passive victim; in their view, both wife and prostitute were subject to male control and sexual coercion.[2]

But beginning in the pre–World War I period and continuing into the 1920s, the notion that women were passionless was crumbling under the weight of scientific investigations such as Katharine Bement Davis's study of premarital sex among college women. Before Davis became Commissioner of Corrections for New York, she had been director of New York's Bedford Hills Reformatory. While there, she researched the sexual experiences of delinquent women. During the 1920s, she turned her attention to the sexuality of women labeled respectable and found that more middle and upper class women were having premarital sex and that they were more aware of sex than in the past. British sex reformer Marie Stopes, perhaps the first popular sexologist, received thousands of letters from couples seeking ways to improve sexual compatibility.[3]

Growing acceptance of the notion that women could enjoy sex and experience sexual ecstasy and sexual intimacy in marriage, separate from procreation, represented a break with the past. But unchanged definitions of male and female roles left the sexual double standard in place. Paula Fass, writing about sexuality on college campuses during the twenties, claims that while youth on campuses experimented with erotic play, they created their own rigid codes against premarital sex and promiscuity. Even in the bohemian circles of Greenwich Village, men's traditional images of women inhibited any change in heterosexual relationships.[4]

Rather than being a "revolution in manners and morals," what occurred in the first decades of the twentieth century was a recasting of women's sexual identity. The recognition of women's erotic heterosexuality represented two steps forward and one step backward. Eroticism between husband and wife was encouraged; even premarital sex with a fiancé was tolerated. But casual sexual encounters, extramarital sex, and homosexuality were taboo.

Psychoanalytic theory and psychology were instrumental in shaping views of female sexual identity during this period. In prescribing normal and healthy sexual responses, these disciplines built upon the older cultural formulas about women's nature as passive and more spiritual than men's. Sigmund Freud, Havelock Ellis, Marie Stopes, and other writers clearly distinguished female from male sexual expression and needs.

More than any other sex theorist of that era, Havelock Ellis was influential in setting forth the ideologies and moral categories that dominated the discourse on sexuality. According to Ellis, women were innately passive in the sexual drama, a biological fact that also determined other facets of women's psychology, such as their modesty. Despite his insistence that sexual passion was distinct from procreation, he concluded that a woman's sexual response suffered when a relationship lacked children. Although Ellis cast off the old formulas about women's purity and sexual inertia, he still gathered most of the Victorian social constructs into his treatises on male and female sexuality.[5]

A popularizer of Ellis, Marie Stopes was interested in increasing women's sexual pleasure. In her manuals, husbands were encouraged to court their wives through sex foreplay and to delay coitus. But she believed that healthy sexual passion was epitomized by a monogamous relationship with the husband as the initator of sex. Although Stopes maintained that the rhythm of sexual activity should be governed by a woman's desires and natural cycle, the man was to be responsible for the art of loving and the outcome of the sex act.[6] Stopes, Ellis, and nearly all the sex manuals of the day reaffirmed the Victorian sexual dichotomies between male-active (or propulsive) and female-passive (or receptive) sexualities. They also continued to assert the traditional view that women's sexual desire was awakened by spiritual feelings, not physical ones, and that women's sexuality was essentially monogamous.

The dominant scientific versions of healthy female sexuality set apart prostitutes and other sexually indiscriminate women as deviant. The woman who sold, bartered, or gave away sex to men in a casual way was acting against her nature and was maladjusted or dysfunctional. The analysts concluded that prostitution, for both men and women, represented a lower form of sexual response—more physical than spiritual—but they perceived promiscuity in women to be deviant.

In his pamphlet *The Prostitute and the Mother Imagio,* psychologist Wilfred Lay postulated that both the prostitute and her patron were social infants. They were autoerotic children who had not gone beyond the stage of satisfying immediate appetites, and they confused sexual expression with animal urges. At the same time, Lay interpreted the male desire for sex with a prostitute to be a natural outgrowth of his search for unconditional acceptance by the mother figure; in his view, a man could never find it in a wife because she would require that he assume responsibilities and take criticism. On the conscious level, Lay argued, respectable men must seek prostitutes because of the taboos against sexual expression among companions of his own class. In contrast, he presented prostitution as a repression of woman's true nature. In order to prostitute herself, a woman must deny her love instinct and maternal love.[7] The male patron was reacting against social and psychological forces that were common to all men reared in Victorian culture; the prostitute was violating her natural biological and psychological makeup, her female identity.

Although psychoanalytic theory accepted women's sexual responsiveness, it did not break the links between female sexuality and female deviance. In fact, it strengthened them at a time when families and communities were losing the power to monitor the sexual experiences of youth. The theorists provided a new language and set of categories that became a part of the female delinquent profile. In some respects, the labels "maladjustment" and "mental incapacity," which emerged in this period, were more insidious than the earlier paradigm of the fallen woman because the new language pretended to be objective and scientific. Perhaps the most dangerous implication for women defined as sexual deviants was the experts' belief that they could predict future behavior. Various preventive measures might include permanent institutional care, sterilization, or taking away a woman's children.

Psychoanalysis provided one of the key mechanisms for enforcing sanctions against women who defied the prescribed normal female sexual response. Psychoanalytic evaluations, along with intelligence testing, were the scientific tools that became institutionalized parts of the criminal justice system. In the case of women, scientific experts took sexual self-control as the major criterion of the normal, healthy, or adjusted woman and recommended treatment terms of supervision and incarceration accordingly.

The case of Ellen Rose,* tried in Boston Municipal Court in 1926, illustrates how much latitude experts had both in their diagnosis of delinquent behavior and in the treatment and punishment they recommended. At age 19, Ellen Rose was sentenced to jail for two months for stealing a dress from a department store. It was her first offense. Most cases of women shoplifting during this period resulted either in probation or in dropped charges if the defendant promised to pay for the item. Ellen's defiant attitude, poor school record, and unwillingness to cooperate with her probation officer influenced the judge's decision to sentence her. But another critical factor was her family's history of delinquency. Ellen's grandmother had died of general paresis (a result of syphilis); her mother

*Names of the principals in this case have been changed.

was a prostitute and had served time in the women's reformatory; her sister was in reform school; and her brother was a well-known juvenile delinquent. Their father was believed to be a bootlegger living illicitly with another women. Eleven social agencies, led by the Family Welfare Society, were involved in supporting the five other children in the family. According to the investigator who collected the facts, both the breed and the breeding determined the criminal careers in this family.

In analyzing Ellen's mental capacities, the medical experts placed her in the "very ignorant" category. Several years before her arrest, her teachers had attempted to have her placed at an institution for the feebleminded. Walter Fernald, who was in charge of the Massachusetts School for the Feebleminded, had examined her at that time and concluded that she had a mental age of eleven and would be a problem for some time. Yet her IQ was listed as 91, nearly average on the standard scale.

Although there was no proof of her sexual delinquency, both social workers and psychiatrists insisted that she was an immoral girl. The court psychiatrist diagnosed her as psychopathic, with "fundamental physical interests, voluptuous in development and a quick, passionate, uncontrolled personality, living at the lowest place of egoism." The doctor who examined her warned that her physical appearance decidedly went against her because she would attract a great many men. Given her family's "primarily physical interests" and lack of moral training, the experts considered her ripe for prostitution. Although Ellen had committed only one offense, that of shoplifting, the experts in this investigation recommended that if she got into any future difficulties she be committed indefinitely to a an institution for the treatment of psychopathic delinquents.[8]

Ellen's history is not unusual for the period. In fact, her profile of family delinquency, poor performance in school, and lack of job stability was typical of those who were processed through the courts during the 1920s. Also, the methods of evaluation took into account all the recent innovations in therapeutic approaches to crime. She was examined by psychiatrists, social workers, and medical doctors, who tested her intelligence and physical health, checked her for venereal disease, and traced her family background and influences.

Ellen's case reveals the degree to which assumptions about gender and class shaped social workers' and psychiatrists' diagnosis of criminality and the treatment they prescribed. Sexual precociousness was still the primary basis for ascribing guilt, as well as for predicting criminal tendencies. Family history and class background were also critical in the labeling of delinquents. Rather than providing more objective evaluations, the scientific tools and methods shrouded ethnic prejudice, sexual bias, and antagonism toward families on public welfare with a cover of psychiatric labels and quantitative measures. Psychiatrists' analyses of prostitution as maladjustment or personality disorder differed little from earlier models of fallen women and female criminality. Scientific testing and the new medical jargon were merely new wine in old bottles: the fallen woman was recast as the psychopathic, feebleminded, or moral defective. Sexual delinquency continued to be a barometer for criminality.

In *The Unadjusted Girl,* Thomas analyzed a prostitute's motivations in terms of universal human desires for new experiences, security, and recognition. He also viewed prostitution as a response to the rising expectations in a modern consumer economy. Prostitutes were women from the lower class who had no means of reaping the rewards of an affluent society and therefore decided to trade sexual favors, some on a casual basis and others with the man they expected to marry. The guiding motivation for prostitutes, according to Thomas, was a yearning for something better than the expected future. Rather than being a physical type or having a defective personality, the prostitute was a natural outgrowth of the tension between individual psychology, a system of values, and the absence of constructive communal forces to channel behavior.[9]

Few social investigators of the 1920s matched Thomas's broad analysis. Furthermore, others placed less emphasis on readjusting society than on remaking individuals to adopt the norms of middle class, native-born Americans. Instead of looking at societal norms as conventions, social scientists investigating crime developed typologies of adjustment and nonadjustment that implied fixed standards of normality concerning intelligence, mental development, and marital and family patterns. Implicit in theories of crime were assumptions that society rewarded the excellent and most gifted and that equal opportunity existed. The experts who examined the criminal population deemed them failures who lacked the capacity to take advantage of life's chances. Social investigators played down environmental forces as the cause of delinquency and focused more and more on innate traits.

The method of investigation in this era, the biographical case study, supported the emphasis on individual responsibility for delinquency and offered a "scientific" basis for politically and socially conservative views.

When Marian Kenworthy, a physician at the New York Bureau of Children's Guidance, wrote about the logic of delinquency, she lumped together male political radicals and promiscuous girls as compensating for personal inadequacies. Agitators were the sons of dominant fathers who could not rebel; sexually active girls lacked skills to achieve and therefore used sex to "put themselves across." Set against these antisocial and abnormal behaviors was the average, normal citizen: hard working, responsible, and gratified with his lot.[10] For the social work professionals, psychologists, and criminologists working with the delinquent population, Babbitt was the unsung American hero.

Although the same scientific labels were applied to both male and female delinquents, antisocial behaviors differed by gender. The paradigm of the psychopathic male personality was the hobo—unattached to workplace, home, or family responsibilities. Social work professionals found its exemplar in the celebrated case of Abraham Bernstein, who had been discovered by a commission that was interviewing 123 homeless men in Chicago in the 1920s. He was a vagrant, long-unemployed worker who became a conman and bilked hundreds of charitable organizations through his shrewdness. Bernstein challenged the essence of the male role in the social system—a success-oriented family man and steady worker.[11]

Analysis of personality defects in female delinquents nearly always revolved around sexual behavior. The psychopathic woman was supposedly unfaithful to her husband, neglectful of her children, and promiscuous. Jenny Edwards,* who was studied in depth by the Harvard Law School Crime Survey, was typical of those classified in this way. She had four or five arrests, all involving moral offenses. Police and probation officers described her as the lowest of types, consorting with all kinds of men. The social worker studying her case drew these conclusions: Jenny was an intelligent but unprincipled young woman, weak and lazy, and easily led into bad relationships. She was indiscriminate in her selection of associates and her "maternal instinct seems a very weak emotion." Jenny was classified as a "psychopathic personality, unstable type."[12]

The most common diagnostic label for female offenders was feeblemindedness. It was the clearest expression of the sex-gender system in the labeling of criminality, for it confused cultural and social factors with innate biological traits. Feeblemindedness in women was linked to early sexual maturation and sexual precociousness, and the theory was posited

---

*Names of the principals in this case have been changed.

that an overdeveloped body signaled an undeveloped mind. No such association was made between men's sexual maturation and activity and mental inferiority. Since promiscuous women arrested by police in American cities came from the poorer classes, the IQ tests that became popular did show a correlation between sexual delinquency and mental ability. However, the pervasiveness and persistence of the feebleminded label among female criminals were based not merely on empirical evidence. Unwed motherhood, dependence, and deviance had a long history of association in the official mind.

Throughout the nineteenth century more women than men had been placed in facilities for the retarded and feebleminded, and women had stayed there longer. In 1875 Robert Dugdale, a charity worker in upper New York State, conducted the first intergenerational study of a family, the Jukes, with a long history of delinquency and social pathology. Dugdale, significantly, followed the degenerative strains through the female line. Three years after the Dugdale study, the first custodial facility for defective women of childbearing age was built in Newark, New York. Massachusetts followed suit, and nearly every state eventually had some separate place for feebleminded women. Women sent to these institutions were deemed moral imbeciles who did not have the wits to say no to vicious men and therefore needed protection. They were considered to be more prolific breeders than normal women, so that they not only drained the state's resources but also threatened to perpetuate a race of unfit persons. With the rise of diagnostic IQ tests, the moral imbecile became the mental defective and the connections between intelligence and deviance were "proved."[13]

The introduction of the Simon and Binet intelligence test in 1908 had enabled criminologists to create "objective" standards of measuring mental capacity and correlating criminal traits with hereditary factors. The very fact that this test was developed at a time when vice commissions were doing surveys of prostitution and when studies were being made of prostitutes detained during the war had the effect of further linking female sexual immorality with low-grade mental performance. Walter Fernald, who was chairman of the Massachusetts Vice Commission as well as director of the state school for the retarded, tested prostitutes in one survey and found that 51 percent were mental defectives.[14] Similar studies were done in the Chicago Morals Court, which determined that 62 percent of the prostitutes were mentally defective.

The feeblemindedness hysteria peaked during World War I, when so many women were interned as venereal disease carriers. Georgia, for example, created a Feeblemindedness Commission and hired a Massachusetts court administrator and expert on testing the feebleminded to come and survey inmates of every institution in the state. Typically, the Georgia commission classified three times more women as feebleminded than men. All the data from federal and state surveys lent support for the already strong belief in the relationship between low mental ability and sexual delinquency; survey results were powerful ammunition for the eugenicists who were asking for stern measures to curb the breeding of the unfit. Between 1913 and the end of the war dozens of states passed sterilization laws, aimed primarily at the female habitual moral offender.[15]

The determination of exactly which intelligence scores or behaviors made an individual incapable of adjusting to the complex demands of society varied with the investigator. It was common to label as feebleminded all those who scored three years below their mental age. Yet all kinds of other standards and criteria were employed, particularly for those in the borderline categories. In most cases very subjective and unscientific measures were employed. In his analysis of borderline defectives Fernald insisted that psychometric tests were not always trustworthy, and he took into account other criteria: the individual's physical appearance, family background, school work, and moral reactions. Green stains on teeth, dissimilar ears, and the inability to do long division were signals of defective personalities. Another was untruthfulness. Fernald cited one case of a women who constantly lied about her sexual relations with men. Yet, given Fernald's prejudice against female promiscuity, this woman showed considerable shrewdness in lying to him. Considering his broad definitions, it is not surprising that Fernald came up with enormously high figures for feeblemindedness: surveys of boy and girl delinquents in Massachusetts reform schools estimated 84 and 97 percent of them, respectively, to be feebleminded.[16]

Fernald was criticized for his lack of methodological sophistication, but the more elaborate causal models of social scientists revealed similar weaknesses. Either they took a criminal's biography and then found causes for his deviant status or they surveyed a criminal population and looked for patterns of causal relationships. Implicit in psychometric tests and psychoanalytic interviews were class, race, and gender biases. The Simon-Binet curves were calculated from scores of average schoolchildren and therefore favored native-born, middle class children. When the tests were given to selected populations with class backgrounds similar to those in criminal institutions, delinquents' scores were comparable to those of nondelinquents. The other criteria—work performance, education, skills, and female chastity—also reflected judgments of middle class investigators.[17]

Typical of the circular reasoning in these studies was psychiatrist Bernard Glueck's 1917 case histories of prisoners in Sing Sing prison in New York. To analyze forces in criminal careers, he developed elaborate bar graphs measuring home life, school performance, work record, previous institutional life, and hereditary influences to explain "antisocial activities." Although these graphic life histories had the appearance of scientific measures, they were not objective instruments for reconstructing the profiles of criminals. The traits he measured were both causes and effects of abnormality. A criminal's lack of capacity for adjustment, according to Glueck, was reflected in the fact that he or she had already served sentences in penal reformatories, and he predicted that the majority would be returned within five years. In effect, they were in prison because they were unadjusted persons; and proof of their constitutional inferiority was that they were in prison. Victor Anderson made the same kind of argument about Georgia prostitutes in his study of feeblemindedness. He reasoned that they turned to prostitution because of their incompetence. Proof of their incompetence was their low position in the industrial market. Therefore they became prostitutes, according to Anderson, because it was more "natural" and "simpler," not because the labor market provided them with few alternatives.[18]

The underlying thesis in both the case evaluations and the criminal surveys of the 1920s and 1930s was that defective individuals committed criminal acts and that aggregate data on persons committed to penal institutions would reveal the kinds of defective traits most often found in deviants. Since average persons did not undergo mental examinations and no clear-cut definition of adjustment existed, studies of delinquent populations tended to validate the researchers' predisposition or theory of criminality. The studies were closed systems, and one could challenge them only by denying the basic premises concerning normality, that is, what constitutes an average life experience in terms of work, marriage, and sexual behavior. Standards of normality for females were more rigid than those applied to males because women's "normal" roles were so much narrower.

More than any other study in the 1920s, Sheldon and Eleanor Glueck's *Five Hundred Delinquent Women* laid the ground rules both for studies of female deviant behavior and for future debates on rehabilitation. The research was a part of the extensive Harvard Law School Crime Survey of all Massachusetts penal institutions. Sheldon Glueck, a recent graduate of the law school and a lecturer at Harvard, became project director. He was neither a pioneer nor the model builder that his brother, Bernard Glueck, was. His work was synthetic, bringing together all the innovations in modern criminology: social work case method, psychiatric evaluation, IQ testing, and the newest of all the sciences, statistics.[19]

Sheldon and Eleanor Glueck took their cases from the records of the Massachusetts Reformatory, which they claimed were the most complete and thorough of any institution in the country. They gathered data on the five hundred delinquents from the reformatory case histories and from parole records; then they hired field workers to gather data on the postparole period. The inmate population in the Massachusetts Reformatory was slightly younger than the average prison population because most chronic recidivists for drunkenness, prostitution, or other misdemeanors were channeled to the local jail. Therefore the group tended to have more sexual offenders, more single women, and fewer recidivists than the jail population.[20]

The analysis of causes of delinquency, not surprisingly, revolved around the question of sexual conformity. Of the five hundred women, 54 percent had been sentenced for specific sexual offenses; but if one includes idle and disorderly charges (nearly always morals offenses in Massachusetts courts) then the figure rises to 77 percent. Sheldon Glueck defended the study's intense scrutiny of illicit sexuality: "Regardless of our views on the soundness or fairness of the laws governing the social control of the sex impulse," society had deemed these offenses harmful and serious.[21] Sexual monogamy and marital fidelity were not merely arbitrary conventional standards for the Gluecks. The number of variables that dealt with illicit sexual behavior and the researchers' view of causality reveal how much sexual behavior—control or lack of control—was the main criterion for judging a woman's mental fitness and social adjustment.

In his theory of delinquency, Glueck conceived of the notion of individual resistance levels, which he claimed resulted from heredity and social upbringing. When he analyzed causes of female deviance, he dwelt on the psychological and hereditary factors, which he implied accounted for women's promiscuity, failed marriages, and criminal records. As it happens, what he considered to be personality defects among the delinquent group were in nearly all instances actually a reflection of class background rather than innate traits.

The delinquent group was compared not with the same socioeconomic class but with upper class college women or the general population. For example, when contrasted with the upper class college women of Davis's study, the reformatory women appeared extremely deviant. While 7 percent of the college women had had premarital sex, 74 percent of the delinquent group had. Moreover, the overwhelming majority of the sexually active college women had sex only with their fiancés. The reformatory women tended to have their first sex experience with a pickup or casual acquaintance.

Delinquent women in the study had begun their sex lives at an early age, which the Gluecks attributed to their early sexual maturity or "hypersexuality." But the mean age for the start of menstruation for the general population was .06 years later, not a very significant amount. In nearly every case the differences between these women and "normal" women were due to different class backgrounds. The women in the study married younger and tended to marry men who had irregular work lives and, often, criminal records. Many of their marriages were cases of premarital pregnancy, where a judge or priest put pressure on the couple to marry. Compared to the general population, few of these women had marriages that endured (81.7 percent failure versus 7.6 percent for the general population). Only 2 out of the 301 marriages were successful, according to the Gluecks' criteria of a successful marriage—fidelity and continued cohabitation.[22]

Although the study revealed a high correlation between delinquency and "abnormal environmental experiences," such as foster home placements, the Gluecks' basic conclusion was that the major cause of delinquency was sexual precociousness: a lack of control of the sex impulse. "Illicit sex practices were extremely common among them, began surprisingly early, and carried in their train disease, illegitimacy, and unhappy matrimony." Management of the sex impulse was the hard task of the reformatory, and in evaluating the graduates of this institution in their postparole period, the study took sexual control as the central criterion for reformation.[23]

An example from the Harvard survey shows how this postparole evaluation operated. A woman was interviewed three years after her parole ended. To all appearances, she seemed to be going straight, being respectably married to a policeman. Ministers and police testified to her good character. Her mother said that she had not committed any immorality. However, the investigator decided to call on a maternal aunt, who confided that the "offender" had been promiscuous before her marriage and had cohabitated with her fiancé. Because of her prior history of sexual immorality, the investigator did not challenge the aunt's version, despite the fact that it was at odds with all the other accounts. Nor did it seem to matter that no hint of sexual immorality existed since her marriage. Her past sexual history convinced this interviewer of her guilt; sexual deviant labels were not easily cast off.[24] What is suggestive about this case is not the prejudice against ex-convicts but the way in which the judgment of failure or success, guilt or innocence, and delinquency or nondelinquency was based on sexual behavior.

According to the statistics on recidivism, the graduates of the reformatory fared better than most ex-convicts: only 16 percent returned to some penal institution. Compared to their situation when entering the reformatory, more of the postparole women were in stable marriages; fewer were dependent upon public aid; more had steady employment. Yet a surprising statistic was the increase in the number of women who became professional prostitutes after a term in prison. At the time of the original study, the majority of sexual delinquents in the group appeared to have been part-time or occasional prostitutes, promiscuous, or unconventional. Professional prostitutes represented only 7 percent of those sentenced but nearly twice as many of those in the follow-up studies.[25]

For the Gluecks and many other criminologists, recidivism was not the fault of the penal system; it was instead a reflection of the characteristics of the offender and poor diagnosis by judges and social workers. Those who did not adjust to society's norms lacked the capacity to be retrained and therefore required either longer supervision or, in cases of feeblemindedness, lifelong care in an institution. At the end of the reformatory study, Sheldon Glueck advocated the following reforms: special tribunals to determine sentences based on the evaluation of experts; institutions or colonies for mentally deficient female offenders of childbearing age; and new kinds of treatment for the habitual chastity offender.[26]

These kinds of sweeping reforms could never have been incorporated into the criminal justice system. They were at odds with the social, political, and legal realities of the day. Gone was the wartime hysteria surrounding venereal disease, and prostitution was no longer a central issue on the political agenda. Consequently, few municipalities or state governments could have convinced taxpayers to foot the bill for building more custodial institutions or for hiring more experts to evaluate and propose treatments for sexual delinquents. Most important, Glueck's program assumed a societal consensus over sexual mores that did not exist.

Inside the courtroom, trials for sexual delinquency dramatized the differences between working class views of sexual propriety and the middle class values of judges, social workers, and lawyers. These cases also revealed the resistance of immigrant working class families to the expanded role of the state in monitoring family life and their rejection of the concept of the court as clinic that emerged in this period. Since judges were elected officials or political appointees, they had to be cautious in sentencing youths to reform schools, removing children from families, and punishing unmarried couples living together. Through ward bosses, working class communities were able to keep juvenile courts and private agencies from intervening in their private lives as much as the laws and institutions might permit; besides, under the patronage system, the city did not always hire scientifically trained personnel for positions of responsibility in the criminal justice system. The Harvard Crime Survey report severely criticized the lack of qualified probation officers and cited a case in which a judge appointed a friendly waitress to the position of probation agent.[27]

Day-to-day justice in municipal courts was not conducive to a "therapeutic" approach to criminal justice. Even in juvenile courts, where the judge was supposedly acting as a counselor and a guide for parents, lawyers often thwarted the system and urged defendants to appeal prison sentences. Miriam Van Waters, who was considered a leading figure in progressive criminology, lamented the lack of cooperation between parents of juveniles and court administrators as she sat in Boston's juvenile court, observing on behalf of the Harvard Crime Survey. Van Waters believed that the court, functioning as clinic, could ideally be able to diagnose the disability as well as to create in the mind of the offender and his family the desire for treatment.[28]

The sheer number of appeals in criminal cases in a state like Massachusetts which automatically granted the right to appeal (trial *de novo* system) suggests how few defendants accepted their sentence as a treatment. Appeals in all cases favored defendants, and sexual offenders were no exception. According to a study of the handling of sexual delinquency in urban courts, bargains were constantly struck between district attorneys and lawyers when cases were appealed. Out of 504 persons charged with sex offenses in Boston's municipal court in 1920 (218 men, 286 women), 83 percent were convicted and, of those, 60 percent were sentenced to some penal institution; yet all but 3—2 men and 1 woman—escaped penal sentence. Only 8 were fined. District attorneys, who were faced with enormous caseloads, dropped these cases. Perhaps they viewed them as less serious than other crimes or merely realized that juries would not convict unless clear-cut professional prostitution could be proved. Whatever the reasons, sex offenders often had ways of circumventing the power of social workers, psychiatrists, and police, as long as they managed to stay out of the institutional system.[29]

In the disposition of cases, judges, rather than paying much attention to mental tests or psychiatric evaluations, usually took into consideration other factors, such as recidivism, family situation, age, and attitude in court. Among women arrested for a sexual offense—whether they were professional prostitutes, charity girls, or married women living with men other than their husbands—the presence of a father or husband in the courtroom often swayed the judge. A comparison of the backgrounds of women on probation with those in the women's reformatory showed little difference in the women's intelligence scores, previous arrest records, or even seriousness of their crimes. Instead, those who got probation were more likely to have had cooperative and supportive husbands or parents. The traditional view of the female delinquent as someone in need of protection and paternal control carried more weight than a psychiatric assertion of a woman's low mental ability or a social worker's assessment of her poor maternal instinct.[30]

Mental tests and expert recommendations did have some bearing on the outcome of a case, and they were crucial when parole was at stake. Inside the institutional system, the concept of adjustment—which for women meant the acceptance of middle class sexual norms and a subservient response to authority—could be more rigorously imposed. Indeterminate sentencing, which was nearly universal in women's reformatories in this period, provided prison administrators with a way of dramatically increasing the terms of confinement for sexual delinquents. The threat of being sent to an institution for defective delinquents or for feebleminded women of childbearing age was a sword of Damocles for habitual offenders and incorrigibles who refused to absorb the ideologies of their keepers.

Psychiatrists and criminologists continued to shape the discourse on prostitution for forty years after World War I. Although the terminology and analysis became more sophisticated, the assumptions remained the same. Causes of prostitution were traced to a woman's sexual frigidity or hypersexuality; psychoanalytic theory had it both ways. Prostitutes appeared as women either governed by masochistic natures or driven by Oedipal revenge. As late as 1958, Harold Greenwald published *The Call Girl,* a psychoanalytic study of case histories of his patients who were prostitutes. From his interviews with about a dozen women, he concluded that the key to prostitution was early deprivation of a mother's love.[31] No trace of the political and social context of prostitution debates from the Progressive years remained. Not until the cultural and social protests of the 1960s and 1970s did prostitution again become an issue of sexual politics or social justice, and many of the conflicts in class and gender politics that had inhibited change in the past would work against change in the future.

"The man said something in the girl's ear, and a moment later the brass-studded door closed behind them." (Page 45.)
(Investigators are at present looking for the girl.)

White slavery narratives presented a world where women mysteriously disappeared. There seemed to be a procurer on every streetcorner. Illustration from H. W. Lytle and John Dillon, *From Dance Hall to White Slavery: The World's Greatest Tragedy* (Chicago, 1912).

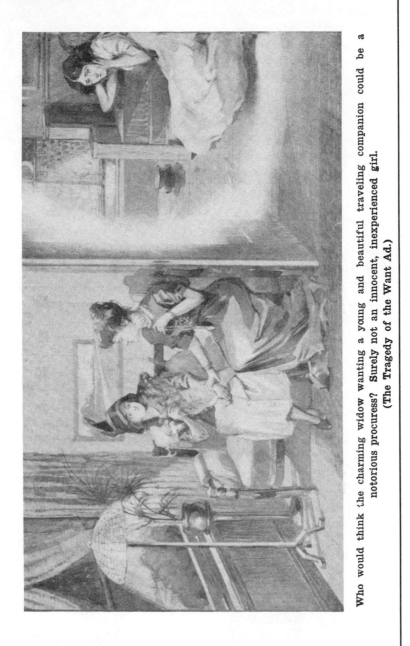

Who would think the charming widow wanting a young and beautiful traveling companion could be a notorious procuress? Surely not an innocent, inexperienced girl. (The Tragedy of the Want Ad.)

As this tale suggests, white slavery narratives were offered as warnings to women considering leaving the wholesome and safe world of small towns. Illustration from Lytle and Dillon, *From Dance Hall to White Slavery: The World's Greatest Tragedy.*

RIGHT: Ethel Dummer embodied the many contradictions within Progressive Era feminism. She espoused women's political and social rights, yet asserted the need for controls and protections. Dummer's disillusionment with the treatment of promiscuous women during World War I led her to turn away from criminal justice reform and toward educational reform. She refused to serve on a War Department committee against venereal disease during World War II. (Courtesy of the Schlesinger Library, Radcliffe College.) BELOW: A typical World War I poster in the campaign against venereal disease and prostitution. (Courtesy of the Social Welfare History Archives, University of Minnesota.)

Go back to them physically fit and morally clean

SOCIAL HYGIENE DIVISION · ARMY EDUCATIONAL COMMISSION

LEFT: In World War II, the U.S. government embarked on a more "hard-sell" campaign against prostitution. In this poster, the prostitute is clearly portrayed as a public enemy to be scorned and distrusted. (Courtesy of the National Archives.) BELOW: Sheldon and Eleanor Glueck worked as a team compiling life histories for five hundred delinquent women at the Massachusetts Reformatory for Women. Their study was considered a definitive work on female delinquency until the 1960s and 1970s, when feminist scholars challenged the sexual norms and prescribed gender roles underlying their theories. (Courtesy of the Harvard Law Art Collection.)

ABOVE: A 1971 feminist demonstration outside a New York City courthouse in support of prostitutes who had to pay high bail while their customers went free. (Photo by Bettye Lane.)

RIGHT: Margo St. James urges women to join a protest against the harassment of prostitutes during the 1976 Democratic Convention. New York City had passed a special anti-loitering law to keep prostitutes out of sight of the convention. (Photo by Bettye Lane.)

ABOVE: Wall painting from a Stockholm subway station. The painter, Sture Nilsson, took this scene from an actual mass demonstration against pornography and prostitution in Stockholm during the mid-1970s. (Courtesy of Sture Nilsson.)

LEFT: Statue of a young girl in the main prostitution thoroughfare in Stockholm. Printed on the statue are lines from a poem titled "Non Serviam" ("I Shall Not Be Used by You") by Gunner Ekeloff, a well-known contemporary Swedish poet. (Photo by Rolf Skog.)

PART IV

Recent Challenges
and Debates,
1970–

9

The Search

for Alternatives

IN THE 1970s prostitution politics once again became part of a reform agenda. Not since the first decades of this century had prostitution issues been debated in the media, on the floors of legislatures, and among feminists. During World War II, prostitution had been an administrative issue—how to keep prostitutes away from soldiers. In the two decades that followed, the problem of prostitution lay buried under postwar complacency, as did other issues of class, race, and gender inequality. In the late 1960s a prostitution reform movement emerged in much the same way as earlier movements had. Prostitution reform once again rode on the coattails of other social movements: in the 1960s these were the civil rights, peace, and—most directly related to prostitution debates—the feminist movements. Much of the reform rhetoric echoed earlier calls for abolishing the sexual double standard. Still, the prostitution agenda was unique in this period. For the first time sexual privacy—freedom to choose sexual partners without interference from the state—became a rationale for prostitution reform. And, never before had prostitutes acted as their own advocates, both challenging false notions about prostitution and offering proposals for reform of the criminal justice system.

Prostitution debates took place in a shifting social and moral landscape. In the United States and western Europe the young challenged the limits of respectability in their dress, music, and lifestyles. In hindsight we know that the hailed and feared sexual revolution never fully materialized. Couples continued to marry; the family did not wither away; and public opinion polls revealed a gap between actual sexual behavior and media images. Nevertheless, the sexual liberation movement of the 1960s profoundly affected perceptions and attitudes about sex; erotic life was being renegotiated.

One could see the eroticization of social life in advertisements, films, and the proliferation of soft- and hard-core pronographic magazines. Even in the field of sexology, new sexual ideologies and norms were being cast. Perhaps the most celebrated sexologists, William Masters and Virginia Johnson, laid to rest Victorian notions of women's sexual passivity and weak sex drive. They said that women had a greater capacity for sexual variety and pleasure than men.[1]

Throughout the 1960s and 1970s all kinds of moral orthodoxies were questioned; legal challenges in the courts reflected the lack of consensus around sexual norms. What was obscene? What kinds of sexual behavior were threatening to society? And what was the state's role in regulating sexual behavior?

More liberal attitudes toward noncommercial sex and changing views of female sexuality influenced the reappraisal of prostitution laws. How could one prosecute a prostitute for peddling sex when, on the same street, one could legally purchase reenactments of sex theater in peep shows and X-rated films? Civil liberties lawyers, feminist activists, and prostitute groups mounted legal challenges, published articles, and held public protests against the social injustice toward the prostitute. Prostitutes appeared on television talk shows; journalists like Gail Sheehy exposed the political corruption in prostitution businesses;[2] and filmmakers portrayed the brutal world of sexual abuse and danger in the prostitute's life. But media interest in prostitution did not lead to any large-scale campaign to abolish antiprostitution laws. Nor did the legal cases result in any significant change in the treatment of the prostitute in the criminal justice system. Courts struck down laws against sodomy, birth control, and abortion, yet prostitution-vagrancy laws remained intact after a decade and half of legal battles.[3]

There was no emotional issue available in the 1960s and 1970s to galvanize the public as white slavery had in the second decade of this century. Feminists supported the prostitute's cause, as did civil liberties groups, but no mass movement coalesced around prostitutes' rights, as did around gay rights and reproductive freedom. Unlike these campaigns, the movement to change prostitution laws lacked a platform and a common strategy for reform. A range of reform groups confronted the prostitution system; they all agreed upon the basic facts about prostitution policy in the United States—that criminal sanctions were ineffective in controlling prostitution, discriminated against women and the poor, and perpetuated oppressive conditions for the prostitute. Civil liberties advocates, feminists, and activist prostitutes were united in their opposition to criminal penalties for prostitution. But they never organized around a specific set of alternative policies. They could not agree on what kind of new system—if any—should replace the old.

Some feminists believed that prostitution enabled women to take control of their sexuality; others viewed all prostitution as sexual slavery. Some feminists considered prostitution a path to economic independence; to others it merely institutionalized women's economic and social dependence.[4] Some civil liberties advocates took a strict libertarian view of prostitution as a private encounter between consenting adults with which the state should not interfere; others, those who defined prostitution as a victimless crime, were not opposed to state licensing or regulation.[5]

In their efforts to uproot prejudice and to rescind criminal penalties, the various groups submerged their differences. They employed the constitutional arguments that had been successful in the landmark cases involving censorship, gay rights, and reproductive freedom. Yet this universalist, gender-neutral strategy could not remove the gender and class bias of antiprostitution laws.

Legal Challenges and Gender Equality

Legal approaches of the 1960s and 1970s represented a departure from previous prostitution reform efforts. In the past nearly all the strategies toward reforming prostitution laws had been based on two ideas: that women needed special consideration in sexual relations and that the state should act as a protector of female chastity. Earlier campaigns to reform prostitution had culminated in laws against seducers and procurers. These gender-specific strategies assumed a basic difference in men's and women's social worlds, sexual natures, and sources of power. In contrast, the recent reform coalition of feminists, prostitute groups, and civil libertarians adopted strategies based on an ideology of gender neutrality. Prostitution laws, they argued, were unconstitutional because they denied free speech, infringed upon a person's right to privacy, and did not provide equal protection under the law for women arrested as prostitutes.[6]

Both the free speech and right to privacy arguments in prostitution cases were couched in gender-neutral language: prosecution of prostitution, like the prosecution of obscenity and homosexuality, represented the state's unjustifiable interference in personal expression and private life. Even in the equal protection argument, which took sex discrimination as its primary focus, the underlying premise was a denial of gender differences. Men and women were both participants in and initators of the sexual exchange, so why should the laws apply only to women? And, more important, why should the means of enforcement (male decoys) perpetuate the false notion that women were the main actors in the prostitution exchange?

But the notion of gender difference was deeply embedded in both the laws and their enforcement. Although male prostitution became increasingly visible in the 1970s, the laws continued to operate as if prostitution was a criminal activity only when women were engaged in it. Louisiana courts claimed that male prostitution was not a social problem in a 1974 case challenging laws that applied only to females living in a house of ill fame. While in some states these gender-specific laws were struck down— recognizing males as both prostitutes and customers—equal protection arguments could not undo the legal convention that prostitution occurred when a woman offered her body indiscriminately to men. Courts, when presented with the undeniable statistics on gender bias in prostitution laws—the proportion of women versus men arrested—did not dispute the discriminatory nature of prostitution laws but maintained that gender was a valid classification in prostitution.[7]

The standard legal argument went as follows: it was reasonable to assume that women were the guilty parties in prostitution because they were the most visible (they did the soliciting); they were the repeat offenders; and they profited from the transaction. But the street life of the city revealed a different story. When police departments employed female decoys, they found that *men* were doing the soliciting in prostitution exchanges. One California city tried an experiment in which female decoys, wired with tape recorders, stood on the sidewalk for two to five hours in the prostitution section. In three months they had received 150 solicitations by men and made 100 arrests, an average of about 8 a week;

male undercover agents testified that they rarely averaged more than 3 arrests a week.[8] On the issue of monetary gain, other persons—that is, pimps, hotel managers, and hotel owners—reaped far greater financial rewards from prostitution than did the prostitute on the street. But the criminal justice system ignored their role in the prostitution system, as it always has.

Activists' attempts to equalize the treatment of men and women in prostitution cases often resulted in new, gender-neutral wording for statutes. However, changes in the letter of the law did not affect the day-to-day practice of enforcement against the female prostitute. When police began arresting male clients in several cities, they made headline news.[9] Even the mildest sanctions—mailing citations to the homes of men charged with patronizing a prostitute—produced angry protests to politicians and did not last long.

Court challenges yielded few, if any, substantive changes in the treatment of prostitution by the criminal justice system. Some states outlawed such practices as quarantine of prostitutes for venereal disease. But in certain municipalities, such as San Francisco, the legal challenges backfired. A California appellate court ruled that the vagrancy laws used for prostitution offenses were vague status offenses and therefore unconstitutional. They were replaced by disorderly conduct laws that made specific references to solicitation and payment of money for lewd behavior. Rather than leading to decriminalization, these new refinements in the law resulted in a greater association between disorderly behavior and prostitution. They also required more police activity—more decoys—to prove without a doubt that solicitation had occurred.[10]

The legal justification for selecting female prostitutes as the guilty parties rested on false dichotomies between public and private acts, and between visible and invisible hands in the operations. Essentially, the terms *public* and *visible,* when translated into actual policies, were gender and status classifications.

To alter the gender identification between prostitution crime and women demanded a more radical break with the past than activists' legal strategies allowed. The prostitution exchange had to be placed in the broad context of sexual relations and women's economic and political power. These are the kinds of issues courts are unable to confront, given their narrow framework of constitutional rights and procedural issues.[11]

Writing in the early 1970s about the politics of prostitution, Kate Millett understood the "vast and elaborate process" needed to undo the deep-seated prejudice against the prostitute. She believed that the women's movement would play a key role as the prostitute's advocate, but she also realized that feminists, though sympathetic, were little aware of the prostitute's situation:

Change would of course involve specific legal reforms, decriminalization, also a redirection in police policy, but it would also imply more basic changes. . . . Essential to bring about such change in attitude is a dramatic shift in perspective in the world of "straight" women, historically divided from the prostitute by their respectability. There must be a new climate of awareness, of trust and self-respect between women, a feeling of community.[12]

The first step in bridging the chasm between prostitutes and straight women, according to Millett, was the inclusion of the prostitute in the debate. In the past, feminist reformers had always spoken for the prostitute; yet few had ever encountered one. Those who had had been their sisters' keepers, in positions of authority as directors of homes for fallen women, as social workers, or as probation officers. On rare occasions during the nineteenth century prostitutes rescued by reformers had been invited to general meetings of women's benevolent organizations to plead for more resources for institutions for fallen women; they came as humble penitents, not women with equal voices. The idea of prostitutes speaking for themselves at a national suffrage meeting or women reformer's convention was implausible. Social barriers were let down in the extraordinary relationship between Maimie Pinzer, the prostitute at the turn of the century whose letters have been preserved, and Fanny, an upper middle class feminist reformer. Even in their intimate and frank letters, the sense of distance and Maimie's deference never totally disappear.[13]

In the early 1970s prostitutes began to attend feminist gatherings, and the fireworks that ensued revealed the longstanding barriers from the past. In 1971 New York area feminists advertised the first feminist conference on prostitution. To their surprise, prostitutes actually attended. As Millett describes it, the conference was a violent and angry encounter, with mutual suspicion and denunciations. Much of the sound and fury came from the prostitutes, who were confronted with panels of experts discussing the "elimination" of prostitution, which meant the elimination of their jobs.[14] The real issues cut deeper and could not be rationalized in terms of immediate strategies and future goals. They touched upon basic questions of sexual identity and social status. Hundreds of years of social stigma against women who violated sexual norms were hard for either side to ignore. Millet concluded that this meeting had occurred too early in the feminist movement, that more exchange between the two groups could result in solidarity and concerted action on the issue of prostitution. In a sense, she was right. Activist prostitutes and feminists did form an alliance, yet many of the tensions that erupted in this first conference continued to bubble beneath the smooth surface of a united front.

During the 1970s feminists and activist prostitutes continued to meet face to face at national conferences. They issued statements of support for mutual goals of prostitutes' rights and the Equal Rights Amendment. Prostitution never became the emotional issue for contemporary feminists that it had been for the feminists of the Progressive Era or of the nineteenth century. But the mainstream women's movement in the United States did place prostitution on its reform agenda, mainly because of the lobbying of activist prostitutes.

Prostitute Unions and Feminist Goals

A prostitute union movement was launched in Lyons in 1975, when local prostitutes took over a church and publicized a list of grievances. A series of violent murders of prostitutes in the city over the preceding months had triggered the prostitutes' church occupation. But their strike was really aimed at the police harassment and repression that arose from revised French prostitution laws, which prohibited trade in hotels, bars, and cities. The law had forced them to work on the streets and left them vulnerable to physical assault and repeated arrest. The Lyons event touched off prostitute protests in other large French cities. What began as a defensive stance against police repression turned into a movement for recognizing prostitutes' right to work and demands for social services, health insurance, and old age pensions.[15] Although the 1975 strikes did not lead to a mass organization of French prostitutes, it raised the public's consciousness about the problems of prostitutes and spawned other prostitute organizations in Europe and the United States.

By calling their organizations unions, prostitutes sought to define themselves as workers and to sever prostitution from its historical association with criminality and deviance. In effect, the notion of a union of prostitutes underscored how institutionalized the sex commerce business had become, even in the United States, where it was a criminal business. Yet these were not trade unions because prostitutes did not set to bargain collectively with pimp managers for higher wages or more autonomy.[16]

When the first wave of prostitute organizations called for better working conditions, they were protesting police harassment and the lack of social benefits such as pensions and unemployment insurance. In the United States, the primary goal of prostitute unions was to eliminate criminal penalties against the women. They functioned as lobbyists or legal advocacy groups, seeking to make their demands heard in the legislatures and through the media. They also provided legal counsel and support for prostitutes who were arrested, and they publicized accounts of police brutality and of abuse by customers.[17]

The first and best-known of the prostitute groups—Call Off Your Old Tired Ethics (COYOTE)—began in San Francisco. Its founder, Margo St. James, a master fundraiser and tactician, is responsible for its success and endurance. She announced the birth of COYOTE on Mother's Day, 1973. To raise funds and get media exposure, she organized hookers' masquerade balls, where the rich and famous mingled with the demimondes of the streets. Her wholesome, athletic look and zany style made her an instant media personality. Newspapers and broadcast talk shows sought out St. James for interviews, and even the established old guard, the San Francisco Barristers Club, invited her to speak about prostitution reform.[18]

Since prostitution is a criminal offense in the United States, to form a prostitute organization was a risky business. *COYOTE Howls,* St. James's newspaper, noted that women known to be union members were singled out by San Francisco police for arrest and harassment. Even with these obstacles, prostitute organizations formed in New York, Massachusetts, Washington State, Hawaii, Colorado, and Florida.

St. James was not representative of the prostitute population. She had graduated from college and even attended law school for a short time. Not only her articulate, witty style but also her message about prostitution was attractive to the media and to the liberal legal establishment. She did not challenge the right of men to have access to prostitutes; nor did she suggest that prostitution was degrading work or harmful to women. On the contrary, she insisted that prostitution was merely a job for most women, and a lucrative one compared to most women's work.

St. James, who called herself chairmadam of COYOTE, became the voice of the prostitute at all national and international forums. As interest in prostitution reform mushroomed, however, grass-roots organizing declined.[19] Instead of building a network of local unions, COYOTE evolved into a political lobbying and research organization, the National Prostitutes' Task Force. The task force found support for its campaign among civil liberties groups, such as the American Civil Liberties Union (ACLU), and the mainstream women's movement. The national ACLU gave prostitution high priority in its Sexual Privacy Project. Several local chapters took on prostitution cases to test the laws. In 1973 the National Organization for Women (NOW) passed a resolution calling for the decriminalization of prostitution; several NOW chapters, particularly in California and Washington, were actively involved in the prostitutes' rights movement. A high point in the movement was the second annual Hookers' Convention in San Francisco in 1975, attended by over a thousand persons—lawyers, celebrities, prostitutes, and their supporters—and panels of experts discussed strategies for altering prostitution laws; the convention was broadly covered on television. *The Politics of Prostitution,* a resource book on prostitution issues, emerged from this activism. It was a testimony to the broad coalition that had formed around the movement, and it was a joint effort of NOW, the ACLU, COYOTE, and feminist researchers.[20]

Prostitutes' rights groups linked their campaign to other campaigns within the feminist movement. Perusing *COYOTE Howls,* one found articles on a range of feminist issues: rape, wife abuse, and lesbianism, as well as prostitution. Feminists also took part in demonstrations for prostitutes' rights. To protest New York City's campaign against prostitutes at the time of the 1976 Democratic National Convention, feminists staged a "loiter in" and experienced firsthand the male–female encounters of the prostitution street scene.[21]

Hookers' Lib became one of the catchphrases of prostitute unions, and they defined their movement as feminist. Unanimously, prostitutes' rights organizations rejected the solution of licensing or any police regulation, which, they insisted, merely increased male control of women's bodies. Mandatory medical examinations for prostitutes only, and not for their male patrons, highlighted the gender and class bias in prostitution policy. These were the same arguments feminists had made against regulation fifty years before.

Activist prostitutes wove feminist arguments into their discussions of causes of and remedies for prostitution. They claimed that prostitution was the best possible option for women who had to support themselves in a discriminatory labor market. One prostitute from the Prostitute Union of Massachusetts (PUMA) asserted that prostitution was an extension of women's economic dependency on men. "The line between paid and unpaid sex is a question of what we get in return." Prostitutes were merely more open about the price of their services than were women who slept with men for the rent or for spending money.[22]

Despite the conscious attempts to define their movement as feminist, the basic philosophy of prostitute unions in the 1970s came in conflict with the long-term goals of many feminists. It was based on a libertarian view of prostitution as a private matter between consenting adults, epitomized by the slogan "My ass is mine." Prostitutes' rights activists characterized prostitution as a service occupation—responding to a legitimate demand for sexual variety—and even claimed that prostitutes were sex therapists. These views echoed an earlier and essentially nonfeminist tradition of prostitution reform. For example, sociologist Kingsley Davis's functional argument in the 1930s favored legalizing prostitution because it bolstered monogamous marriage. In a similar vein, Harry Benjamin and Robert Masters, two physicians writing about prostitution in the 1960s, contended that American society should legalize prostitution since men would always demand the service for erotic desires that wives could not satisfy.[23] Both rationales assumed that men have a greater sex drive than women and that indiscriminate and impersonal sex is in fact normal for men, though abnormal or uncommon in women.

The unions' claim that prostitution was a sexual service for men seeking variety among sex partners struck a dissonant chord among radical feminists attacking the social constructions of male and female sexuality. Moreover, to treat prostitution strictly as a right to privacy issue undermined feminist critiques of the gender bias within legal definitions of private and public. At the very same time that St. James and other prostitutes' rights activists were bringing cases using the sexual privacy doctrine, feminist lawyers were attacking the state's failure to intervene in the private sphere of marital rape and child and wife abuse.[24]

In the name of a common front against unjust prostitution laws, neither feminists nor prostitute union organizers acknowledged ideological differences. Yet the two groups had unresolvable differences in ideology and long-term goals. Beneath the voices of solidarity—that all women are prostitutes, dependent on men for economic support—was both a vast divide in social experiences and a conflicting sexual politics.

Prostitute unions sought to create a sex commerce that followed the rules of the marketplace. Local governments might issue licenses, like cab or peddler licenses, but there should be no restrictions on who could become a prostitute, whom she chose to be her manager, and where she chose to practice her trade. In this kind of setting, they argued, prostitution would provide women with financial rewards and the freedom to shape their work environment.[25]

Many feminists, while strongly supporting the unions' goals of decriminalization, still felt uncomfortable with a position that tended to institutionalize prostitution or even to define it as women's work. To do so was to suggest that women would always lack economic opportunities and thus would serve men as sex objects. Anticipating this uneasiness around prostitution, the writers of *The Politics of Prostitution* identified what they called the "feminist dilemma":

As feminists, many of us are idealistic when we first encounter the issue of prostitution. Because of the sexual exploitation involved in prostitution, we are tempted to initially say that this is an improper use of human beings. Prostitution, we say, should be eliminated, not legislated.[26]

The authors then asked feminists to cast aside their naiveté and "enter reality": "To speak only to the ideal of no sexual exploitation—in the face of current sexual, economic, and legal realities—is self-serving." The resolution of the dilemma, therefore, is to recognize freedom of choice, that many women choose to be a prostitute for a dollar a minute rather than a clerk-typist for two dollars an hour.[27]

A similar argument appeared in a Seattle newspaper. The issue of legalizing prostitution had been placed on the agenda of the local county council during a period when law enforcers were attempting to widen police powers in prostitution arrests. At a hearing Jill Severn, of Seattle Radical Women, argued that legalized prostitution was a temporary expedient to erase legal discrimination against women. Of course, she asserted, the "wonderful solution" was an end to the sexual double standard and the creation of "a social and cultural system which will accept women as equals."[28]

One finds the same conflict between immediate strategies and long-term goals in NOW's resolutions supporting decriminalization. On the one hand, they urge as an "interim measure" an end to laws relating to the act of prostitution. On the other hand, they insist that to repeal such laws "is not to make a judgment that prostitution is morally good."[29]

Feminists in the 1970s were caught in a maze of contrary positions. Women who wished to ally themselves with the sexual liberation movement often felt uncomfortable accepting the idea of prostitution as a sexual service or therapy for men. Yet these feminists wanted to break with the tradition of feminism that dwelt exclusively upon women's passivity and victimization in sex and thus had portrayed the prostitute as an enslaved woman. On the other side, those who insisted that prostitution was sexual exploitation and who rejected a free-market approach to prostitution wanted to distinguish their position from the antifeminist attack on prostitution, abortion, gay rights, and women's liberation issues in general.[30]

The divisiveness within the feminist movement over sexual politics and the ambivalence of feminists toward the prostitute's cause may explain why no campaign around prostitution has materialized within the American feminist movement. Feminists in earlier prostitution reform campaigns made no distinction between voluntary and involuntary prostitution. Their world view was simple: men controlled women's bodies in the home and in the marketplace. Sexual freedom was therefore a male prerogative only. In the 1970s and 1980s women still lack power in economic, political, and social spheres. But the women's movement during these years has brought about greater diversity in economic and social roles for women. And by this time women can explore the erotic without being labeled whores—or fast, easy, bad girls. Curiously, sexual liberation has had the dual effect of breaking down many of the social barriers between prostitutes and straight women while constructing ideological barriers between them. For many feminists sexual liberation meant eliminating the power dynamics in sexual relations. But prostitutes in their trade must implicitly accept them and use them to advantage; this is the essence of "turning a trick."

The prostitution reform movement in the United States has become increasingly divided along these ideological lines. Among activist prostitutes, one finds two opposing factions. A number of prostitute unions, in a group calling itself the United States Prostitutes' Collective, have joined forces with the Wages for Housework movement. Under the rubric "No bad women, only bad laws," they present prostitution as a legitimate work choice for women in a capitalist economy. Furthermore, they claim, prostitution actually increases the value of women's time outside the home, since prostitutes are high paid.[31]

Challenging some of the basic assumptions within the prostitute union movement, a collective of prostitutes formed a new organization in 1985, Women Hurt in Systems of Prostitution Engaged in Revolt (WHISPER). WHISPER's attack on systems of prostitution represents a thorough rejection of the notion that prostitution offers economic independence. Editors of their newsletter separated themselves from the libertarian movement in prostitution:

We will no longer whisper furtively about the ways that we have been used and hurt by men, while they brag about, celebrate and profit from our abuse. We also reject the self appointed "experts" or spokespersons who pimp prostitution as a pleasurable, lucrative, economic alternative that women freely choose, while they decline this "choice" for themselves.[32]

The newsletter's graphic accounts of women held in ropes and chains, burned with cigarettes, and sexually degraded in prostitution and the provocative stance of WHISPER constitute a conscious effort to offer an antidote to the view of the prostitute as woman empowered and sexually liberated. This is the overriding picture that emerges from Arlene Carmen and Howard Moody's study of New York street prostitutes in 1985. Prostitutes appear as women liberated from sexual moralism on the cutting edge of the feminist movement:

In a society where women are at the threshold of equality with men, beginning not only to enjoy sex but also to decide when and with whom to have it, the prostitute becomes the embodiment of that freedom which until now has been only a fantasy.[33]

Carmen and Moody's *Working Women* maintains that prostitutes freely choose their careers and that pimps, contrary to the stereotypes, do not coerce women into prostitution or have absolute power over them; a prostitute can always find another man. But WHISPER repudiates the notion of voluntary prostitution in a prostitute–pimp relation.

In denying the distinctions between voluntary and involuntary prostitution, the members of WHISPER echo feminist views of prostitution in the nineteenth and early twentieth century, which portrayed prostitutes as sexual slaves. Yet WHISPER represents prostitutes speaking for themselves and from their own experience. Moreover, unlike earlier constructs of sexual slavery, their position is rooted in a much broader structural analysis of women's economic powerlessness and social dependence. Still, this view is somehow lost in the pages of *WHISPER,* where not gender or class systems but pimps and johns appear as the source of the problem of prostitution. One member of the collective has advocated criminalizing the customer as a solution to prostitution, a strategy that in the past has unleashed greater repression against prostitutes.[34] Since policy makers continue to justify incarcerating juveniles and prostitutes as a measure for their protection, there is implicit danger in portraying prostitution as sexual slavery.

The tensions over protection and rights have erupted in struggles over pornography and censorship among feminists. The feminist movement has become divided into two ideological camps, and this factionalism reverberates into prostitution politics. One side contends that the social hierarchy of gender relations translates the right to sexual expression into the right to rape and abuse women. In the name of free speech, images of pornography construct a violent sexual world for women. The other side claims that protective strategies have affected all women negatively and have inhibited the struggle for sexual equality. To view sexuality as fraught with danger is to deny women sexual pleasure, according to the defenders of unrestricted free speech. Leaders of the antipornography campaign believe that sexual domination enforces women's subordination. Their opponents, the libertarians, counter by saying that sexual exploitation is a symptom of women's more encompassing social and economic dependence.[35]

Neither group has applied its reasoning to prostitution policy, however. Feminists who have portrayed any kind of censorship as a threat to women's sexual freedom have been unwilling to make a parallel argument about prostitution. They say that antiprostitution campaigns have led to repression of women's sexuality, but they have not favored a laissez faire market in prostitution. Similarly, those involved in the antipornography movement have not urged a campaign against prostitution. They realize that the enforcement of prostitution laws reflects the inequalities in the system through punishing only women, mainly poor and black women.

In Sweden and Norway, feminists, who have become deeply engaged in the prostitute's cause, have been able to galvanize the women's movement around prostitution politics; tensions have been submerged in their campaigns against rape, pornography, and prostitution. Rape has not been viewed as a middle class issue and prostitution as a working class issue; both are seen as different faces of male power and domination. Scandinavian socialist feminists have analyzed pornography and prostitution as class and gender issues, reflecting both women's weak economic position and social constructions of women as sexual commodities.

Swedish feminists defined prostitution as a collective female and *male* problem. Serving on the government's commission on prostitution, Rita Liljeström, the leading feminist scholar in Sweden, characterized prostitution as an erotic war between the sexes that expressed the separation of female and male gender roles into reproduction and production, respectively. Feminist writer and psychotherapist Hanna Olsson, secretary of the prostitution commission, used the phrase "the non-sexuality of sexuality," to describe the dehumanization of both customer and prostitute in the sexual exchange. These feminists were instrumental in diffusing a movement that was building among radical social work groups and one segment of the Social Democratic party to create penalties for customers.[36]

Unlike their American sisters, Scandinavian feminists did not have to contend with a right-wing antifeminist campaign against women's sexual liberation. Nor did they face a challenge from a prostitute union movement that presented prostitution as a legitimate work choice. Consequently, they were able to build a consensus on prostitution issues and remedies within their society. The remedies were clear cut in the case of prostitution: greater penalties for profiteers in prostitution; no penalties against prostitutes or customers, but rather more social work support systems; and more education about sexual relationships and equality between the sexes.[37]

Among the Americans, in contrast, there were different strategies for prostitution reform: should there be halfway houses and social work remedies for prostitutes, or unions of prostitute workers? Was the prostitute a powerful and rebellious woman rejecting the low-paying, low-status work of most women and using her sexual prowess to subdue men? Or was she a sexual victim abused by a pimp and forced to degrade herself daily for men who felt nothing but contempt for her? But neither those who cast the prostitute as victim nor those who viewed her as empowered could create an ideological consensus on prostitution policy.

Finding Practical Solutions

The same conflicts over sexual freedom and protection from abuse emerged in general debates on prostitution remedies. In 1977, when a New York judge, Margaret Taylor, threw out a prostitution case involving a fourteen-year-old girl, she caused a furor by describing prostitution as recreational sex for a fee. Syndicated columnist Ellen Goodman, who is opposed to the present laws against prostitution, found Taylor's ruling unsettling. To view prostitution as merely casual sex for pay or to argue that a prostitution career was a lifestyle ignored some of the hard facts about life on the street, particularly in the case of juvenile prostitution, Goodman pointed out.[38]

Physical and emotional abuse by pimps, drug addiction, and juvenile prostitution called out for some kind of intervention or support systems. However, the legal hook of the state had always used protection as a pretext to incarcerate and stigmatize women. Was not the best strategy therefore to eliminate all forms of intervention?

A judge in Boston's municipal court, who daily faced prostitution cases, admitted that she could never resolve the tensions between society's obligation to intervene in cases of sexual exploitation and the unjust outcomes when it did:

> The pull is that it always seems as if you can do something when you are sitting there, that you can turn this life around—can get this woman off the street. The pull in the other direction is that criminalization only enhances the oppression of the institution, which is especially true for black prostitutes. The race factor makes them more vulnerable to arrest, to police harassment, and to prejudice in the courts as black defendants.[39]

When it came to finding practical solutions for prostitution, the issues became extremely complicated. They involved not only the prostitute, pimp, and customer, but also neighborhoods where prostitution existed and the society in general. An individual might express a tolerance toward prostitution in the abstract, but the reality of solicitation in one's own community often produced a shift in one's ideological ground.

A survey of Boston residents, businesses, and police during 1977 and 1978 revealed conflicts between libertarian attitudes toward prostitution and practical solutions for neighborhood problems. While a majority of the respondents were in favor of some form of legalized prostitution through licensing or zoning, the overwhelming majority found it offensive to have prostitutes in their neighborhood. The message in these responses was that prostitution was okay in someone else's backyard. Only a small minority (14 percent) considered prostitution immoral, and most conceded that prostitution could neither be eliminated nor significantly reduced. Yet the associations of prostitution with crime, venereal disease, and neighborhood decay, which have existed for over a hundred years, remained fixed in the minds of most residents of that city.[40]

Throughout the 1970s lawyers and social scientists attempted to prove that these were false associations. They offered empirical evidence (1) that venereal disease is more often spread by nonprofessionals; (2) that only a small percentage of prostitutes commit other crimes, often after they have been labeled criminal through a prostitution arrest; and (3) that prostitutes come into a neighborhood that is already in decline. They argued that most of the negative aspects of prostitution were side effects caused by its illegal status. European cities with legalized prostitution therefore offered models for change.[41]

European Models

Maintaining that moves to decriminalize prostitution have been stymied by the lack of satisfactory policy alternatives, some American legal experts explored the West German experience. They found that civil controls were in fact more effective in policing prostitution than were criminal sanctions. State regulation in Germany, according to Barbara Yondorf, had reduced prostitution-related crime and venereal disease, and it had even increased state revenues (since prostitutes have to pay taxes).[42]

Those who felt that the state should not be directly involved in the business of prostitution found the Dutch system more appealing. There a zoning system existed in the major cities, but state intervention was minimal. Many of the distasteful aspects of regulation were absent. Women did not have to be publicly inscribed; the district did not have the sense of being cut off from the city; and since all policies were unofficial, the state was not acting as a manager or pimp in prostitution.

Harvard Law School dean James Vorenberg and his wife, Elizabeth, who had worked on the Vera Institute Diversionary Justice Program, visited the red-light districts of many European cities. They concluded that the Dutch response to prostitution was the most enlightened. It fit best with views of the American legal establishment: sexual relations were considered a private matter; public order and safety were the business of the state. Police concerned themselves with confining public solicitation to one area, and they maintained an informal record of who was in the business of prostitution.[43] The Vorenbergs characterized the red-light district in Amsterdam as a clean, well-lighted place, where three-story prostitution hotels existed side by side with family homes, shops, churches, and restaurants. The Vorenbergs noted that there was a long history of peaceful coexistence between residents and prostitutes in Amsterdam's red-light district. They set out to convince Americans that other systems were feasible; ironically, Holland's long tradition of toleration, rather than any specific policy, had created the country's more benevolent prostitution system.[44]

TRANSPLANTING EUROPEAN APPROACHES

Interviewed in a *Time* magazine article on prostitution, ACLU attorney David Goldberger also cited Amsterdam as an example of legalized prostitution that "really works." In the same article Florida prosecutor Leonard Glick warned that the Puritan heritage of Americans would never accept legalized prostitution.[45] Yet even in the heart of Puritanical Boston, as the 1977–78 survey reveals, not morality but anxiety over crime, property values, and pride in neighborhood were uppermost in the minds of city residents. When Boston police instituted an experimental zoning system in its prostitution section, known as the Combat Zone, the peaceful coexistence of residents, businesses, and prostitutes found in Amsterdam's red-light district was never realized.

The decision to create an adult entertainment zone in Boston did not represent a recognition of prostitution as a legitimate form of recreation or a means for women to earn their livelihood. Nor did local politicians consider the zone a permanent solution to the problems surrounding prostitution or a model for other cities. The idea was to contain prostitution in one corner of the city and to minimize its negative consequences on urban development. But in contrast to rationales for zoning prostitution in the past, politicians saw the zone as a first step toward banning prostitution from the rest of the city altogether. Their long-term scenario had prostitution moving to neighboring cities with less to lose economically.[46]

A logical site for the district was chosen. A prostitution trade already existed in the area, and police and politicians regarded it as blighted and rundown, not viable for economic development. Equally important, the contiguous residents, the Chinese, had little political clout. But policy makers did not foresee the building boom that would come to downtown Boston in the 1970s, making the area more attractive to investors. Nor did they realize that prostitutes from all over the country would be attracted to an area of tolerated prostitution. The murder of a Harvard football star during an incident in the zone ignited a municipal campaign against clubs in the Combat Zone, but business lobbies had already laid the groundwork for its dismantling.[47]

The Boston experience highlights the difficulty of importing European approaches. Prostitution policy cannot be decided on a community-by-community basis, since cities with legal prostitution would be overrun by prostitutes from other areas. Furthermore, the violence and crime that have evolved in prostitution culture in the United States would not necessarily disappear were prostitution legalized or classified as "adult entertainment." Last, urban development and the gentrification of downtown areas in many American cities have set in motion a rethinking of the ecology of prostitution among reform-minded policy makers: Should prostitution be concentrated in one section, dispersed throughout the city, or allowed to exist in cities at all?

The Nevada experience offers another lesson in what happens when European systems are transplanted directly to American soil. In 1971 the Nevada state legislature passed a local option law that enabled any counties with a population of less than 200,000 to license, tax, or prohibit brothels in cities and towns. Four rural counties legalized prostitution. One finds some of the worst features of legalized prostitution in the Nevada system. Prostitutes are isolated in remote areas, and they are subject to all kinds of infringements on their personal liberties.

In Lyon county, for example, brothels must be located in uninhabited areas at least five miles from a city, town, mobile home park, or where people generally reside. A local sheriff can limit the work hours, days of business, number of prostitutes in a house, and size of the building. Other ordinances restrict prostitutes' activity outside the brothel. They are often confined to certain sections of town and permitted out only at certain times of day. One municipality prevents prostitutes from leaving brothels on Sundays. This town limits when prostitutes can shop and the establishments they can frequent. Although prostitution is defined as legal entertainment and perceived by residents to be a local business, prostitutes are pariahs in these communities, an untouchable caste kept apart from the institutions and daily life of the "permanent" residents. Even the language used to describe prostitutes in the legal codes ("inmates") underscores their marginal status.[48]

Thus legalized prostitution does not in itself necessarily result in the integration of prostitutes into communities or the acceptance of prostitutes as service workers. When the state becomes a manager of prostitution, the stigma and isolation of prostitutes can become even greater. This was the message of nineteenth-century abolition, and it is still relevant to present-day American prostitution policy. The Nevada case, as well as proposals for local-option prostitution laws, supports this view. The local-option proposals seek to place prostitution in remote areas outside large cities and thus, as with the isolated ranches in Nevada, the goal is to limit the social and geographical spaces prostitutes inhabit, rather than to allow prostitutes greater freedom to pursue their trade. The policy debates on the 1986 New York Bar Association's local-option proposal are revealing. Essentially they viewed the licensing proposal as a means of limiting prostitution to areas where it least affected residences and businesses and of providing law enforcers with more control, with less expense and greater efficiency than in the past. Although that initiative died after pressure from feminists and activist prostitutes, a group of businessmen in Portland, Oregon—the Portland City Club—began lobbying city officials for a similar law. Their proposed legislation went even further in abridging prostitutes' civil rights: it had a provision for the mandatory testing of prostitutes for AIDS.[49]

Prostitute unions, feminists, and civil libertarians have all found the Nevada system an unattractive alternative. Yet neither prostitute activists nor legal experts have abandoned their interest in promoting European-style approaches.

REEVALUATING THE EUROPEAN PROSTITUTION EXPERIENCE

A changing prostitution economy in Europe has led to the reevaluation of regulatory policies. In Berlin, for example, a policy of unofficial toleration has been in effect since World War II.[50] According to Rose-Marie Giesen, author of a recent study, prostitution has become tougher and more brutal. Over the past decade more prostitutes have been on the street and most have been working full time. Pimping has become increasingly dominated by immigrant groups from countries where prostitution is highly organized. Giesen maintains that it has become almost impossible for a woman to be an independent prostitute.[51]

In Dutch cities, the peaceful coexistence between prostitutes and neighborhood residents has begun to erode. Behind the lace curtains and postcard views of prostitutes reading and knitting in the windows of Amsterdam's red-light district are the invisible hands of a highly organized and tightly controlled sex commerce industry. By the time the Vorenbergs made their tour, these changes had already begun. Drugs have had a major impact. The spread of heroin increased street prostitution; prostitutes high on drugs often conducted business in forbidden areas. More juveniles joined the ranks of prostitutes. Many heroin dealers have bought houses in the prostitution centers in Dutch cities, which may be an indication of a permanent transformation in sex commerce.[52]

Prostitution had been accepted in working class neighborhoods in Dutch cities because it was low-key, small-scale, and run by locals. In Rotterdam, police ended a long tradition of tolerating prostitution after a series of violent incidents between pimps and families living in the red-light district. According to one report, the sex industry expanded dramatically in the 1970s; sex clubs began staying open twenty-four hours a day. Pimps did not care about maintaining good contacts in the neighborhood. When local residents complained about the nuisance of the prostitution trade, pimps retaliated by shooting at some of the leaders of the protest. At one point local authorities were considering a floating brothel district in the waterways around the city, but the idea found little support among prostitutes or the general public.[53]

The Amsterdam city council, which has considered legalizing all prostitution businesses, is currently in a quandary over the growing street prostitution trade. One hotly contested issue is what to do about neighborhood protests. Should street prostitution be moved to other neighborhoods, dispersed over several streets, or eliminated altogether (the position taken by Amsterdam's mayor)? In fact, the mayor's view captures the ambivalence of the Dutch authorities: he maintains that prostitution must be accepted as a normal profession and prostitutes not stigmatized; yet he insists that other considerations—such as order and property values—be taken into account. These considerations, however, undermine the very idea of prostitution as a "normal profession."[54]

Despite pressures from prostitutes' rights groups, police and other authorities continue to pay more attention to neighborhood residents' demands for removing prostitutes from the streets, especially in areas undergoing renovation and gentrification. Moreover, the links to drugs and organized crime, particularly in the street prostitution trade, reveal the difficulty of implementing prostitutes' rights proposals that seek to treat prostitution as a service profession or a licensed trade.

These tensions surrounding prostitution policy in Holland underscore the importance of understanding the organization of the prostitution economy in a particular society before implementing a change in regulatory policy. It is essential to consider the management of prostitutes' labor as well as the ways in which women enter and leave prostitution. This caveat is highly relevant to the prostitutes' rights movement, which has aimed its struggle at the policy makers at the top, while ignoring managers and businesses.

IDEOLOGICAL CROSSCURRENTS IN EUROPE

At present two ideological crosscurrents dominate the prostitution discourse in Europe. One advocates the greater integration of prostitution into a legitimate business enterprise and work environment. I call this the Dutch model because Holland is its ideological center. The other favors repression against sex commerce as a business enterprise and offers social work remedies for prostitutes. I call this approach the Swedish model because it has been most influential there.[55] Underlying these two positions is a radically different sexual politics.

Holland is the home of the movement to promote a legitimate prostitution work culture. In 1985 Amsterdam was the host city for an international meeting of prostitutes' rights groups, informally called the "whores' congress." Despite its small membership, the Red Thread, the Dutch prostitute union, has received a great deal of media attention and has had an impact on prostitution debates. Many feminists have actively supported the Red Thread's demands for recognition as legitimate professionals.[56]

Prostitutes' rights groups also have had strong advocates in parliament and in local city councils. The Dutch government has become more receptive to the proposal that all laws against the business of prostitution be repealed. The stated objective of such legislation would be to allow prostitutes to make contracts with their employers, something they cannot do if the activity is illegal. A proposed change in the Dutch criminal code would nullify an earlier statute against promoting prostitution and pimping, replacing it with one that would prosecute only those cases in which a person has been coerced or "deluded" into prostitution and brings the complaint herself.[57]

Much of the prostitutes' rights activism in Holland can be traced to the de Graaf Stichting Society in Amsterdam, a quasi-governmental agency partially funded by the Ministry of Culture, Recreation, and Social Work. The society functioned until the late 1960s as a shelter for prostitutes wanting to leave the trade. It has now taken on the role of an advocacy group for "emancipation of the prostitute." This means, according to the director, John Visser, removing prejudice against prostitution in general and providing prostitutes with the same protections and benefits as all Dutch workers have, that is, pensions, health insurance, and so on.[58]

The proposed reforms do not address these grass-roots issues, however. The proposed criminal code reform protects the rights of pimps and managers in sex commerce to operate freely, rather than addressing prostitutes' rights per se. Prostitutes' rights groups, such as the de Graaf Stichting and the Red Thread, maintain that legalizing prostitution businesses will make it easier for prostitutes to make contractual agreements with their employers and will thus improve their working conditions.

Yet these policy initiatives come at a time when sex commerce is becoming more organized, and when there have been more documented cases of coercion in Holland, particularly among the substantial immigrant prostitute population. Defenders of the law that would legalize pimping and brothelkeeping argue that the revised code actually punishes more severely those who "delude" or "coerce" women into prostitution. They neglect to mention, however, that it places the burden on the prostitute to make the complaint against her exploiter. For immigrant women, the fear not only of reprisals from pimps but also of deportation will inhibit such complaints.[59] The elimination of laws against promoting prostitution thus allows the state to sidestep the more disturbing issue of what free choice means in prostitution, especially in the sociopsychologically dependent relationship between pimp and prostitute.

The Dutch movement to emancipate the prostitute takes for granted certain premises regarding gender roles and the empowerment of women. It assumes that women's economic and social dependence will ensure a continual supply of prostitutes who are managed by pimps. Furthermore, its advocates argue that the demand for prostitution will never disappear and that the best course is to give it legitimacy and institutional support. Beyond these ideological underpinnings, it is also important to place Dutch prostitution politics within a larger socioeconomic context: among Western industrialized nations, the Netherlands has the lowest level of female participation in the labor force, and Holland also has one of the highest overall unemployment rates in Europe.

Emancipation of the prostitute has a totally different meaning in Swedish society. Architects of Swedish prostitution policy in the 1980s have concluded that to turn prostitution into a legitimate business and to give prostitutes the status of workers would not emancipate prostitutes but would merely allow prostitution's managers to extend their control over the market. During the mid-1970s a Swedish government commission recommended legislation—similiar to the proposed Dutch reform—that would have removed from the criminal code all existing laws against pimping and promoting prostitution. But their rationale was different. They assumed that sex for hire would inevitably disappear in a sexually liberated society. Their predictions were not borne out, and in 1977 another government commission concluded that this liberal sexual climate had actually increased the supply, demand, and number of businesses in prostitution. One Swedish criminologist compared the marketing of prostitution to the selling of soft drinks: both were commodities for which demand could be created and expanded.[60]

Much of the impetus behind prostitution reform in Sweden has come from those who work closely with prostitutes in halfway houses or as counselors in government-funded programs. Swedish prostitution policy rests on a foundation of generous state investment in social programs. Some well-funded municipal programs, which have been able to provide money for prostitutes to start new lives, have helped reduce prostitution in Swedish cities. But in an era of scarce state subsidies and demands for other social services, such programs are now in jeopardy; it is therefore difficult to predict the future of prostitution reform.[61]

Underlying prostitution politics in Sweden is a core ideology, based on the assumption that sexual and social inequality produce prostitution and that inequality is rooted in economic and social institutions that can be changed. Although most Swedes in prostitution reform see this goal as visionary, it is nonetheless a goal. As I have described earlier, Swedish feminists have asserted that an institutionalized system of prostitution would work not only against economic and social change for women but also against their goal of emancipating men.[62]

Prostitution reform groups in Holland and Sweden have been able to link their campaigns to cultural traditions and political ideologies, and consequently they have achieved a certain degree of consensus. In Sweden, prostitution politics could be translated into state intervention to protect the weaker party, a longstanding position of the Swedish welfare state. Also, Swedish policy initiatives regarding social problems in the private sphere have provided a context for the discussion of sexual exploitation. In Holland, support for legitimizing prostitution could be placed alongside a laissez faire policy toward family relations and private life as well as a liberal tradition toward sexuality and pornography.

At first glance, the arguments for legitimacy and integration put forth by the de Graaf Stichting and prostitute unions may seem more likely to gain acceptance than do long-term programs to eliminate prostitution by restructuring class and gender systems. But perhaps it is no less visionary to assume that by some sleight of hand the age-old prejudice and disdain for the woman who sells sex will disappear. To completely integrate prostitution into mainstream social and economic life would require a radical transformation in the way society views sexual relations, women, and the poor. Those advocating legitimacy expect people to cast aside romantic images of sex and love and to view sexuality totally instrumentally—with a price set for different sexual functions. Both the free love movement of the 1960s and the reaction against it in the 1970s held a mystique about sexual expression. In fact, rather than decreasing romantic expectations of sexual love, the sexual permissiveness of our era has increased them. Equally relevant to prostitution reform is the contemporary feminist movement, which has generated a new set of expectations about what is possible for women. Consequently, institutionalized prostitution appears to be a step backward to an earlier era of women's dependence and submissiveness. Acceptance of prostitution implies a deep cynicism over women's chances for empowerment in economic and social life.

Conclusion

In the United States, present policies toward prostitution seem far removed from emancipation of the prostitute in either the Dutch or Swedish sense. Rather than worrying about prostitutes' rights or protection, lawmakers in American cities voice concern about the rights and protection of taxpayers and property owners. The boom in urban development over the last few years has resulted in campaigns against street-walking in business districts and tougher penalties against prostitutes. But these campaigns have not cut down on the prostitution trade; instead, prostitutes have moved into new neighborhoods or dispersed throughout the city.

After numerous legal challenges, scientific investigations, and public discussion, prostitution policy remains at an impasse. Among the various reform groups are completely divergent interpretations of the most fundamental issues: Is prostitution a matter of sexual privacy and free speech? Or is prostitution sexual domination and exploitation? Does prostitution exist because of sociobiology or because of the social construction of sex roles? Is prostitution a product of a patriarchal system or of a capitalist one?

These competing views cut across the ideological fault line in the United States between equal rights (equality of opportunity) and social rights (equality of results). Thus legalized prostitution appears as a form of institutional inequality, yet the social and economic measures that might reduce prostitution are not enacted. The line has fractured social life into public and private domains so that selling sexual services on the street is a criminal offense but acting in a pornographic film or viewing sex acts in a movie theater or on home video is not. Finally, it has placed those who profit from prostitution indirectly—owners of places of prostitution (hotels or clubs), publishers of newspapers that run ads for prostitution, and so forth—as outside the boundaries of crime and those who solicit or pimp as within them.

The prospect that some consensus on prostitution reform can be found seems more remote as various reform groups construct a world of dualisms: between sexual pleasure and sexual danger, between economic exploitation and sexual domination, between public and private spheres, between sexual freedom and protection from sexual abuse. Yet the long, complex history of prostitution policy offers the strongest argument for the need to create a synthesis in the dialectic of rights and protections.[63] Prostitution reform movements over the last hundred and fifty years have assumed that women needed protection from male aggression; however, policies based on protection led to greater intrusion and control of women's sex lives instead of to the punishment of exploitative men. Because protective strategies have resulted in a denial of women's sexual rights, there is a tendency among prostitution reform groups to brush aside the violence and coercion in prostitution and pornography. The Progressive reform portrait of the prostitute as woman enslaved was simplistic, but the present-day representation of prostitutes as women entrepreneurs is equally naive.

The image of the prostitute as working woman, featured in films, books, and television and radio talk shows of the 1980s seeks to demystify prostitution—to strip away the glamour and sensationalism. Prostitution appears as a work option for women who would otherwise be trapped in the welfare system or stuck in the lowest paying jobs. Some of the most recent portraits of prostitutes in films such as *Chicken Ranch,* or *Working Girls,* present prostitution not as a positive career choice but as routinized, isolating, and alienated labor. These images represent a conscious attempt to repudiate the portrayal of prostitutes as outcast women, deviant actors, and criminal types prevalent in the popular literature and scientific journals of the last century and a half. To view prostitutes as working women is an indictment of the hypocrisy in a society that charges with a criminal offense prostitutes in a multimillion dollar, visible industry. But these images of prostitution also reveal a retreat from an era of social justice campaigns that sought through economic and social programs to remove the sources of prostitution. Moreover, to characterize prostitution as work is to sever the prostitution exchange from sexuality.

A society that institutionalizes prostitution as a work option for the poor makes a statement about its position on inequality. One can see this in the policy toward prostitution in countries like Korea, and until recently, the Philippines. There governments have sought to legitimize prostitution as work and even elevated it to a patriotic endeavor, since sex commerce has brought in foreign tourism and reduced the national debt. Recent American policy initiatives for legalized prostitution in zoned, isolated districts of cities suggest more a return to the nineteenth-century ghettoization of prostitutes than a step toward the integration of prostitutes into mainstream social and economic life. They reveal the dangers of treating prostitution as a narrow, single-issue campaign. Remedies for prostitution need to be linked to social policy reforms around poverty, unemployment, and child welfare; more specifically, the growing feminization of poverty—as a result of divorces and nonmarital pregnancies—needs to be addressed. Changing the course of prostitution history will require beginning with a recognition that prostitution is not a private contract between consenting adults but an issue that is intrinsically bound up with long-term agendas for social and sexual equality.

NOTES

Introduction

1. Sue Gronewold, *Beautiful Merchandise: Prostitution in China, 1860–1936* (New York, 1982); Mary E. Perry, "Lost Women in Early Modern Seville: The Politics of Prostitution," *Signs,* 4 (Feb. 1978), 195–213; and Philip F. Riley, "Women and Police in Louis XIV's Paris," *Eighteenth-Century Life,* 4 (1979), 37–42.

2. I am using a general definition of gender in this book which assumes that gender relations are based upon perceived differences between the sexes and are structured through institutions and power representations. Joan Scott's view of the reciprocal nature of gender and society is highly relevant to my work: she asserts that "politics construct gender and gender constructs politics." See Joan W. Scott, "Gender: A Useful Category of Historical Analysis," *American Historical Review,* 91 (Dec. 1986), 1053–75.

3. Recent examples include Bernard Cohen, *Deviant Street Networks: Prostitution in New York City* (Lexington, Mass., 1980); and Eleanor F. Miller, *Street Women* (Philadelphia, 1986).

4. St. Louis in the mid-nineteenth century briefly experimented with regulated prostitution: see John C. Burham, "Medical Inspection of Prostitutes in America in the Nineteenth Century: The St. Louis Experiment and Its Sequel," *Bulletin of the History of Medicine,* 45 (May 1971), 203–18.

Chapter 1

1. Josiah Quincy, *A Municipal History of the Town and City of Boston during Two Centuries from September 17, 1630 to September 17, 1830* (Boston, 1852), p. 103; *Massachusetts Special Laws,* 5 (1814–22), 1821, chap. 110, sec. 14. Arrests of prostitutes calculated from Suffolk County, Mass., Police Court Docket, 1822–23.

2. Walter Muir Whitehill, *Boston: A Topographical History,* 2d ed. (Cambridge, Mass., 1968), chap. 4; Peter R. Knights, *The Plain People of Boston, 1830–1860: A Study in Growth* (New York, 1971); Oscar Handlin, *Boston's Immigrants: A Study in Acculturation* (Cambridge, Mass., 1959), chap. 1; Robert A. McCaughey, "From Town to City: Boston in the 1820's," *Political Science Quarterly,* 88 (June 1973), 191–214.

3. "To the Selectmen of the Town of Boston," April 4, 1820, Petition by West End residents, quoted in William Jenks's diary, Aug. 1, 1820, Jenks Family Collections, Massachusetts Historical Society, Boston.

4. Edward H. Savage, *Recollections of a Boston Police Officer: Boston by Daylight and Gaslight* (Boston, 1865), p. 57.

5. Manuscript census of Boston, 1820, and manuscript tax registers, 1820, both in the Boston Public Library.

6. *A Brief Account of the Boston Female Society for Missionary Purposes . . . with Extracts from the Reports of Reverend James Davis and Reverend Dudley Rossetter* (Boston, 1818), p. 8.

7. Quincy's third mayoral address was reprinted in *Bowen's Newsletter,* Jan. 7, 1826, p. 31; see also April 8, 1826, and June 17, 1826.

8. William Collier, "Report of Ministerial Labors," in The Society for Religious Purposes, Annual Report of 1820, p. 36; and West End petition "To the Selectmen."

9. "The Subcommittee Appointed to Make Enquiry Respecting the Necessity of Establishing a Penitentiary in this Town," (Boston, n.d.), n.p.

10. Eli Faber, "The Evil That Men Do: Crime and Justice in Colonial Massachusetts" (Ph.D. diss., Columbia University, 1974), pp. 73–74.

11. Carl Bridenbaugh, *Cities in the Wilderness: The First Century of Urban Life in America, 1625–1742* (New York, 1955), pp. 388–89. Douglas Greenberg gives evidence for the same trend in eighteenth-century New York: *Crime and Law Enforcement in the Colony of New York 1691–1776* (Ithaca, N.Y., 1976), pp. 142–45.

12. Horatio Woodman, *Report of Criminal Cases Tried before the Municipal Court of the City of Boston before Peter Oxenbridge Thatcher, Judge of the Court from 1823–1843* (Boston, 1845), pp. 8–13. *Commonwealth v. Sosa,* Police Court Docket, 1827. The case is summarized in William E. Nelson, *Americanization of the Common Law: The Impact of Legal Change on Massachusetts Society, 1760–1830* (Cambridge, Mass., 1975), p. 90.

13. Douglas L. Jones, "Poverty and Vagabondage: The Process of Survival in Eighteenth-Century Massachusetts," *New England Historical and Genealogical Register,* 133 (Oct. 1979), pp. 249–54; and Jones, "Female Vagabonds in Eighteenth-Century Massachusetts" (Paper presented at the Conference on Women in the Era of the American Revolution, Washington, D.C., July 25, 1975).

14. Josiah Quincy, *Remarks on Some of the Provisions of the Laws of Massachusetts Affecting Poverty, Vice and Crime; Being from General Topics of a Charge to Grand Jury of the County of Suffolk in March Term, 1822* (Cambridge, Mass., 1822), p. 4. Two reports on pauperism: Boston Committee on Pauperism, *Report of the Committee on the Subject of Pauperism and a House of Industry in the Town of Boston, March 1821* in "Report of the Committee on Pauper Laws of this Commonwealth, Massachusetts General Court, 1821," in *Poverty U.S.A.: The Historical Record,* ed. David J. Rothman (New York, 1971). See also Redmond Barnett, "From Philanthropy to Reform: Poverty, Drunkenness, and Social Order in Massachusetts" (Ph.D. diss., Harvard University, 1973), chap. 2.

15. *Miscellaneous Remarks on the Police of Boston; as Respects, Paupers; Alms and Work House; Classes of Poor and Beggars; Laws Respecting Them; Charitable Societies; Foreign and Domestic Missionary Societies; Evils of the Justiciary, Imprisonment for Debt, Remedies* (Boston, 1814), pp. 4, 5, 30–32.

16. Prosecution cases reported in and rates computed from Suffolk County municipal and police court dockets; *Commonwealth v. Gilmore* and other cases from the 1822 Boston Police Court Docket.

17. *Acts and Resolves Passed by the Massachusetts Legislature in the Year 1787,* chap. 54, sec. 2; *1821,* chap. 109, sec. 2.

18. "Report of the Committee Appointed by the Board of Guardians of the Poor of the City and Districts of Philadelphia to Visit the Cities of Baltimore, New York, Providence, Boston, and Salem" (Philadelphia, 1827), in *Poverty U.S.A.,* p. 19.

Notes

19. U. R. Q. Henriques, "Bastardy and the New Poor Law," *Past and Present*, 37 (July 1978), 105–14.

20. *Brief Account*, p. 24. Social backgrounds of these reformers are traced in Barnett, "Philanthropy," pp. 260–61. Female Missionary Society officers were married to men from the same class of new entrepreneurs: Barbara M. Hobson, "Sex in the Marketplace: Prostitution in the American City, Boston, 1820–1880" (Ph.D. diss., Boston University, 1981), p. 139. See also "Annual Report," Boston Society for the Religious and Moral Instruction of the Poor (Boston, 1819).

21. Patrick Colquhoun, *A Treatise on the Police of the Metropolis* (London, 1798), p. x; E. P. Thompson, *The Making of the English Working Class* (New York, 1966), p. 56. See also David Sugarman, "The Criminal Law as an Instrument of Class Politics in Nineteenth-Century England" (Paper presented at the International Conference on the History of Crime and Criminal Justice, College Park, Md., Sept. 4–7, 1980).

22. Collier, "Report of Ministerial Labors," pp. 26–27.

23. No newspaper coverage of the event exists. The account is taken from Jenks's diary. See June 23, 1820; Sept. 18 and 23, 1820; and Oct. 11, 1820.

24. For accounts of the Beehive Riot, see Savage, *Recollections*, pp. 107–16; *Boston Courier*, July 28, 1825 and Aug. 15, 1825; and *Columbian Centennial*, July 30, 1825.

25. Occupations of the rioters were traced in the Boston city directories, 1820–26. They were as follows: two victualers, one cooper, one mariner, one laborer, one miner, two truckmen, one blacksmith, one housewright, one merchant.

26. Woodman, *Municipal Court Cases*, p. 119.

27. *Bowen's Newsletter*, Jan. 28, 1826.

28. Summaries of the riots can be found in these sources: for Portland, *American Violence: A Documentary History*, ed. Richard Hofstadter and Michael Wallace (New York, 1970), pp. 441–50; for Cincinnati, *Friend of Virtue*, 5 (Nov. 1, 1842), 324; for St. Louis, John C. Schneider, "Riot and Reaction in St. Louis, 1854–56," *Missouri Historical Review*, 68 (Jan. 1974), 171–85; and for Minneapolis, Paul Lucas, "Congregationalism in Minnesota, 1850–1900," *Minnesota History*, 44 (Summer 1974), 62.

29. Richard Tansey, "Prostitution and Politics in Antebellum New Orleans," *Southern Studies*, 18 (Winter 1979), 457–59.

30. Marion S. Goldman, *Gold Diggers and Silver Miners: Prostitution and Social Life in the Comstock Lode* (Ann Arbor, Mich., 1981); Jaqueline B. Barnhart, "Working Women: Prostitution in San Francisco from the Gold Rush to 1900" (Ph.D. diss., University of California, Santa Cruz, 1976), pp. 70, 75.

31. Christine Stansell distinguished the working class view of prostitution from middle class attitudes. She makes the point that a woman's turning to prostitution meant a loss to the family economy, but one cannot ignore the sense of shame that set this family misfortune apart from other misfortunes among the working poor; see *City of Women: Sex and Class in New York, 1789–1860* (New York, 1986), pp. 178–79.

Chapter 2

1. Some of the best known in the last decades are Vern L. Bullough, *The History of Prostitution* (New York, 1964); Harry Benjamin and R. E. L. Masters, *Prostitution and Morality* (New York, 1964); and John F. Decker, *Prostitution, Regulation, and Control* (New York, 1979).

2. For France, see Jill Harsin, *Policing Prostitution in Nineteenth-Century France* (Princeton, N.J., 1986); for Italy, see Mary Gibson, *Prostitution and the State in Italy, 1860–1915* (New Brunswick, N.J., 1986); and for England, see Judith R. Walkowitz, *Prostitution in Victorian Society: Women, Class, and the State* (Cambridge, 1980).

3. Alain Corbin, "Commercial Sexuality in Nineteenth-Century France: A System of Images and Regulations," *Representations,* 14 (Spring 1986), 215–16.

4. *Directory to Seraglios in New York, Philadelphia, Boston, and All Principal Cities in the Union* (New York, 1859); and "Pomp, Pandemonium, and Paramours," *Register of the Kentucky Historical Society,* 81 (Summer 1983), 274–86.

5. David H. Flaherty, "Law and Enforcement of Morals in Early America," *Perspectives in American History,* 5 (1971), 203–53; and William E. Nelson, *The Americanization of the Common Law: The Impact of Legal Change on Massachusetts Society* (Cambridge, Mass., 1975), chaps. 3, 4.

6. *Boston Daily Bee,* Dec. 2, 1845, p. 4.

7. *Massachusetts Revised Statutes,* 1836, chap. 130, sec. 4 (lewdness); chap. 143, secs. 5, 6 (nightwalking). The same statutes still apply: *Annotated Laws of Massachusetts,* chap. 272, sec. 53.

8. Thomas Clyde Mackey, "Red Lights Out: A Legal History of Prostitution, Disorderly Houses, and Vice Districts, 1870–1917" (Ph.D. diss., Rice University, 1984), pp. 30–31; and G. W. Mueller, *Legal Regulation of Sexual Conduct* (New York, 1968), p. 49.

9. Thomas E. James, *Prostitution and the Law* (London, 1951). Walkowitz maintains that solicitation was not illegal and that a constable's authority over streetwalkers was minimal: *Prostitution in Victorian Society,* p. 14.

10. William Lloyd Garrison, "Abominations of the Theater," *Friend of Virtue,* 9 (Dec. 1846), 7.

11. Boston Police Court Dockets, 1826, 1830, 1840, and 1850.

12. Ibid., July 23, 1830.

13. Report of the Chief of Police, City Document 8 (1871), pp. 62–63.

14. Boston Police Court Docket, 1830; an account of the raid can be found in *Friend of Virtue,* 4 (Sept. 1842), 271.

15. Cited in Mackey, "Red Lights Out," p. 41.

16. Joel Best, "Keeping the Peace in St. Paul: Crime, Vice, and Police Work, 1869–74," *Minnesota History,* 47 (Spring 1980), 244–45.

17. David C. Humphrey, "Prostitution and Public Policy in Austin, Texas, 1870–1915," *Southwestern Historical Quarterly,* 96 (Apr. 1983), 500–501.

18. The class/race bias in policing prostitution is documented in Richard Symanski, *The Immoral Landscape: Female Prostitution in Western Societies* (Toronto, 1981); and Bernard Cohen, *Deviant Street Networks: Prostitution in New York City* (Lexington, Mass., 1980).

19. Brenda E. Pillors, "The Criminality of Prostitution in the United States: The Case of San Francisco, 1854–1919" (Ph.D. diss., University of California, Berkeley, 1984), pp. 113–14; Richard Tansey, "Prostitution and Politics in Antebellum New Orleans," *Southern Studies,* 18 (Winter 1979), 474–75.

20. The conviction rates are computed from data gathered from the Boston Police Court Dockets, 1822–50.

21. *Boston Daily Bee,* Nov. 6, 1845, p. 2.

22. Ibid.

23. Peter R. Knights, *The Plain People of Boston, 1830–1860: A Study in Growth* (New

Notes

York, 1971), chaps. 2, 4; and Oscar Handlin, *Boston's Immigrants: A Study in Acculturation,* rev. ed. (Cambridge, Mass., 1959), chaps. 3–5.

24. *Friend of Virtue,* 8 (Dec. 1845), 360–62.

25. Josiah Quincy, *A Municipal History of the Town and City of Boston during Two Centuries from September 17, 1630 to September 17, 1830* (Boston, 1852), p. 380.

26. *Acts and Resolves of the Massachusetts Legislature Passed in the Year 1852,* chap. 322; and Michael B. Katz, *The Irony of Early School Reform: Educational Innovation in Mid-Nineteenth-Century Massachusetts* (Cambridge, Mass., 1968), pp. 12–13.

27. For a summary of ordinances passed, see Address of the Mayor to the City Council of Boston, City Document 1 (1848), p. 7.

28. Commitments for brothelkeeping rose from 34 per 100,000 between 1835 and 1846 to 54 per 100,000 between 1847 and 1854. Christine Stansell found that commitments to jails quadrupled during this period (1849–60) in New York City. She maintains many were prostitution cases: "Women of the Laboring Poor in New York City, 1820–1860" (Ph.D. diss., Yale University, 1980), p. 191.

29. Report of the Chief of Police, City Document 4, (1852), pp. 12–13.

30. Edward H. Savage, *Recollections of a Boston Police Officer: Boston by Daylight and Gaslight* (Boston, 1865), pp. 257–62; *Boston Daily Times,* Apr. 23–25, 1851; *Boston Daily Atlas,* Apr. 25, 1851.

31. Address of the Mayor (1848), p. 7.

32. A series of court cases during the 1850s and 1860s emerged as a result of this changing view of the brothel. See, for example, *Commonwealth v. Kimball, Gray,* 7 (1856), 330; *Commonwealth v. Edward Gannett, Massachusetts Reports,* 83 (1851), 7–8; and *Commonwealth v. Lambert, Massachusetts Reports,* 94 (1866), 77–79.

33. *Massachusetts Acts and Resolves,* 1855, chap. 405, secs. 1, 4; and Report of the Chief of Police, City Document 5 (1851), p. 20. The 1851 attorney general's report listed three cases of letting a house for a brothel; it also showed one case of letting furniture to a brothel; Attorney General's Report, Massachusetts House Document 72 (1851), p. 17; in 1856, one year after the statute was passed, there were four cases in municipal court of letting houses for brothels: Attorney General's Report, Massachusetts House Document 70 (1856), p. 22.

34. Report of the Chief of Police, 1866, 1869, 1870; *Directory to Seraglios,* pp. 17–18.

35. Statistics on the racial and ethnic background of keepers were derived from statistical analysis of the Boston House of Correction and House of Industry registers, 1858–65.

36. *Massachusetts Acts and Resolves,* 1855, chap. 405, sec. 1; Report of the Chief of Police, City Document 5 (1851), p. 20; see also Mackey, "Red Lights Out," pp. 99–132, for summary of the case law on public nuisance and brothelkeeping.

37. Report of the Chief of Police, 1866, 1869, 1870.

38. "Boston By-Ways to Hell, A Visit to the Dens of North Street" (Boston, 1867), pp. 4–5; and Benjamin O. Flower, *Civilization's Inferno* (Boston, 1893).

39. Report of the Chief of Police, City Document 9 (1862), p. 29.

40. Prostitution case statistics were derived from my sample of Boston Municipal Court cases, 1870–90; Eric C. Schneider, "In the Web of Class: Youth, Class, and Culture in Boston, 1840–1940" (Ph.D. diss., Boston University, 1980), p. 14; Report of the Chief of Police, 1866, 1869, 1870.

41. Boston Municipal Court Dockets, 1873–93, sample data. The rise in unresolved cases is documented in Michael S. Hindus, Theodore M. Hammett, and Barbara M.

Hobson, *The Files of the Massachusetts Superior Court, 1859–1959: A Plan for Action* (Boston, 1979). Massachusetts has a trial *de novo* system, which grants defendants unconditional appeal rights.

42. Joel Best, "Careers in Brothel Prostitution: St. Paul, 1865–1883," *Journal of Interdisciplinary History,* 22 (Spring 1982), 597–619.

43. James L. Wunsch, "Prostitution Policy: From Regulation to Suppression, 1858–1920" (Ph.D. diss., University of Chicago, 1976); and Tansey, "Prostitution and Politics."

Chapter 3

1. Nancy F. Cott, *The Bonds of Womanhood: "Woman's Sphere" in New England, 1780–1835* (New Haven, 1977), pp. 197–206; and Barbara Welter, "The Cult of True Womanhood, 1820–1860," *American Quarterly,* 28 (Summer 1966), 150–74.

2. *Friend of Virtue,* 4 (March 1841), 93.

3. Donald Scott, *From Office to Profession: The New England Ministry, 1750–1850* (Philadelphia, 1978), pp. 54–57, 113–39.

4. See, for example, *Friend of Virtue,* 10 (July 1847), 212; 7 (Aug. 1844), 188; 3 (Dec. 1840), 360–63. See also *Illuminator,* Mar. 30, 1836, p. 86.

5. *McDowall's Journal,* 2 (1834), 3.

6. *Illuminator,* Nov. 23, 1836, p. 91.

7. For other examples of female moral reform activism, see Carroll Smith-Rosenberg, "Beauty, the Beast, and the Militant Woman: A Case Study in Sex Roles and Social Stress in Jacksonian America," in her *Disorderly Conduct: Visions of Gender in Victorian America* (New York, 1985), pp. 109–28; and Mary P. Ryan, "The Power of Women's Networks: A Case Study of Moral Reform in Antebellum America," *Feminist Studies,* 5 (Spring 1979), 66–86.

8. Aileen Kraditor, *Means and Ends in American Abolitionism: Garrison and His Critics on Strategy and Tactics, 1834–1850* (New York, 1969); Marlou Belyea, "Hesitant Reformers" (unpublished paper, 1975). Nancy A. Hewitt underscores the differences within women's activism in this era: *Women's Activism and Social Change: Rochester, New York, 1822–72* (Ithaca, N.Y., 1987).

9. "Soliloquy of the Libertine," *Friend of Virtue,* 7 (Oct. 1844), 305.

10. Ibid.

11. Ibid., 10 (November 1847), 321–23.

12. " 'Susan Miller,' A Story by F. G. A., A Lowell Operative," in *Root of Bitterness: Documents of the Social History of American Women,* ed. Nancy F. Cott (New York, 1972); and Lucy Larcom, *A New England Girlhood Outlined from Memory* (Boston, 1889), p. 200.

13. *Friend of Virtue,* 2 (Sept. 1839), 251–52.

14. Ibid., 1 (Nov. 1838), 175; 10 (Jan. 1847), 244.

15. Some corroborating evidence can be found in Janet Golden, "From Breasts to Bottle: The End of Wet Nursing in Boston, 1867–1927" (Ph.D. diss., Boston University, 1983). See also John R. Gillis, "Servants, Sexual Relations and the Risks of Illegitimacy in London, 1801–1900," in *Sex and Class in Women's History,* ed. Judith L. Newton, Mary P. Ryan, and Judith R. Walkowitz (London, 1983), pp. 114–45; and Judith R. Walkowitz, *Prostitution and Victorian Society: Women, Class, and the State* (Cambridge, 1980), p. 17.

16. Daniel Scott Smith and Michael S. Hindus, "Pre-Marital Pregnancy in America:

Notes

An Overview and Interpretation," *Journal of Interdisciplinary History*, 5 (1975), 531–71. Smith admits in a later article that no data for American cities exists comparable to the European: Daniel Scott Smith, "The Long Cycle in American Illegitimacy and Prenuptial Pregnancy," in *Bastardy and Its Comparative History*, ed. Peter Laslett, Karla Oosterveen, and Richard M. Smith (London, 1980), p. 370.

17. Maris A. Vinovskis, "An Epidemic of Adolescent Pregnancy? Some Historical Considerations," *Journal of Family History*, 1 (1981), 205–30; see also Joan Brumberg's study " 'Ruined' Girls: Changing Community Responses to Illegitimacy in Upstate New York, 1890–1920," *Journal of Social History*, 18 (Winter 1984), 247–72.

18. Alice Kessler-Harris, *Out to Work: A History of Wage-Earning Women in the United States* (New York, 1982), pp. 34–39.

19. *State v. Martin Peters*, Massachusetts Supreme Judicial Court, summarized in the *Boston Daily Mail*, Dec. 17, 1845, p. 2. See also Linda Gordon, *Woman's Body, Woman's Right: A Social History of Birth Control in America* (New York, 1977).

20. Christopher Smout, "Aspects of Sexual Behavior in Nineteenth-Century Scotland," in *Bastardy and Its Comparative History*, p. 215; and Margareta R. Matović, "The Stockholm Marriage: Extra-Legal Family Formation in Stockholm, 1860–1890," *Continuity and Change*, 1 (1986), 385–413.

21. Lemuel Shattuck, *Report to the Committee of the City Council Appointed to Obtain the Census of Boston for the Year 1845* (Boston, 1846), p. 45.

22. *Friend of Virtue*, 9 (Sept. 1846), 259–60.

23. *Friend of Virtue*, 3 (Dec. 1840), 262–63; 10 (May 1847), 158–59; 4 (Mar. 1841), 65–66; (July 1841), 336; 9 (Sept. 1846), 259–60.

24. Deposition of Mary Clark of Boston taken at the jail, Aug. 14, 1863, *Commonwealth v. Fanny Moore*, Files of the Superior Court, Suffolk County, Mass.

25. Ibid.

26. *Friend of Virtue*, 4 (Nov. 1841), 331; 9 (June 1846), 171; 10 (July 1847), 198–99.

27. Carol Lasser, "Mistress, Maid, and Market: The Transformation of Domestic Service in New England, 1790–1820" (Ph.D. diss., Harvard University, 1981), p. 12; and William W. Sanger, *History of Prostitution: Its Extent, Causes, and Effects throughout the World* (New York, 1858), pp. 517–18.

28. *Friend of Virtue*, 9 (May 1846), 157; 7 (Apr. 1844), 121–22.

29. Thomas Dublin, "Women, Work and the Family Economy: Textiles and Palm Leaf Hatmaking in New England, 1830–1850," *Tocqueville Review*, 5 (Fall/Winter 1983), 279–316; and Kessler-Harris, *Out to Work*, pp. 48–51.

30. *Friend of Virtue*, 9 (September 1846), 259–60; and *Prisoner's Friend*, 1 (August 1849), 253.

31. Faye E. Dudden, *Serving Women: Household Service in Nineteenth Century America* (Scranton, Pa., 1983), pp. 12–43; Lasser, "Mistress, Maid, and Market," chap. 1; and *Friend of Virtue*, 2 (Mar. 1839), 49.

32. Lasser, "Mistress, Maid, and Market," chap. 3.

33. *Friend of Virtue*, 5 (Jan. 1842), 25.

34. *Address of the Mayor in the City of Boston*, City Document 1 (1848), pp. 12–13.

35. The major civil actions in this area were seduction, loss of consortium, or breach of promise to marry; see Michael S. Hindus, Theodore M. Hammett, and Barbara M. Hobson, *The Files of the Massachusetts Superior Court, 1859–1959* (Boston, 1979), pp. 172–84.

36. An Act to Punish Seduction, Massachusetts House Document 26 (1845).

37. *Acts and Resolves of the Massachusetts Legislature Passed in the Year 1845*, chap. 216.

38. *Commonwealth v. Cook, Massachusetts Reports,* 53 (1847), 93–103.

39. The Pennsylvania state legislature passed a seduction law in 1853, but Marcia Carlisle maintains that this kind of remedy was used by the middle class, not the working class. "Prostitutes and Their Reformers in Nineteenth-Century Philadelphia" (Ph.D. diss., Rutgers University, 1982).

40. *Friend of Virtue,* 34 (Jan. 1872); 36 (July 1876).

41. Lyle H. Wright, *American Fiction, 1774–1850: A Contribution toward a Bibliography,* 2d rev. ed. (San Marino, Cal., 1969), pp. 52–57; and Margaret Wyman, "The Rise of the Fallen Woman," *American Quarterly,* 3 (Summer 1951), 167–77.

42. Charles Loring Brace, *The Dangerous Classes of New York and Twenty Years' Work among Them* (1872; reprint, New York, 1964), pp. 117–18; and Mrs. Mulock [Dinah Marie Craik], *Woman's Thought upon Women* (London, 1858), p. 297.

43. *The Journal of Richard Henry Dana Jr.,* ed. Robert F. Lucid, vol. 1 (Cambridge, Mass., 1968), pp. 76–83; quotation on p. 80.

44. Edward H. Savage, *Boston by Daylight and Gaslight: Recollections of a Boston Police Officer* (Boston, 1865), pp. 171–78; quotation on p. 174.

45. The facts of this case appear in Barbara M. Hobson, "A Murder in the Moral and Religious City of Boston," *Boston Bar Journal,* 22 (Nov. 1978), 9–21.

46. *The Life and Death of Mrs. Maria Bickford, A Beautiful Female, Who Was Inhumanely Murdered in the Moral and Religious City of Boston* (Boston, 1846).

47. The Amelia Norman case is summarized in the *Friend of Virtue,* 7 (Mar. 1844), 75–79 (reprint from the *Boston Courier*).

48. Lynn Weiner, *From Working Girl to Working Mother: The Female Labor Force in the United States, 1820–1980* (Chapel Hill, N.C., 1985), pp. 51–61.

Chapter 4

1. William Tait, *Magdalenism: An Enquiry into the Extent, Causes, and Consequences of Prostitution in Edinburgh* (Edinburgh, 1842), pp. 190–96.

2. The references throughout to Boston and Philadelphia prostitutes are derived from statistical analysis of the Boston House of Correction and House of Industry Registers, a data set of 1,165 cases coded for the years 1858–65; and the Philadelphia City Hospital Register of Prostitutes, 1861–63. The Philadelphia data was gathered in 1976 by Janet Glass of Bryn Mawr College.

3. William W. Sanger's statistics on age in *The History of Prostitution: Its Extent, Causes, and Effects throughout the World* (1858; reprint, New York, 1974), p. 484; Alexandre Jean-Baptiste Parent-Duchatelet's findings in *De la prostitution dans la ville de Paris (Prostitution in Paris)* (Paris, 1836); Mary Gibson offers some of the strongest evidence for the age-specific character of prostitutes using nineteenth-century Italian data: *Prostitution and the State in Italy* (New Brunswick, N.J., 1986), p. 107; see also Judith Walkowitz's pioneer study of prostitution in Britain: *Prostitution and Victorian Society: Women, Class, and the State* (Cambridge, 1980). For Dutch prostitution, see F. A. Stemvers, *Meisjes van plezier de geschiedenis van de prostitutie in Nederland* (Utrecht, 1985).

4. Christine Stansell, *City of Women: Sex and Class in New York, 1789–1860* (New York, 1986), pp. 185–87.

5. Jennifer James, "Mobility as an Adaptive Strategy," *Urban Anthropology,* 4 (1975), 349–64.

Notes

6. Marion S. Goldman, *Gold Diggers and Silver Miners: Prostitution and Social Life in the Comstock Lode* (Ann Arbor, Mich., 1981); and Joel Best, "Careers in Brothel Prostitution: St. Paul, 1865–1883," *Journal of Interdisciplinary History*, 12 (Spring 1982), 611–12; Walkowitz, *Prostitution in Victorian Society*, pp. 193–96; and Gibson, *Prostitution and the State in Italy*, pp. 160–63, 179.

7. Gunilla Johansson, "Prostituerade kvinnor i Stockholm under reglementationsperioden 1859–1918" (dissertation in progress; hereafter cited as "Stockholm Prostitutes"); and Gibson, *Prostitution and the State in Italy*, p. 113.

8. Joel Best, "Keeping the Peace in St. Paul: Crime, Vice, and Police Work, 1869–74," *Minnesota History*, 47 (Spring 1980), 244–45; and Brenda E. Pillors, "The Criminality of Prostitution in the United States: The Case of San Francisco, 1854–1919" (Ph.D. diss., University of California, Berkeley, 1984), pp. 92–98.

9. Sanger, *History of Prostitution*, p. 476; and Hasia R. Diner, *Erin's Daughters in America: Irish Immigrant Women in the Nineteenth Century* (Baltimore, 1983).

10. Sanger, *History of Prostitution*, pp. 255, 259; sample data gathered from Boston Municipal Court Probation Files, 1813–23.

11. U.S. Census Abstract, Eighth Census (1860), 508. See also Maris A. Vinovskis, *Education and Social Change in Nineteenth-Century Massachusetts* (New York, 1980), tables A 2.5, A 5.7.

12. On the importance of family networks for jobs, see Thomas Dublin, *Women and Work: The Transformation of Work and Community in Lowell, Massachusetts, 1826–1860* (New York, 1979).

13. Sanger, *History of Prostitution*, pp. 461, 465–67.

14. The subject of the status of the artisan in New England is treated in depth in Gary Kornblith, "From Artisans to Businessmen: Master Mechanics in New England, 1799–1850" (Ph.D. diss., Princeton University, 1982).

15. Sanger, *History of Prostitution*, p. 456; Gibson, *Prostitution and the State in Italy*, p. 126; Walkowitz, *Prostitution in Victorian Society*, pp. 16–17; and Duchatelet, *Prostitution in Paris*, p. 107. Peter Uhlenberg estimates the strong chance of being orphaned in the nineteenth century: "Changing Configurations of the Life Course," in *The Family and the Life Course in Historical Perspective*, ed. Tamara K. Hareven (New York, 1978), pp. 78–79.

16. Matthew Carey, *Letters on the Condition of the Poor* (Philadelphia, 1835). Michael Katz documents the grave consequences for working class families from the loss of the major breadwinner: *The People of Hamilton, Canada West: Family and Class in a Mid-Nineteenth Century City* (Cambridge, Mass., 1975), chaps. 1, 2.

17. Sanger, *History of Prostitution*, p. 460.

18. Ibid., p. 467.

19. The best overviews for these changes in women's work outside the home during the first half of the nineteenth century can be found in Carol Lasser, "Mistress, Maid, and Market: The Transformation of Domestic Service in New England, 1790–1870" (Ph.D. diss., Harvard University, 1981), pp. 80–84.; Alice Kessler-Harris, *Out to Work: A History of Wage-Earning Women in the United States* (New York, 1982), chap. 2; and Stansell, *City of Women*, pp. 106–14.

20. Lucy Larcom, *A New England Girlhood Outlined from Memory* (Boston, 1889); and Harriet Hanson Robinson, *Loom and Spindle, or, Life among the Early Mill Girls* (New York, 1898).

21. Dublin, *Women and Work*, pp. 192–93; and Ava Baron, "Women and the Making

of the American Working Class: A Study of Proletarianization of Printers," *The Review of Radical Political Economics*, 4 (Fall 1982), 23–42.

22. Stansell, *City of Women,* p. 227; see also Clyde Griffen and Sally Griffen, *Natives and Newcomers: The Ordering of Opportunity in Mid-Nineteenth Century Poughkeepsie* (Cambridge, Mass., 1978); and Carol Turbin, "Reconceptualizing Family, Work, and Labor Organizing: Working Women in Troy, 1860–1890," *Review of Radical Political Economics,* 16 (1984), 1–16.

23. For estimates of women in the labor force, see W. Elliot Brownlee and Mary M. Brownlee, *Women in the American Economy: A Documentary History, 1675–1925* (New Haven, 1976), p. 3.

24. David M. Katzman, *Seven Days a Week: Women and Domestic Service in Industrializing America* (New York, 1978), calculates yearly average wages of domestics and factory workers; see table A-23 (from the Massachusetts Bureau of Labor Statistics), p. 313. See also his figures on the low unemployment rates of domestic servants, table A-24, p. 314.

25. Lucy M. Salmon, *Domestic Service* (1897; reprint, New York, 1972), pp. 98–103

26. Lasser, "Mistress, Maid, and Market," p. 166.

27. Kessler-Harris, *Out to Work,* p. 135; and Lori Rosenbery, "The Wayward Worker: Toronto's Prostitute at the Turn of the Century," in *Women and Work: Ontario, 1850–1930,* ed. Janice Acton, Penny Goldsmith, and Bonnie Shepard (Toronto, 1974), p. 39.

28. Carroll D. Wright, *The Working Girls of Boston,* from the 15th Annual Report of the Massachusetts Bureau of Statistics of Labor for 1884 (reprint, Boston, 1889), pp. 124–25.

29. George J. Kneeland, *Commercialized Vice in New York City* (1913; reprint, Montclair, N. J., 1969), pp. 256–62.

30. Wright's figures (pp. 124–25) appear very high in contrast to the combined aggregate figures from seven cities (Boston, Chicago, Cincinnati, Louisville, New Orleans, Philadelphia, and San Francisco) surveying prostitutes in the 1884 census; 68 percent listed a former occupation: see Brownlee and Brownlee, *Women in the American Economy,* p. 195.

31. Kneeland has the most complete data on this: *Commercialized Vice,* pp. 249, 256, 262.

32. Mary K. Conyngton, "Relation between Occupation and Criminality of Women," U.S. Congress, Senate Document No. 645, 61st Congress, 2d Session (1911).

33. Jau Don Ball and Thomas Hayward, "A Sociological, Neurological, Seriological, and Psychiatric Study of a Group of Prostitutes," *American Journal of Insanity,* 74 (1918), 656–58.

34. Conyngton, "Occupation and Criminality," pp. 70–71.

35. Thomas Dublin, ed., *Farm to Factory: Women's Letters, 1830–1860* (New York, 1981); and Kessler-Harris, *Out to Work,* pp. 34–35.

36. Duchatelet, *Prostitution in Paris,* p. 100; and Sanger, *History of Prostitution,* p. 149.

37. Sanger, *History of Prostitution,* p. 488.

38. Ibid., pp. 491–92.

39. Henry Mayhew, *London Labour and the London Poor: Cyclopedia of the Condition and Earnings of Those That Will Not Work,* vol. 3 (London, 1862), pp. 210–11.

40. Sanger, *History of Prostitution,* p. 488. Duchatelet, *Prostitution in Paris,* p. 107.

41. See Johansson, "Stockholm Prostitutes," chap. 4; Walkowitz, *Prostitution and Victorian Society,* pp. 17–18; and Vice Commission of Philadelphia, "Report on Existing Conditions" (Philadelphia, 1913), p. 92.

Notes

42. Johansson, "Stockholm Prostitutes"; Duchatelet, *Prostitution in Paris,* p. 79; and Sanger, *History of Prostitution,* p. 477.

43. Jennifer James, *Juvenile Female Prostitution: Final Report* (Seattle, 1979); and Mimi H. Silbert and Ayala M. Pines, "Entrance into Prostitution," *Youth and Society,* 13 (June 1982).

44. Sanger, *History of Prostitution,* p. 529.

45. Edward J. Bristow, *Prostitution and Prejudice: The Jewish Fight against White Slavery* (New York, 1983), pp. 148–49.

46. Barbara Heyl, *The Madame as Entrepreneur* (New Brunswick, N.J., 1979).

47. Eleanor F. Miller, *Deviant Street Women* (Philadelphia, 1986).

48. These figures were derived from data gathered by Gunilla Johansson; see her "Stockholm Prostitutes."

49. *The G'hals of Boston, or Pen and Pencil Sketches of Celebrated Courtezans by One of Em* (Boston, 1850), pp. 18–23. Though embellished, these portraits seem to contain accurate details and real addresses of Boston Brothels. Several of the names appeared in John Augustus's papers, Harvard Law School Archives.

50. Both accounts are in *The G'hals of Boston,* pp. 35–38.

51. William Acton, *Prostitution Considered in Its Moral, Social & Sanitary Aspects, in London and Other Large Cities, with Proposals for the Mitigation and Prevention of Its Attendant Evils* (1857; reprint, New York, 1968), pp. 59, 72–73.

52. Charles Washburn, *Come into My Parlor: A Biography of the Aristocratic Everleigh Sisters of Chicago* (New York, 1936); and Nell Kimball, *Autobiography by Herself,* ed. Stephen Longstreet (New York, 1970).

53. Best, "Careers in Brothel Prostitution," 617.

54. Joan Hori, "Japanese Prostitution in Hawaii during the Immigration Period," *Hawaiian Journal of History,* 15 (1981), 113–23; and Lucie Cheng Hirata, "Free, Indentured, Enslaved: Chinese Prostitutes in Nineteenth-Century America," *Signs,* 5 (Autumn 1979), 3–29.

Chapter 5

1. Francis Lieber, Introduction to *On the Penitentiary System in the United States, and Its Application in France,* by Gustave de Beaumont and Alexis de Tocqueville (Philadelphia, 1833), pp. xiv–xvi; quotation, p. xv.

2. Ibid., p. xv.

3. *Friend of Virtue,* 9 (May 1846), 146.

4. William Acton, *Prostitution Considered in Its Moral, Social & Sanitary Aspects, in London and Other Large Cities, with Proposals for the Mitigation and Prevention of Its Attendant Evils* (1857; reprint, New York, 1968), p. 119.

5. Joseph Tuckerman, *A Letter Addressed to the Hon. Harrison Gray Otis, the Mayor of Boston, Respecting the House of Correction and the Common Jail in Boston* (Boston, 1830), pp. 14, 15, 17.

6. Michel Foucault, *The History of Sexuality,* trans. Robert Hurley, vol. 1 (New York, 1980), p. 55.

7. For a recent discussion of this paradox, see Thomas Laquer, "Organism, Generation,

and the Politics of Reproductive Biology," *Representations,* 14 (Spring 1986), 30–31; see also John S. Haller and Robin M. Haller, *The Physician and Sexuality in Victorian America* (Urbana, Ill., 1974).

8. Bram Stoker, *Dracula* (1897; reprint, New York, 1965).

9. Enoch C. Wines and Theodore W. Dwight, *Report on the Prisons and Reformatories in the United States and Canada* (New York, 1867), p. 327.

10. See Elizabeth Fee, "The Sexual Politics of Victorian Anthropology," in *Clio's Consciousness Raised: New Perspectives on the History of Women,* ed. Mary Hartman and Lois W. Banner (New York, 1974), pp. 86–102.

11. Mary Poovey, "Scenes of an 'Indelicate Character': The Medical Treatment of Victorian Women," *Representations,* 14 (Spring 1986), 145; and Charles Rosenberg and Carroll Smith-Rosenberg, "The Female Animal: Medical and Biological Views of Woman and Her Role in Nineteenth-Century America," *Journal of American History,* 60 (Sept. 1973), 332–56.

12. Linda Gordon, *Woman's Body, Woman's Right: A Social History of Birth Control in America* (New York, 1976); Nancy F. Cott, "Passionlessness: An Interpretation of Victorian Sexual Ideology, 1790–1850," *Signs* (1978), 219–36.

13. Elizabeth Blackwell is one of the most noteworthy among this group of doctors: see *Essays in Medical Sociology* (1902; reprint, New York, 1972), pp. 56, 61.

14. For an analysis of this terminology in recent prostitution debates, see Barbara Millman, "New Rules for the Oldest Profession: Should We Change Our Prostitution Laws?" *Harvard Women's Law Journal,* 3 (Spring 1980), 9–11.

15. "Report of the Committee Appointed to Investigate Alleged Abuses in the House of Reformation and the House of Correction," City Document 35 (1864), p. 16.

16. "Report of Inspectors of the House of Reformation," City Document 6 (1840), pp. 8–9.

17. Ibid.

18. See the testimony of Judge Russell of Boston Police Court in support of a reformatory for girls: Massachusetts House Document 20 (1856), p. 39; and Police Chief Tukey's appeal to the state legislature in *Friend of Virtue,* 12 (July 1849), 200.

19. Stanley Nash, "Prostitution and Charity: The Magdalen Hospital. A Case Study," *Journal of Social History,* 17 (Summer 1984), 617.

20. *A Short Account of the Penitent Females' Refuge in the City of Boston* (Boston, 1834); and *Annual Report of the Directors of the Penitent Females' Refuge* (Boston, 1830).

21. Penitent Females' Refuge Inmates Register, New England Home for Little Wanderers, Archives, Boston, Mass., 1822–45. I located sixteen women from the institution who were sent back to the House of Correction and House of Industry.

22. Minutes of the Ladies Auxiliary Quarterly Meetings, February 22, 1835, New England Home for Little Wanderers, Archives, Boston, Mass. *Annual Report of The Directors of the Penitent Females' Refuge* (Boston, 1835).

23. Steven Ruggles, "Fallen Women: The Inmates of the Magdalen Society Asylum of Philadelphia, 1836–1908," *Journal of Social History,* 16 (Summer 1983), 67.

24. The reference to the Glasgow Lock Hospital appeared in *Friend of Virtue,* 30 (Aug. 1867), 249–50; William Blackmore, *Moonlight Cruises: A Brief Sketch of the Establishment and Operations for the Female Temporary Home for the Higher Class* (London, 1854).

25. *Brief History of the Rise and Progress of The Penitent Females' Refuge Instituted January 12, 1825* (Boston, 1849), p. 14.

26. For numbers of women in the home, see Barbara M. Hobson, "Sex in the Marketplace: Prostitution in the City, Boston, 1820–1880" (Ph.D. diss., Boston University, 1981), p. 263.

27. *Friend of Virtue,* 29 (July 1866), 5; see also 10 (June 1847), 203; 27 (Feb. 1864), 58–59; and 28 (Sept. 1865), 280–81.

28. *Friend of Virtue,* 5 (Jan. 1842), 29.

29. The Dedham Asylum received $1,800 for the year 1867; the Temporary Home received $600: "Sixth Annual Report of the Board of State Charities," Public Document 17 (1869), p. 9.

30. Carroll Smith-Rosenberg, *Disorderly Conduct: Visions of Gender in Victorian America* (New York, 1985), pp. 173–75.

31. *Prisoner's Friend,* 3 (Jan. 1851), 228.

32. Barbara M. Brenzel, *Daughters of the State: A Social Portrait of the First Reform School for Girls in North America 1856–1905* (Cambridge, Mass., 1983), pp. 151–53; and Eric C. Schneider, "In the Web of Class: Youth, Class and Culture in Boston, 1840–1940" (Ph.D. diss., Boston University, 1980), pp. 217–28.

33. *Prisoner's Friend,* 2 (Apr. 1850), 340–42.

34. Estelle Freedman's study of women's prisons is the classic in this area: *Their Sisters' Keepers: Women's Prison Reform in America, 1830–1930* (Ann Arbor, Mich., 1978); see pp. 79–81 for inmate statistics.

35. I am grateful to Estelle Freedman for sharing the facts of this case with me.

36. "Reformatory Prison for Women," Massachusetts Commissions of Prisons Report, Public Document 13 (1881), p. 18.

37. Freedman interprets prison administrators' decision to stick to domestic training as both pragmatic and ideological: *Their Sisters' Keepers,* pp. 88–99.

38. A good example of the madam's role can be found in *Madeleine: An Autobiography* (New York, 1909), pp. 108–10.

39. Sue Davidson and Ruth Rosen, eds., *The Maimie Papers* (Boston, 1977), pp. 195–96, xxvi.

40. Eleanor F. Miller, *Deviant Street Women* (Philadelphia, 1986), pp. 45, 44–54.

41. Samuel G. Howe, *A Letter to J. H. Wilkins, H. B. Rogers, and F. B. Fay, Commissioners of Massachusetts for the State Reform School for Girls* (Boston, 1854), pp. 31, 21.

42. Freedman, *Their Sisters' Keepers,* pp. 207–8.

43. Schneider, "In the Web of Class," pp. 217–28.

44. Wines and Dwight, *Report on Prisons,* pp. 273–74; and "Sixth Annual Report of the Board of State Charities," Public Document 17 (1869), p. 28.

45. *Acts and Resolves of the Massachusetts Legislature Passed in the Year 1855,* chap. 69, sec. 1; Michigan statute appears in "Board of State Charities," p. 30.

46. The most developed theories of criminal types appear in Cesare Lombroso and William Ferraro, *The Female Offender* (New York, 1900); see also Peter L. Tyler, " 'Denied the Power to Choose the Good': Sexuality and Mental Defect in American Medical Practice, 1850–1920," *Journal of Social History,* 10 (June 1977), 472–89.

47. John Augustus, *A Report of the Labors of John Augustus for the Last Ten Years, in Aid of the Unfortunate* (Boston, 1852), tables, p. 41; names and addresses of those he posted bail for can be found in the archives of the Harvard Law Library, Cambridge, Mass.

48. Ibid., pp. 48–50. For a comparison of Augustus's methods with later institutionalized probation, see Barbara M. Hobson and Theodore M. Hammett, "The Transformation of American Criminal Courts: The Case of Massachusetts, 1890–1959" (Paper

presented at the International Conference on the History of Crime and Criminal Justice, College Park, Md., 1980), p. 5.

49. This general summary of probation emerged from my statistical analysis of probation records from the Boston courts, 1913–23; see also George E. Worthington and Ruth Topping, "Summary and Comparative Study of the Specialized Courts in Chicago, Philadelphia, Boston, and New York," *Journal of Social Hygiene*, 9 (June 1923), 348–66.

50. Probation Files, Boston Municipal Court, 1923.

51. Ibid., 1913.

52. Ibid.

53. Over 25 percent of sex delinquents in Philadelphia and Boston had probation extended: George E. Worthington and Ruth Topping, *Specialized Courts Dealing with Sex Delinquency* (New York, 1923), pp. 230–32.

54. "State Welfare Agencies," Miriam Van Waters Papers, Harvard Law School Survey of Crime and Criminal Justice in Boston, Harvard Law Library Archives, Cambridge, Mass.

55. Schneider, "In the Web of Class," p. 342.

56. Worthington and Topping, *Specialized Courts*, p. 156.

Chapter 6

1. Herbert D. Croly, *The Promise of American Life* (New York, 1909). See also two classic studies of these tendencies in Progressive reform: Samuel Haber, *Efficiency and Uplift: Scientific Management in the Progressive Era, 1890–1920* (Chicago, 1964); and David J. Rothman, *Conscience and Convenience: The Asylum and Its Alternatives in Progressive America* (Boston, 1980).

2. Howard B. Woolston, *Prostitution in the United States, Prior to the Entrance of the United States in the First World War* (1921; reprint, Montclair, N.J., 1969), p. 31; and Edward J. Bristow, *Prostitution and Prejudice: The Jewish Fight against White Slavery* (New York, 1983), p. 41.

3. Ruth Rosen, *The Lost Sisterhood: Prostitution in America, 1900–1918* (Baltimore, 1981); and Mark T. Connelly, *The Response to Prostitution in America* (Chapel Hill, N.C., 1980), pp. 8–9. See also Egal Feldman, "Prostitution, the Alien Woman and the Progressive Imagination," *American Quarterly*, 3 (Summer 1967), 192–206; and Richard Symanski, *The Immoral Landscape: Prostitution in Western Societies* (Toronto, 1981). Some exceptions to this position are: Roy Lubove, "The Progressive and the Prostitute," *The Historian*, 24 (1962); and Eric Anderson, "Prostitution and Social Justice, Chicago, 1915," *Social Service Review*, 48 (June 1974), 203–28.

4. Margaratha Jarvinsen, "Prostitution in Finland—Accepted or Condemned?" (M.A. thesis, University of Helsinki, 1984); and *Prostitution beskrivining analys* (Stockholm, 1981).

5. Studies of organized crime in this period provide the most convincing arguments for these changes: David R. Johnson, *Policing the Urban Underworld: The Impact of Crime on the Development of the American Police, 1880–1887* (Philadelphia, 1979), pp. 116–19; Mark H. Haller, "Organized Crime in Urban Society: Chicago in the Twentieth Century," *Journal of Social History*, 8 (Winter 1971–72), 210–34; and Bristow, *Prostitution and Prejudice*.

Notes

6. A complete description of the case appears in Michael Pearson, *The Age of Consent: Victorian Prostitution and Its Enemies* (London, 1972).

7. United States Immigration Service (USIS) reports, National Archives, box 52483, file 1b; box 52809, file 7, and box 52809, file 7e; ethnic backgrounds of prostitutes can be found in New York and Massachusetts reports: George J. Kneeland, *Commercialized Vice in New York City* (1913; reprint, Montclair, N.J., 1969), pp. 209–11; "Report of the Commission for the Investigation of the White Slave Traffic, So Called" (1913); reprinted in *Prostitution in America: Three Investigations* (New York, 1976), pp. 37–39. Court decision summarized in "Women Not Immune," *Washington Post*, Feb. 2, 1915; and Bristow, *Prostitution and Prejudice*, pp. 111–81.

8. Sue Gronewold, *Beautiful Merchandise: Prostitution in China, 1860–1936* (New York, 1982).

9. Lynn Weiner, *From Working Girl to Working Mother: The Female Labor Force in the United States, 1820–1980* (Chapel Hill, N.C., 1984); and Kathy Peiss, *Cheap Amusements: Working Women and Leisure in Turn-of-the-Century New York* (Philadelphia, 1986).

10. Sven-Axel Månsson, *Könshandelns profitörer* (Stockholm, 1981).

11. Flexner was told by European police that between 80 and 90 percent of prostitutes had pimps. *Prostitution in Europe* (New York, 1914), p. 32. See also Woolston, *Prostitution in the United States*, p. 83; and Stephen Longstreet, ed., *Nell Kimball: Her Life as an American Madam by Herself* (New York, 1970), pp. 232–33.

12. Kneeland, *Commercialized Vice*, pp. 88–89.

13. Maude E. Miner, *The Slavery of Prostitution: A Plea for Emancipation* (New York, 1916), p. 105.

14. Walter C. Reckless, *Vice in Chicago* (1933; reprint, Montclair, N.J., 1969), p. 43.

15. Bernard Cohen, *Deviant Street Networks: Prostitution in New York City* (Lexington, Mass., 1980).

16. Kneeland, *Commercialized Vice*, p. 6; USIS, box 52484, file 8b; and Bristow, *Prostitution and Prejudice*, pp. 139, 168–69, 207.

17. Reckless, *Vice in Chicago*, found this pattern in Chicago beginning the late twenties; see also Ivan S. Light, "The Ethnic Vice Industry, 1880–1944," *American Sociological Review*, 42 (1977), 469–75. On the dominance of immigrants in the vice trade during this period, see Haller, "Organized Crime," 216–19; and Johnson, *Policing the Urban Underworld*, pp. 116–19.

18. A summary of the Soviner brothers example appears in Bristow, *Prostitution and Prejudice*, p. 152; see also Daniel Bell, "Crime as an American Way of Life," *Antioch Review*, 13 (Summer 1953), 131–54.

19. Statistics on Chicago are found in Reckless, *Vice in Chicago*, pp. 260, 290; for New York, see Kneeland, *Commercialized Vice*, pp. 163–70; and for San Francisco, see Neil L. Shumsky, "The Municipal Clinic of San Francisco: A Study of Medical Structure," *Bulletin of the History of Medicine*, 52 (Winter 1978), 554.

20. E. R. A. Seligman, "The Social Evil of Prostitution," in *Prostitution in America: Three Investigations* (1902; reprint, New York, 1976), p. 245; and Harold Cross (a public health officer in San Francisco during the Progressive Era), *The Lust Market* (London, 1959), pp. 21–24.

21. John C. Burnham, "Medical Inspection of Prostitutes in America in the Nineteenth Century: The St. Louis Experiment and Its Sequel," *Bulletin of the History of Medicine*, 45 (May 1971), 203–18; and Thomas C. Mackey, "Red Lights Out: A Legal History of Prostitution, Disorderly Houses, and Vice Districts, 1870–1917" (Ph.D. diss., University of Texas, 1984), pp. 144–45, 160–73.

22. Woolston, *Prostitution in the United States,* pp. 27–31; and Shumsky, "Municipal Clinic," 555.

23. The law is summarized in Mackey, "Red Lights Out," p. 176; see legal challenges to the law, pp. 177–84.

24. The Houston case and community response appears in ibid., pp. 192–232.

25. Neil Shumsky, "Vice Responds to Reform," *Journal of Urban History,* 7 (Nov. 1980), 31–47; see also Shumsky, "Municipal Clinic."

26. The National Purity Crusade as chronicled in David J. Pivar, *Purity Crusade: Sexual Morality and Social Control, 1868–1900* (Westport, Conn., 1973); Mary Jo Buhle outlines the socialist movement's involvement with antiprostitution in *Women in American Socialism, 1870–1920* (Urbana, Ill., 1981), pp. 249–54; and see Anderson, "Prostitution and Social Justice," for a discussion of the social justice impulse in the movement.

27. Rosen, *Lost Sisterhood,* pp. 51–67.

28. Pivar, *Purity Crusade,* pp. 85, 137. See Paula Baker for an analysis of women's political culture in this era: "The Domestication of Politics: Women and American Political Society, 1780–1920," *American Historical Review,* 89 (June 1984), 625–47.

29. Antoinette Blackwell, "Immorality of the Regulation System," in *The National Purity Congress: Its Papers, Addresses and Portraits* (New York, 1896), pp. 25–26.

30. Ibid., p. 26.

31. This argument is made by Swedish health officer Anders Linblad's study *Prostituerade kvinnors levnadshistorier: reglementeringsutredningen* (Stockholm, 1910).

32. Pivar, *Purity Crusade,* pp. 85–88; and Burnham, "Medical Inspection of Prostitutes," pp. 207–9.

33. A series of exchanges appear in *Boston Surgical and Medical Journal,* July 11, 1895, pp. 29–31, 42–45. See also Connelly, *Response to Prostitution,* pp. 67–74.

34. Allan M. Brandt, *No Magic Bullet: A Social History of Venereal Disease in the United States since 1880* (New York, 1985), pp. 19–37.

35. Flexner, *Prostitution in Europe:* on the medical dangers, see 204–65; for statistical comparisons on disease control, see pp. 304–94.

36. Ibid., pp. 269–70.

37. Ibid., p. 284.

38. Jane Addams, *A New Conscience, and an Ancient Evil,* (New York, 1913), pp. 218–19.

39. Data from the Women's Education and Industrial Union survey of one hundred prostitutes in Boston, Women's Educational and Industrial Union Papers, the Schlesinger Library, box 8, file 62. For a discussion of the Women's Educational and Industrial Union's activities, see Buhle, *Women in American Socialism,* pp. 58–60.

40. James F. Gardiner, Jr., "Microbes and Morality: The Social Hygiene Crusade in New York City, 1892–1917" (Ph.D. diss., Indiana University, 1974), pp. 229–30.

41. "Investigation of the White Slave Traffic," p. 65.

42. Miner, *Slavery of Prostitution,* p. ix.

43. Joseph Mayer, *The Regulation of Commercialized Vice: Analysis of the Transition from Segregation to Repression in the United States* (New York, 1922), pp. 6–7; 45–46; New York Committee of Fourteen, *Annual Report* (New York, 1921), pp. 6–9. Massachusetts passed some of the most stringent laws: *Acts and Resolves of the Massachusetts Legislature Passed in the Year 1914,* chap. 624; and *Massachusetts Acts and Resolves,* 1910, chap. 424, sec. 5.

Notes

44. Quoted in James Marchant, *The Master Problem* (1917; reprint, New York, 1979), p. 8.

45. Reckless, *Vice in Chicago*, p. 13. Several scholars conclude that the main effect of antiprostitution was dispersal of prostitutes: Connelly, *Response to Prostitution*, pp. 26–27; Neil L. Shumsky and Larry M. Springer, "San Francisco Zone of Prostitution 1880–1934," *Journal of Historical Geography*, 7 (1981), 83–84; and Richard Symanski, *The Immoral Landscape: Prostitution in Western Societies* (Toronto, 1981).

46. Reckless, *Vice in Chicago*, pp. 95–97; 78–79. See also Haller, "Organized Crime in Urban Society," 212–13, 215.

47. Mark H. Haller, "Urban Crime and Criminal Justice: The Chicago Case," *Journal of American History*, 57 (Dec. 1970), 628–36; USIS, box 52484, file 15A; and Woolston, *Prostitution in the United States*, p. 207.

48. George E. Worthington, *Developments in Social Hygiene Legislation from 1917 to Sept. 1, 1920*, American Social Hygiene Association publication no. 313; and Miner, *Slavery of Prostitutes*, p. 126.

49. New York Committee of Fourteen, *Annual Report*, (New York, 1917), p. 47.

50. "Investigation of the White Slave Traffic," p. 61; New York Committee of Fourteen, *Annual Report* (New York, 1917), p. 47.

51. George E. Worthington and Ruth Topping, *Specialized Courts Dealing with Sex Delinquency: A Study of Procedures in Chicago, Boston, Philadelphia, and New York* (New York, 1925), p. 12; and "Investigation of the White Slave Traffic," p. 62.

52. George E. Worthington and Ruth Topping, "Summary and Comparative Study of the Specialized Courts in Chicago, Philadelphia, Boston, and New York, *Journal of Social Hygiene*, 9 (June 1923), 348–66.

53. Indeterminate sentencing was introduced for prostitute recidivists; see New York Committee of Fourteen, *Annual Report* (New York, 1921), pp. 6–9, 21–23. For statistics on sex discrimination, see Willoughby Cyrus Waterman, *Prostitution and Its Repression in New York City 1900–1931* (New York, 1932), pp. 73–75.

54. Symanski, *Immoral Landscape*, pp. 179–206; Connelly, *Response to Prostitution;* and Lisa Dugan, Nan Hunter, and Carole S. Vance, "False Premises: Feminist Anti-Pornography Legislation in the U.S.," in *Women against Censorship*, ed. Verda Burstyn (Vancouver, 1985).

55. A detailed account of the Swedish campaign and a comparison of the crusades can be found in Barbara M. Hobson, "The Politics of Class and Gender: Prostitution in Historical and Comparative Perspective" *Working Papers*, University of Tampere, Finland, 6 (1986), 1–22; and "Antiprostitution: Swedish and American Responses" (Bunting Institute Working Paper, Harvard University, 1983).

56. Taped interviews with experts on the Swedish government commission, Hanna Olsson, Sven Axel Månsson, Rita Liljeström, Anders Nelin, and Inga Artin. I am thankful to the Swedish Institute for supporting my research visit in Sweden during the summer of 1982.

57. Lavina L. Dock, *Hygiene and Morality: A Manual for Nurses and Others Giving an Outline of the Medical, Social, and Legal Aspects of Venereal Disease* (New York, 1910), p. 97.

58. Kathryn Kish Sklar, "Hull House in the 1890's: A Community of Women Reformers," *Signs*, 10 (Summer 1985), 658–77.

59. Ronnie Steinberg, *Wages and Hours in Twentieth-Century America* (New Brunswick, N.J., 1984).

60. Walter Lippmann, *Preface to Politics* (New York, 1913), p. 189.

61. Articles summarized in Waterman, *Prostitution and Repression,* pp. 61–62.

62. Agnes Maude Royden, *Downward Paths: An Inquiry into the Causes Which Contribute to the Making of the Prostitute* (London, 1916), pp. vii–xiii.

Chapter 7

1. Allan M. Brandt, *No Magic Bullet: A Social History of Venereal Disease in the United States since 1880* (New York, 1985), pp. 73, 76–77.

2. Estelle Freedman, *Their Sisters' Keepers: Women's Prison Reform in America, 1830–1930* (Ann Arbor, Mich., 1978); and Eric Monkkenon, *The Dangerous Class: Crime and Poverty in Columbus, Ohio, 1860–1885* (Cambridge, Mass., 1973), pp. 40–72.

3. No reliable estimates of the disease in the period exist, according to Brandt, *No Magic Bullet,* pp. 12–13; he cites the admission rate for new army recruits in 1909 as close to 200 per 1,000 men.

4. Local health departments carried out the war policy, but they were funded and regulated by a federal agency, the Interdepartmental Social Hygiene Board; see Mary M. Dietzler, *Detention Houses and Reformatories as Protective Social Agencies in the Campaign of the United States Government against Venereal Disease* (Washington, D.C., 1922), pp. 10–20.

5. Decisions of State Supreme Courts on the Subject of Venereal Disease Laws: National Archives, RG 90, file 273, pp. 6–7. I am indebted to Allan Brandt for giving me access to this material.

6. Court cases challenging incarceration and medical inspection without trial can be found in Ibid. pp. 1–9. The 1890 case of *Union Pacific Railway Company v. Botsford,* 141 U.S., p. 250, formed the basis for the *Roe v. Wade* abortion decision in 1973.

7. Linda Gordon, *Woman's Body, Woman's Right: A Social History of Birth Control in America* (New York, 1976); and David J. Pivar, *Purity Crusade: Sexual Morality and Social Control, 1868–1900* (Westport, Conn., 1973). Lawrence D. Longo and Christina M. Thomsen, "Prenatal Care and its Evolution in America," *Proceedings of the Second Motherhood Symposium of the Women's Studies Research Center,* University of Wisconsin, Apr. 9–10, 1981. I would like to thank Judy Leavitt for pointing out this reference to me.

8. *Survey,* Apr. 10, 1910, p. 179.

9. Ibid., May 28, 1910, p. 354.

10. Ibid., July 8, 1910, p. 596. For other discussions of the Page Law, see Brandt, *No Magic Bullet,* pp. 36–37; and James F. Gardiner, "Microbes and Morality: The Social Hygiene Crusade in New York City, 1892–1917" (Ph.D. diss., Indiana University, 1974), pp. 196–98.

11. Bushnell, "What's Going On," pp. 4–10. Ethel Sturges Dummer Papers (hereafter ESD Papers), the Schlesinger Library, Radcliffe College, Cambridge, Mass., A-127, box 24, file 380. For the British response, see David J. Pivar, "Cleansing the Nation: Prostitution, 1917–21," *Prologue,* 28 (Spring 1980), 34–36.

12. Brandt, *No Magic Bullet,* pp. 74–75.

13. Maude E. Miner, *The Slavery of Prostitution: A Plea for Emancipation* (New York, 1916), pp. 283, 290–91, 295.

14. Ethel S. Dummer, *Why I Think So: The Autobiography of a Hypothesis* (Chicago, 1937), pp. 80–82; "Steps on Path Leading to Interest in Securing Justice for the Prostitute

Notes

Arrested by Government Order during the War," ESD Papers, box 24, file 375. See Robert M. Mennel's biographical note on Ethel Dummer in *Biographical Dictionary of Social Welfare in America,* ed. Walter Trattnor (Westport, Conn., 1986), pp. 254–57.

15. ESD Papers, box 24, files 375, 377.

16. Ibid., box 24, file 378; and Dummer, *Why I Think So,* p. 82.

17. ESD Papers, box 24, file 379.

18. *Manual for Various Agents of the United States Interdepartmental Social Hygiene Board* (Washington, D.C., 1920), p. 21; Dietzler, *Detention Houses,* p. 33; and Dummer, *Why I Think So,* p. 104.

19. New York Vice Commission data showed the average age of prostitutes to be 23.5 years and age at first sex experience, 17.5; the mean age of women in the Interdepartmental Board of Social Hygiene statistics was 22.5 years and the age at which they had their first sexual experience, 16.4. In both reports the majority of chastity offenders had been employed in factory work, domestic work, and waitress work. Less than half were employed at the time of arrest. Case records of women detained during the war were calculated from *Manual for Various Agents,* tables VI, IX, XV, XVII. New York data appear in George J. Kneeland, *Commercialized Vice in New York City* (1913; reprint, Montclair, N.J., 1969), tables X, XIV, pp. 222, 226.

20. *Manual for Various Agents,* p. 25.

21. ESD Papers, box 24, file 381.

22. Dietzler, *Detention Houses.*

23. ESD Papers, box 24, file 379.

24. Ibid.; Martha P. Falconer, "The Part of the Reformatory Institution in the Elimination of Prostitution," *Social Hygiene,* 5 (Jan. 1919), 4.

25. ESD Papers, box 24, files 378, 380.

26. Ibid., box 26, file 402; and Dummer, *Why I Think So,* pp. 94–95.

27. *Fit to Fight* (Washington, D.C., 1918), pp. 4, 8; Gardiner, "Microbes and Morality," pp. 372–73; Brandt, *No Magic Bullet,* pp. 64–68, 110–11.

28. Brandt, *No Magic Bullet,* pp. 85–111, 92.

29. Misconduct Rule of the Bureau of Social Hygiene; the law giving immunity for servicemen in paternity suits: "An Act to Extend Protection to the Civil Rights of Members of Military and Naval Establishments," in ESD Papers, box 24, file 381.

30. ESD Papers, box 24, file 375.

31. Storey quoted in Dietzler, *Detention Houses,* p. 4; and Dummer, *Why I Think So,* p. 106.

32. ESD Papers, box 24, file 375; box 16, file 235; and Dummer, *Why I Think So,* p. 88.

33. Dummer, *Why I Think So,* p. 105–7; and ESD Papers, box 24, file 390.

34. The World War II debate on venereal disease control and prostitution appears in series of articles in one issue of *Federal Probation,* 7 (Apr.–June 1943); Brandt, *No Magic Bullet,* pp. 161–70.

Chapter 8

1. W. I. Thomas, *The Unadjusted Girl,* ed. Benjamin Nelson (1923; reprint, New York, 1967), pp. 230–31. For a discussion of popular images of the new woman in film, see Majorie Rosen, *Popcorn Venus: Women, Movies and the American Dream* (New York, 1973), pp. 59–67.

2. Linda Gordon and Ellen Dubois, "Seeking Ecstasy on the Battlefield: Danger and Pleasure in Nineteenth-Century Feminist Sexual Thought," *Feminist Studies,* 9 (Spring 1983), 7–27; and Barbara Epstein, "Family, Sexual Morality, and Popular Movements at the Turn of the Century in America," in *Powers of Desire: The Politics of Sexuality,* ed. Ann Snitow, Christine Stansell, and Sharon Thompson (New York, 1983), pp. 117–30.

3. Katharine B. Davis, *Factors in the Sex Lives of Twenty-Two Hundred Women* (New York, 1929). For an analysis of the letters Marie Stopes received from persons seeking sexual advice, see Ellen M. Holtzman, "Marriage, Sexuality, and Contraception in the British Middle Class: Correspondence of Marie Stopes" (Ph.D. diss., Rutgers University, 1982).

4. Paula Fass, *The Damned and the Beautiful: American Youth in the 1920s* (New York, 1977), pp. 363–75; and Ellen K. Trimberger, "Men and Modern Love: Greenwich Village, 1900–1925," in *Powers of Desire,* pp. 131–52.

5. While admitting that Freud's intellectual doctrines had more lasting influence, Paul A. Robinson argues that Ellis was the central figure: *The Modernization of Sex: Havelock Ellis, Alfred Kinsey, William Masters and Virginia Johnson* (New York, 1977), pp. 2–3, 10–11; see also Jeffrey Weeks, *Sex, Politics, and Society: The Regulation of Sexuality since 1800* (London, 1981), pp. 148–52.

6. Holtzman, "Marriage, Sexuality, and Contraception," p. 153; Weeks, *Sex, Politics, and Society,* pp. 165–210.

7. Wilfred Lay, *The Prostitute and the Mother Imagio* (New York, 1919), pp. 14–24. Ethel Dummer found this work, originally a conference paper, so intriguing that she paid for its printing and circulation.

8. Case studies, Harvard Law School Survey of Crime and Criminal Justice in Boston (hereafter HCS), Sheldon Glueck Papers, Harvard Law School Library.

9. Thomas, *Unadjusted Girl,* pp. 4–5, 118–22.

10. Marian E. Kenworthy, "The Logic of Delinquency," *Papers and Proceedings of The Americal Sociological Society,* 16 (Chicago, 1921), 17–19.

11. Dorothy Embry Cross, *A Behavior Study of Abraham Bernstein, A Psychopathic Personality in Search of Change, Security, and Recognition* (Chicago, 1924).

12. Case Studies, HCS. The case worker recommended she be segregated in an institution for psychopathic delinquents. Since no such institution existed in Massachusetts, she was sent to the house of correction.

13. Peter Tyler, "Denied the Power to Choose the Good: Sexuality and Mental Defect in the American Medical Practice, 1850–1920," *Journal of Social History,* 10 (June 1977), 472–89; and Charles Rosenberg, *No Other Gods* (Baltimore, 1978), pp. 25–54.

14. Statistics on feebleminded prostitutes in Massachusetts appear in "Report of the Commission for the Investigation of the White Slave Traffic, So Called" (Mass. House Document 2281), in *Prostitution in America: Three Investigations* (1913; reprint, New York, 1976).

15. "Mental Defect in a Southern State: Report of the Georgia Commission on Feeblemindedness," *Mental Hygiene,* 3 (Oct. 1919), 559. For an analysis of the ideology surrounding sterilization, see Rudolph J. Vecoli, "Sterilization: A Progressive Measure," *Wisconsin Magazine of History,* 43 (Spring 1960), 202.

16. Walter E. Fernald, "The Growth of Provisions for the Feebleminded in the United States," *Mental Hygiene,* 1 (1917), 34–59; see also Fernald, "Borderline Defectives," in ibid., 220.

17. Jerome Michael and Mortimer J. Adler, *The Report of a Survey Conducted for the*

Notes

Bureau of Social Hygiene under the Auspices of the School of Law of Columbia University (New York, 1932), pp. 137–40.

18. Bernard Glueck, *Some Mental Problems at Sing Sing,* Reprint of *Reports and Addresses of the National Conference on Social Work* (Pittsburgh, 1917), pp. 1–3; and "Mental Defect in a Southern State," p. 546.

19. The study was a part of an extensive study of all Massachusetts penal institutions and procedures, initiated by Roscoe Pound, at that time Dean of the Harvard Law School.

20. Discussion of the methods of the study appear in "Massachusetts Reformatory," HCS, pp. 3–4; for comparisons with women offenders in the jail population, see tables on pp. 3, 5, 8, 12–13.

21. Sheldon Glueck and Eleanor Glueck, *Five Hundred Delinquent Women* (Boston, 1934), p. 88.

22. Glueck claimed that no estimates of sexual unconventionality for the general female population in the socioeconomic class of these women were available. Statistics comparing sexual experiences, marriage, and domestic situations can be found in Glueck and Glueck, *Five Hundred Delinquent Women,* p. 91.

23. Ibid., p. 97.

24. Ibid., p. 355.

25. Ibid., pp. 226–34.

26. Ibid., p. 283; and "Massachusetts Reformatory," HCS, p. 30.

27. Probation studies, HCS, pp. 5–6. The incident referred to can be found in HCS, August 23, 1926, pp. 10–11.

28. Juvenile court survey, HCS, Miriam Van Waters Papers, pp. 183–84. Of 122 cases that came before the court investigators, only 12 were brought by parents or relatives. Ibid., pp. 26–30.

29. George E. Worthington and Ruth Topping, *Specialized Courts Dealing with Sex Delinquency* (New York, 1925), p. 241.

30. From a 10 percent sample of Boston Municipal Court Probation department for the years 1913 and 1923, I found that commitment to an institution was based more on number of offenses, age of delinquent, and most important, the willingness of husbands or fathers to oversee a female delinquent's behavior during probation.

31. There is a vast literature on psychological views of prostitution. Some of the most noteworthy are: on the frigidity of prostitutes, Helen Deutsch, *The Psychology of Women* (New York, 1945); and on prostitution as a defense against homosexuality, Frank S. Caprio, *Female Homosexuality* (New York, 1954). See also Harold Greenwald, *The Call Girl* (New York, 1958), case studies on pp. 31–90 and analysis on causes, pp. 94–98.

Chapter 9

1. William H. Masters and Virginia E. Johnson, *Human Sexual Response* (Boston, 1966); for a summary of sex literature of the period, see Meryl Altman, "Everything They Always Wanted You to Know: The Ideology of Popular Sex Literature," in *Pleasure and Danger,* ed. Carole S. Vance (Boston, 1984), pp. 115–30.

2. Gail Sheehy, "The Landlords of Hell's Bedroom," *New York,* Nov. 20, 1972, pp. 67–80; and Sheehy, *Hustling: Prostitution in Our Wide-Open Society* (New York, 1971).

3. A recent Supreme Court decision suggests a retreat from gay rights: *Bowers v. Hardwick,* 106 S.Ct. 2841 (1986).

4. Kathleen Barry, *Female Sexual Slavery* (New York, 1979), represents one end of the spectrum. The public stance on prostitution of Wages for Housework, which sees it as empowering women, is at the other end.

5. The American Civil Liberties Union takes the strict libertarian view: see Marilyn Haft, "Hustling for Rights," *Civil Liberties Review,* 1–2 (Winter 1974), 8–26; and ACLU, Board Minutes, March 5–6, 1977, policy no. 210. Other legal experts using civil libertarian arguments do not reject outright licensing or regulation: see John F. Decker, *Prostitution: Regulation and Control* (New York, 1979); and John Kaplan, "The Edward G. Donley Memorial Lecture: Non-Victim Crime and the Regulation of Prostitution," *West Virginia Law Quarterly Review,* 79 (1976–77), 597–605.

6. For a discussion of legal strategies in the 1970s, see Jacqueline Boles and Charlotte Tatro, "Legal and Extra-Legal Methods of Controlling Female Prostitution: A Cross-Cultural Comparison," *International Journal of Comparative and Applied Criminal Justice,* 2 (Spring 1978); and Nan Aaron, "Court Challenges and Legislative Approaches to Prostitution Laws" (paper presented at the ACLU Biennial Conference, Philadelphia, June 10–13, 1976.

7. *State of Louisiana v. Derall,* 302 So. 2d 909 (La. 1974); Anne M. Jennings, "The Victim as Criminal: A Consolidation of California's Prostitution Law," *California Law Review,* 64 (1976), 1281; and Aaron, "Court Challenges," p. 4.

8. Jennings, "Victim as Criminal," 1281.

9. *New York Times,* June 26, 1978, p. 1; *Boston Globe,* June 26, 1978, p. 2.

10. *Reimer v. Jensen,* 17 Crim. L. Rep. 2042 (Cal. 1975); and Jennings, "Victim as Criminal," 1241.

11. Catharine A. Mackinnon, "Feminism, Marxism, Method, and the State: Toward Feminist Jurisprudence," *Signs,* 8 (Summer 1983), 640–58; and Frances E. Olsen, "Statutory Rape: A Feminist Critique of Rights Analysis," *Texas Law Review,* 63 (Nov. 1984), 387–432.

12. Kate Millett, *The Prostitution Papers* (New York, 1971), p. 13.

13. Ruth Rosen and Sue Davidson, eds., *Maimie Papers* (Boston, 1977).

14. Dorothy Tennov, "Prostitution and the Enslavement of Women," *Women Speaking* (Apr.–June 1972), 10–12; and Millett, *Prostitution Papers,* pp. 15–16.

15. Claude Jaget, "Hookers in the House of the Lord"; and Margaret Valentina and Mavis Johnson, "On the Game and on the Move," both in *Prostitutes, Our Lives,* ed. Claude Jaget (Bristol, England, 1980).

16. Many pimps were said to be supportive of prostitutes forming unions: "Responses to Prostitution," 17th National Conference on Women and the Law, Chicago, March 20–23, 1986.

17. See *ASP Whoreganizer,* Apr. 1983 and July 1983. A good example of the campaigns against police attacks on prostitutes appears in *COYOTE Howls,* 4 (Autumn 1977), 1–4.

18. Margo St. James, "What's a Girl Like You . . .?" in *Prostitution, Our Lives,* p. 217; and Carol R. Silver, "What Price Prostitution?" *Barrister's Baliwick,* 8 (Feb. 1974), 1–4.

19. A critique on this direction in COYOTE appears in *Berkeley Barb,* Oct. 18–31, 1979.

20. See Haft, "Hustling"; and Jennifer James et al., *The Politics of Prostitution: Resources for Legal Change* (Seattle, 1977).

21. *Majority Report,* Aug. 6, 1976, pp. 1, 6.

Notes

22. *Boston Phoenix*, Dec. 16, 1975, p. 32.

23. Kingsley Davis, "Prostitution," in *Contemporary Social Problems: An Introduction to Sociology, Deviant Behavior, and Social Organization,* ed. Robert K. Merton and Robert A. Nesbit (1937; reprint, New York, 1961); and Harry Benjamin and R. E. L. Masters, *Prostitution and Morality* (New York, 1964), pp. 435–47.

24. Frances E. Olsen, "The Politics of Family Law," *Law & Inequality: A Journal of Theory and Practice,* 2 (Feb. 1984), 1–18; Olsen, "The Myth of State Intervention in the Family," *Michigan Journal of Law Reform,* 18 (Summer 1985), 835–64; see also Catherine A. Mackinnon, "Pornography, Civil Rights, and Speech," *Harvard Civil Liberties Review,* 30 (Winter 1985), 20–42.

25. Eileen McLeod, *Women Working: Prostitution Now* (London, 1982); and James et al., *Politics of Prostitution,* pp. 4–6.

26. James et al., *Politics of Prostitution,* p. 1.

27. Ibid., pp. 3, 5.

28. Rick Anderson, "Making Prostitution Legal Is a Tricky Business," *Seattle Post Intelligencer,* Jan. 9, 1972.

29. *National Organization for Women Policy Manual* (1982), pp. 5, 6, 100.

30. This was the theme of a meeting of prostitution reformers in Rotterdam in 1983: see *International Feminist Networking against Female Sexual Slavery: Report of Global Feminist Workshop to Organize against the Traffic in Women, Rotterdam, April 6–15, 1983* (New York, 1984).

31. "Hookers and Housewives Come Together," *COYOTE Howls,* 4 (Autumn 1977), 1. "Money for Prostitutes Is Money for Black Women," Margo St. James Papers, Manuscript collection, Schlesinger Library, Radcliffe College, Cambridge, Mass.; and McCleod, *Women Working,* p. 3. Not all prostitute activist groups have done so. PUMA, for example, retained its independence from other political groups: see "Responses to Prostitution."

32. *WHISPER,* 1 (Winter 1985–86), 1.

33. Arlene Carmen and Howard Moody, *Working Women: The Subterranean World of Street Prostitution* (New York, 1985), p. 80.

34. Taped interview with Sara Wynter, April 1986.

35. Mackinnon, "Pornography, Civil Rights, and Speech"; Andrea Dworkin, "Against the Male Flood: Censorship, Pornography and Equality," *Harvard Women's Law Journal,* 8 (1985), 1–29; Lisa Dugan, Nan Hunter, and Carole S. Vance, "False Premises: Feminist Anti-Pornography Legislation in the U.S.," *Women Against Censorship,* ed. Verda Burstyn (Vancouver, 1985); and Ann Snitow, "Retrenchment versus Transformation: The Politics of the Anti-Pornography Movement," in *Women Against Censorship,* pp. 107–20.

36. Taped interview with Gunilla Molloy, one of the organizers of the radical feminist Group Eight Collective, July 1982; *Prostitution som fond problem* (Conference Papers of the Trondheim Conference, April 10–11, 1985), ed. Trondheim Commune (Oslo, 1985). See also Rita Liljeström, *Erotiska Kriget* (Stockholm, 1981).

37. Taped interviews with Hanna Olsson and Rita Liljeström, July 1982.

38. "A Case of Futility," *Boston Globe,* Dec. 4, 1977, p. 1; and Ellen Goodman, "Prostitution and the Law," *Boston Globe,* Dec. 4, 1977, p. 4.

39. Taped interview with Judge Margaret Burnham, April 4, 1986.

40. Barbara Millman, "New Rules for the Oldest Profession: Should We Change Our Prostitution Laws?" *Harvard Women's Law Journal,* 3 (Spring 1980), appendix A: 85

percent said prostitution produced criminal activity; 75 percent said it was bad for business; 85 percent believed prostitutes caused venereal disease.

41. Millman, "New Rules," 7–36; Boles and Tatro, "Legal and Extra Legal Methods," 71–84; and Richard Symanski, *The Immoral Landscape: Female Prostitution in Western Societies* (Toronto, 1981), pp. 41–48.

42. Barbara Yondorf, "Prostitution as a Legal Activity: The West German Experience," *Policy Analysis,* 5 (Fall 1979), 417–33; see also Haft, "Hustling for Rights," p. 23, where she refers to West Germany as the country with the most open mind toward prostitution.

43. Elizabeth Vorenberg and James Vorenberg, "The Biggest Pimp of All: Prostitution and Some Facts of Life," *Atlantic Monthly,* Jan. 1977, pp. 27–38.

44. Ibid., p. 145.

45. "Unhappy over Hookers," *Time,* Oct. 2, 1978.

46. Peter Langer, "Downtown Neutrality: The Case of Boston's Combat Zone" (unpublished paper, 1983).

47. Ibid.; and Boles and Tatro, "Legal and Extra-Legal Methods," 79.

48. Richard Symanski, "Prostitution in Nevada," *Annals of American Geographers,* 64 (Sept. 1984), 359–77. Madams and brothel owners are respected entrepreneurs according to Symanski.

49. *WHISPER,* 2 (Spring 1986); and *WHISPER,* 5 (forthcoming).

50. Because of its unusual political status, West Berlin is one of the few West German cities that does not have licensed prostitution. To institute such a policy, West Berlin would have to get American, French, and British approval.

51. Rose-Marie Giesen and Gunda Schumann, *An der Front despatraichats: Berict vom langen Marsch durch das Prostitutions Milieu* (Frankfort, 1980); and taped interview with Rose-Marie Giesen, June 1984.

52. Interview with Jon Visser, director of a prostitution research and advocacy group in Holland, the de Graaf Stichting Society, June 1982; interviews with prostitution researchers Fred Stemvers and Hans Menlenbroek, June 1982 and April 1987.

53. F. A. Stemvers, *Meisjes van plezier, de geschiedenis van de prostitutie in Nederland* (Utrecht, 1985), pp. 90–95, 134–43; and Luc Overman, *Prostitutie in Woonbuurten* (Amsterdam, 1982), pp. 49–62.

54. "Advies om tippelzone niet langer te gedogen," *NRC Handelsblad,* Sept. 30, 1986, p. 3; and "Van Thijn blijft tegenstander van tippelzone," *NRC Handelsblad,* Oct. 23, 1986, p. 1.

55. Norway has also taken an anti-institutional approach to prostitution but has not been as active in prostitution reform as Sweden.

56. For a discussion of the prostitute movement and the 1985 congress in Amsterdam, see: Sharon Beldon, "Prostitution," *The Paper,* Mar. 1984, p. 1; "We worden overal gedescrimineerd," *Het Vraie,* Feb. 15, 1985; "Amsterdam, vitrine du premier congrès mondial des prostituées," *Libération,* Feb. 16, 1985.

57. The legal reform may be more symbolic than real—the criminal code section on pimping and promoting prostitution (250B) has not been enforced in the past: see Stemvers, *Meisjes van plezier.*

58. The society was established at the turn of the century by de Graaf, an activist in the movement to abolish regulated prostitution; see "To the Committee on Pornography and Prostitution" and "The View of Mr. A. de Graaf Stichting on Prostitution," from the files of the society; also interview with Jon Visser, June 1982.

Notes

59. Hans Menlenbroek, "Prostitution and the Law," *NRC Handelsblad,* forthcoming (July 1987).

60. Taped interviews with Leif Persson, Swedish criminologist, and Anders Nelin, former Stockholm police chief, July 1982 (both were members of a government prostitution commission); see also Leif G. W. Persson, *Horor, hallickar och torskar* (Stockholm, 1981).

61. The Malmö program has had the most written about it; taped interviews with Stig Larsson and Sven Axel Månsson, July 1982.

62. See the Prostitution Commission report, *Prostitution: beskrivning analys förslag till åtgärder* (Stockholm, 1980); taped interviews with commission experts: Hanna Olsson, Rita Liljeström, Anders Nelin, Leif Persson, Sven Axel Månsson, June–July 1982.

63. Frances Olsen, "Feminism and Critical Legal Theory: An American Perspective" (unpublished paper); see also Olsen, "Statutory Rape," 429–31.

NAME INDEX

Name Index

Name Index

SUBJECT INDEX

267

Subject Index

Subject Index